The
Porn User's Guide
to
Enlightenment

Psychosexuality and
the Erotic Imagination

Drew Wynn

A catalogue record for this book is available from the National Library of Australia

Psychosexuality Series, Volume 2, 2009
Second Edition 2021
First Printed by Ganieda Press
Perth, Australia

X X X
PGR

Linellen Press
265 Boomerang Road
Oldbury, Western Australia
www.linellenpress.com.au

Warning!

This book contains material of a sexually-explicit nature.
Some readers may find this offensive.

What has become of human sexuality in the West?

After nearly two thousand years of Church repression, assisted with guilt and shame, we have the denial and objectification of sex with the scientific era culminating in Freud. We are in a sorry state.

With the turning of the tide of the nineteen-sixties and the mixed blessings of feminism, we are now visited with the enormous and volcanic depiction of sexuality on the Internet. Where do we stand with this? How do we guide our youth?

Drew Wynn believes the pornographic phenomenon represents more than a reactive and degenerative view of sexuality and is in danger of reinforcing the opinion of the shrinking moral minority. He traces seeds of renewal and initiation that may guide us into a more enlightened perspective for our sexual and cultural health.

Using tools such as creativity, autobiography and fiction embedded in mythic and magical paths to sexual fulfilment, he wishes nothing more than to help in the establishment of a "Tantra for the West", and draws on the tradition of alchemy in this quest. Drew believes that our sexual health is imperative in a world-view governed by fear, illness and death, and that this will re-establish a modern perspective of soul that will inform our creative future.

This book is far more than a discussion of the pornographic phenomenon; it is a window into the volcanic and transformative power of sex.

*****

Drew Wynn has spent his life preoccupied with sex, for which he makes absolutely no apology.

In this book, Drew presents a distillation of his ideas and feelings, fashioning them into a creative whole that he wishes to share with the troubled majority of the population in these matters. This work continues his series of writing and other creative output in this exciting field.

Preface

The modern-day judgement of pornography that serves the prevailing moral minority and other vested interests I find concerning and deplorable. Surely pornography is, at the very core, a primal reaction to such repression? Aren't we mature enough as a society, culture or even species to at least dispassionately look at what I would suggest is a daunting and overwhelming phenomenon that simply demands examination? What is it that so polarises people in their view of pornography? What is its relationship to sexuality in our society and what is it telling us of our fundamental sexual nature and its future?

I think these are some of many demanding questions that need to be directed toward the pornographic phenomenon and which I will attempt to answer, as well as keeping the consumer very much in the loop. Why? Because I am a consumer of erotic material, which by modern definition forms a continuum to the pornographic, with some subtle differences that we will be exploring. But mainly because the consumer is too often left out of the equation for a variety of seemingly obvious reasons: This I wish to redress.

My interest in human sexuality and its fundamental involvement in the journey of our individual existence and health has been lifelong. Yet, in my latter years, I have become increasingly surprised that whilst I was and am closely involved in disciplines and professions that were heavily informed by sexuality, there was little in the way of its creative integration within them. Further, I was contributing to this lack, even with my reasonably considerable personal and professional experience.

This lack is closely associated with the erotic imagination and the pornographic phenomenon in particular, which forms the main background theme of this book. I have chosen this emphasis to rectify a personal omission, not only in my own development, but also to assist others who may have and maybe still are wrestling with the sort of issues I have had to confront. This is why I have taken the main thrust into this work from the perspective of the consumer and tried to negotiate the sort of difficulties that he or she faces in integrating this consumption within the mainstream of their – our – lives.

The initial chapters of the book will look through the personal lens of my upbringing and, therefore, they are autobiographical. Well, not entirely, there's a little fiction. Is this to protect others? To some extent, and I discuss this in the Introduction. But there is also some fiction in this autobiographical section to mirror and complement the personal experience that is embedded in the larger fictional component that follows. This is because sexuality – or psychosexuality as I define it – is profoundly linked to the imagination and, from there, to our creativity and spirituality.

In relation to the factual material of an impersonal nature, personally experienced or research-derived, this is as accurate as recall or corroboration permits. Memory suffers – or enjoys – the ravages of the creative imagination. Metaphor is often turned to humour or irony and is sometimes more tongue-in-cheek than I originally intended, even to the point of satire. A mixed bag, really, but guided by the creative imagination with the intent to restore psychosexuality to its full place in our Western culture and to take pornography away from the pathological view that seems inevitably to follow, watch, criticise and judge it.

The title has gone through various metamorphoses. The

original title was *The Money Shot*, and you may be amused that it was a female colleague who suggested it, but it seemed too 'obvious', in more ways than one. Then, as I used the Pandora myth as an introduction, I came to *Opening Pandora's Box* as a title, but decided against this when I saw how the myth and name are being represented – or misrepresented – in the public domain. *The Porn User's Guide* is an elaboration and conveys not a guide through pornographic material, but a guide into your consumption, or an understanding of someone close to you who is a consumer, and where it may lead.

But why "Enlightenment"? Because sexuality has traditionally been the cornerstone of man's journey of discovery in the meaning of his or her existence and the pathways that map it. That this connection has suffered serious disruption in the West is beyond doubt. That much healing in mental and physical disease rests on this awareness is also beyond doubt. That both these positions are not fully appreciated in our modern Western culture is a serious cause for concern.

I have been challenged in this work in a way that has not occurred before in my writing. I have found creative and spiritual dimensions to have emerged from the writing itself in ways that I have marvelled at. I have thoroughly enjoyed writing it, yet I remain more than a little nervous about its entry into the public domain. Somewhat paradoxically, I am also proud of it. If this book gives you or someone close to you an appreciation of what the erotic imagination is and can mean, then it has done its job. If it inspires you to a full and open acceptance of your sexuality free from current constraints and informs others similarly, I will be doubly proud.

Contents

Introduction

Opening Pandora's Box

There are some major unresolved issues surrounding both pornography and the pornographic industry with its established position in modern Western culture. By now there can be little argument that it does have such a position, but it is distorted and rendered incomplete by these unresolved issues.

I will mention some, although there are many more:

- That it is a huge modern phenomenon is obvious to all but the blind, yet its acceptance and integration within society is still governed by a relative state of denial.

- Approaches that examine it are from the outside looking in: academic, cultural, or journalistic studies, not to mention the input from politics and religion with varying levels of criticism, prejudice, and moral judgment.

- The most vociferous commentators are usually quite emotive and negative, and use ethical issues and value judgement to support their positions, often in a self-righteous manner.

- Many of these studies and commentaries are quite

vicarious and conceal voyeurism or consumerism on the part of the author(s).

- The inside looking out perspective is primarily of the industry expressing itself through its own genre, maybe with some input from the performing artistes of usually questionable value. This position has all sorts of inherent distortions.

- The admission of consumerism is negligible, for varied yet seemingly obvious reasons, and as a result lacks a significant voice in the overall debate.

Regarding the last point, I have yet to read a significant appraisal from the consumer's perspective or one that gets beyond the immediate criticisms of the phenomenon – masturbatory, fantasy-land, morally suspect, mentally disturbed, dirty old men, sick puppies and so on – to explore the depth to which pornography may well be pointing, which I believe it is. Trivialising and demeaning pornography allows us as a culture to avoid examining where it may be leading us, because my position is that it would demand a fundamental re-visioning of where Western culture is headed. I do not believe that pornography itself is leading us toward moral decrepitude, although by denying its existence and importance it might. In fact, it may do quite the opposite, if we can embrace the challenges that it raises.

Elsewhere I have promoted the primacy of what I call the Great Cycle of Existence. The Great Cycle encompasses the period from birth – or maybe conception – to death. In more detail it could be considered as conception, life, birth, sex, marriage, family, ageing and death. (Note the important differentiation of sex and marriage.) This latter expanded view is open to alternative and branching pathways, some of which we will be exploring in more detail. I will be summarising the Great Cycle as birth, sex and death as, after all, the topic under discussion here is basically sex. However, I want to, and from the onset, indicate the very important close relationship of sex to birth and death: the first being relatively obvious, the second less so. I also want to offer the intuition that birth, sex and death leads to rebirth, either literal or symbolic.

Why do I consider the Great Cycle of Existence to be primary? Because I believe it is the fundamental pattern that underpins our existence in this day-to-day reality. What reinforces such a belief? The fact that it is these elements that have been used from time immemorial in magical and mystical traditions as a means of ritual and initiation into the mysteries and complexities of life. Further, that if the elements within this primal pattern are removed from our presence and contact, we are left psychologically impoverished, even divided, and at the mercy of whatever agency – political, social or religious – that would use such measures for power and control.

Strong words? Well, have a quick look at how all this operates in the current era: In the West, birth and death have been excluded from our presence within the confines of modern medicine and placed in hospitals. Sex? Ignored by medicine, it has been left to the conventional religions with the psychological tools of guilt and shame.

Somewhat light-heartedly, let's take a look at the shadow or undercurrent to this pattern in the modern idiom of 'sex 'n' drugs 'n' rock & roll' to examine some of these issues and as a sort of lead in to the book as a whole. When we lose contact with the deeper patterns of the Great Cycle within ourselves, we may disconnect from their creative functions as agents of initiation, but they do not go away. These patterns slip into the shadows and re-emerge in a more nefarious manner. This could be considered to have happened and promoted 'sex 'n' drugs 'n' rock & roll' as a modern phenomenon. Yet, precisely because it contains these deeper patterns, it is also ancient; we just need to search a little for it.

Drugs of the mind-altering variety would be a good place to start. As well as the moral issues surrounding illicit drugs, there is also the medical position. Modern medicine has attempted to associate such drugs with mental health issues under the title of co-morbidity. The paradox that such drugs may be therapeutic whilst also illicit (as, for example, with amphetamines) is yet to be addressed beyond the limited neuroscientific perspective. I can assure you that this co-morbidity is not a good fit, as the evidence that drugs actually cause insanity is tenuous at the best. This simply represents a desire for establishment control of an issue that inevitably cannot be dealt with in such a fashion.

Drugs can be agents of initiation. In their natural and hallucinogenic aspect, they are an integral part of traditional religion and its patterns of ritual and ceremony. In their modern form, they represent a thwarted attempt at the same by many: Thwarted by the increasingly chemical content and mode of administration, as well as being usually taken outside of a ritual setting. Well, not entirely, as some have been used in the modern rave phenomenon, which brings in the 'rock & roll'. It is telling and somewhat ironic that it is usually the drug 'ecstasy' that is commonly used: The term ecstasy is used to describe the shaman on his journey in an altered state of consciousness, usually for the purposes of healing a sick person. Similarly, you may not be surprised that there is an ancient correlation between drumming, music and dancing, which were also tools of religion and initiation in times past, and still present in some cultures. And, of course, they are both associated – strongly – with sex. We'll be coming back to all the above issues in the course of the book, but let's get the focus back onto sex. Or, more specifically, pornography – as this is probably why you have this book in your hand in the first place.

Maybe you, like I, are a consumer and you want to get the consumer's angle on your attraction – or even compulsion. Because it is a central thesis of mine that, buried deep in pornography, are issues of spirituality and initiation, and much more ... and that it may be this that fundamentally attracts you to pornography. Also, maybe sometimes it is – though not always – a poorly guided attempt to obtain a broader and more complete appreciation of yourself as a sexual human being, and even to have this exposure initiate you into a more wholesome and spiritual world-view. There you go, I've done it again; I've placed the conclusion of the book right at the beginning: Don't despair, though; the journey may be much more fun than the conclusion!

Some clarification of my orientation may be in order. I am positioning myself, first and foremost, with respect to this work as a consumer. As a consumer, I can see many flaws, distortions and negativity, specifically within pornography, as well as sexuality in the West in general, which pornography may reflect, parallel and even promote. As pornography spearheads the explosive re-emergence of sexuality as an issue that has effectively negated earlier attempts at control, and for which I suppose we have the Internet to thank, it has also brought to light all that is not good, truthful or beautiful about sexuality. My critical position is that it is this differentiation we must undertake if we are to discover the creative roots buried deep within the pornographic phenomenon.

My primary interest is to discover what is erotic, creative, artistic and spiritual within pornography. Further, this is also to include sexuality in all its varied forms. It also highlights the fundamentally important position of the imagination in the psychic economy. Beyond this, I hope to clarify the deeper and more mystical patterns that we can connect to, so that we do not remain psychically divided as a result of vested interests and groupings within our society. Indeed, it is these patterns I believe we need to connect with so that we can transform our society and free ourselves of those restrictive and inhibitive influences.

There are going to be some challenges and limitations. One challenge would be how to illustrate the text without lapsing into making the book subject to the charge that it is actually a work of pornography in and of itself. This is a risk; whilst I have some creative ideas about this and will see how they emerge in the writing of this work; I will restrict myself to verbal illustration only. Such creative artwork would involve others as part of a larger project that may follow this book. This work is, first and foremost, an act of creation in its own right. At the time of writing, I have a general idea of the outline and the points I want to cover, but the specifics of the writing in terms of genre are relatively vague.

There is one important consideration with respect to the fictional component of the book, which I would like you to consider as you read it. I will be describing the sexuality as if it was being portrayed in front of you, something like watching a pornographic movie. If taken at face value and literally, it could be described as *pornographic*, but it is actually more than that. A simple descriptive portrayal could be considered so and this is the very nature of most pornography, which may lead to repetition and potentially addiction, although I will be arguing that there are sections of the industry that do incite a more subjective involvement. To overcome this difficulty, I make use of the technique of 'voice-overs' as a way of introducing, even if somewhat artificially, the physical and emotional responses of the performers so connecting you, as the reader, with their subjective states and hence, or as well as, your own. The overall effect of this is to connect you with the sexual portrayal in a subjective manner and involve you in the sexual content.

There are also many limitations: I will outline just two. The first is that, apart from being a consumer, I have very little in the way of direct contact with the industry. I have never met a porn performer or been near a porn set: that is, not unless something was being filmed in the bushes when I have walked the dogs! By the way, I'll generally use the term *performer*, rather than actor to avoid any gender issues and bias, not necessarily because it is the best term. Alternatively, I will use the industry-favoured *porn star*. I have tried to enlist the cooperation of one major pornography company but with no success. So, I am on my own. The material in this work is a result of my own consumption, reflection and integration of it within my life as a whole. It is thus personal, with all the inherent bias that position eschews, and is largely autobiographical from the narrative perspective.

The second limitation is the range of material I will use and what I shall exclude. As the book is autobiographical, it will contain my own sexual orientation and proclivities, plus those of people I have come into contact with. (The pun is intended, and there will inevitably more of these puns and innuendoes as we proceed; sex is like that if you hadn't noticed!) While we may go to the edges and discuss such issues as homosexuality, this will not be in any significant detail. Fetishism will be looked at, particularly as it highlights issues of performance and acting, as well as engaging other genres such as the fashion industry, for example. BDSM (bondage and discipline, sadomasochism) will receive a bit more attention, as I will be using it to further explore the more contentious issue of power and its relationship to sexuality. I won't be taking all this into a detailed examination of what is and is not a perversion, as this will pathologise a creative venture and has been more than adequately done to date by others.

We will be touching on some morally sensitive issues: that is, moral beyond the ethical standards of a society that the pornographic genre as a whole seeks to challenge, either directly or indirectly. These include some dimensions of the seemingly ubiquitous 'money shot' (the visual display of male ejaculation usually onto at least one female body), multiple and complex sexual penetration, then, on occasion, making brief reference to urination and the use of large sex toys, hands or fists in genital penetration. We will be only looking at rape, incest and paedophilia in a cursory manner when it supports a position or argument and to disentangle the sexual elements from other probably more significant factors. Extreme practices such as bestiality and necrophilia are questionable as primarily sexual practice, so their exploration will be avoided and they would be mentioned only when they support an argument in a related area.

The pornographic lens I shall use will include photography as an important, although not of recent times, the largest feature, as well as video, DVD and the Internet. There will be some significant references to creativity and artistic production to explore the boundaries between pornography, eroticism and art. As we do this, the various political, feminist, academic, medical and religious perspectives will be included and elaborated on. The main feature, however, will be the inner perspective that pornography inspires within the consumer. This will be significant and detailed, moving into a range of associated areas and occasionally looking at individuals who, for one reason or another, have been prominent. We will be looking more at performance than the performers as individuals. Whilst it has become an increasing trend to provide the thoughts and feelings of performers, maybe to reinforce 'acceptability' and to counter issues of coercion and even abuse, reference will only be to those who are considered significant in the thrust of my overall thesis.

In the above, I have tended to treat the terminology

associated with pornography somewhat formally. There are difficulties with this as, depending on the term employed, it may tend to categorise the discussion, such that it may appear medical or religious in orientation. This may present some difficulties. The pornographic industry has a range of terminology that informs the mainstream and has been informed itself from the confines of the bedroom. In general, it is this terminology I will use, unless otherwise indicated by the demands of any discussion being undertaken. In the male domain, for example, ejaculate could be referred to as semen, sperm, spunk or cum; ejaculation itself as orgasm, the cumshot or money shot. I will try and refrain from unnecessarily vulgar and prejudicial terms that, I believe, demean the genre. By contrast, I will also try to re-establish the authenticity of some terms that have become generally demeaned in the broader culture itself. I will attempt to use the terms to match the mood and tone of the subject under discussion. So, please be prepared.

The title to the Introduction: *Opening Pandora's Box?* I have always had a preference for symbolic titles, so when the Pandora title based on the Greek myth occurred to me it seemed to stick, even to consideration as a title to the book itself. As there will be significant references to mythology in the book, it seemed appropriate. Here is one version of the Pandora story:

> *(Outraged by Prometheus, who stole fire from the gods to give to men) Zeus sent a fresh calamity to men. He ordered Hephaestus (the blacksmith of Olympus) to fashion clay and water into a body, to give it vital force and a human voice, and to make therefrom a virgin whose dazzling beauty would equal that of the immortal goddesses. All the divinities heaped their*

especial gifts on this new creature, who received the name of Pandora. Hermes (the trickster god), however, put perfidy (treachery) into Pandora's heart and lies in her mouth. After which Zeus sent her as a gift to Epimetheus. Although his brother Prometheus had warned him against accepting any gift from the ruler of Olympus, the imprudent Epimetheus was enchanted by Pandora's beauty, welcomed her, and made a place for herself among men. Unhappy imprudence! For Pandora brought in her arms a great vase – which is incorrectly called 'Pandora's box'. She raised its lid, and the terrible afflictions with which the vase had been filled escaped and spread over the earth. Hope alone did not fly away. Thus, with the arrival of the first woman, misery made its appearance on earth.

(From: *New LaRousse Encyclopedia of Mythology*)

Note the parallels to Eve of the Garden of Eden, as well as the implication that the primal Fall is related to sexual desire. This is further reinforced by the modern duplicity in the term box, as a symbol. As with the Garden of Eden story, the myth of Pandora is deeply symbolic with many levels of appreciation. If taken at the obvious level it seems somewhat sexist and to reinforce the feminist perspective that is pro-censorship and anti-pornography. This is further reinforced by the obvious patriarchal tone of the myth. (These two perspectives have more in common than is generally appreciated.)

At another level, Pandora could be pornography itself and I invite you to look at the myth through that lens. Yet there is much more to this myth, to which we will return in the company of some others that reflect on the topic, when we do more than open the box; we actually go inside.

This book is not only about my personal journey through this world. Whilst I will be describing some of my experiences, it is the fact that my journey is that of many – estimated to comprise at least one-third of the adult population – that captures my imagination. So, my journey will be used as an illustration to lead into this world of the pornographic and erotic, and from this basis to radiate out into the wider world of the imagination. We will be wandering down roads of the artistic, mythic and spiritual to provide a wider and more holistic framework into which the modern pornographic flood – or explosion – properly fits.

Of the various intersecting themes that comprise this work, the autobiographical presents some unique challenges and ethical concerns. It is my decision to explore the morality of consumerism, as I believe such an examination is indispensable to the wider debate. However, being significantly autobiographical it will encompass others and particularly those with whom I have had sexual contact or a relationship. Avoiding names will negotiate many of the concerns of this unless it suits the discussion to use one, in which case I will use a pseudonym. I will refer to any sexual relationships as such, alternatively as connections or even partnerships. I take license to disguise anyone involved in whatever way I can to preserve confidentiality without sacrificing the point or argument I am trying to make, unless permission has otherwise been obtained. I will use fiction to augment this position. I won't identify either marriages or children.

Initially, there will be a need to look at pornography as a modern cultural phenomenon and explore the political, legal and social issues, although the psychological, medical and religious dimensions necessitate more scrutiny and will be referred to throughout. I do not want to spend much time on this initial perspective, as, like you may wish to, I want to get into the 'real stuff'. It is not that these dimensions are not relevant, they most certainly are. However, they have been done to death by others to the point of confusion and obfuscation, so it is my intention to cover them briefly and concisely to move on to the more relevant and, I think, interesting aspects of the pornographic phenomenon. It will be my thesis that unless and until we get to these other artistic, mythic and spiritual aspects, we will not come to a full appreciation of the phenomenon.

More than that: I believe that, without appreciating these artistic, mythic, and spiritual aspects, we will not fully understand the pornographic phenomenon and will remain confused and psychically in conflict, particularly if attracted to it. Ultimately, I believe such an expanded perspective can heal such psychic turmoil and provide a basis for the correct use of the imagination and its relationship to both soul and spirit.

A point about the research that I have undertaken for this book: there hasn't been much and this is quite deliberate, if you take out the laziness argument! I had intended to work and write in a more detailed even academic way about sexuality, as well as the association with subjects such as physical and mental health, creativity and spirituality. I still intend to, but after reading only a couple of works on the subject of pornography I realised that was not the way to proceed in this work. I already had a considerable amount of intellectual appreciation of the subject matter from my professional interests and my personal experience as a consumer.

So, I decided that a work based on this background and not too influenced by other critics and commentators – at this early stage in what is emerging as a much larger project – would be of value in its own right. It may be relatively unsophisticated and available to criticism at many levels beyond my position as a consumer, although any criticism may be covertly just because of this fact! This position, with its lack of sophistication, may provide the material in a relatively raw manner from the subjective viewpoint. My impression is that this has not been done in this way, except by the porn industry itself, which is somewhat tautological.

The subject matter of sexuality is complex and dense if it is approached at any significant depth, which is what this enquiry aims to do. The text will then give an impression of speed, even haste, as the issues rise from the depths and demand an audience. Although seemingly intellectual, there is little in the way of formal thought involved, it is more like the rapid brush strokes and palette knife work of an art canvas. Because the depth is archetypal (more of this term later ...) it is not linear and ordered. It also contains a variety of subject matters and disciplines, leaving the reader with the impression that there are several books rolled into one.

In truth, this may be the case, as I suspect this work is seminal and will lead to further exploration, although I also suspect that the style will remain. As an artist, this is how I approach the canvas in front of me, and the feeling is more like I am a channel of information rather than its originator. This overall impression is reinforced by the fact that the subject matter has been under my sometimes-detailed attention for several decades, so there is a lot to express, and which I would like to cover in one work. Consequently, the style of the book is deliberately circular and layered, much like a tapestry. As such we will be revisiting points from differing angles as we build up the debate; I hope you enjoy this style.

As a young boy I remember being ejected from the school choir because I "didn't have a voice". I think the actual words were that I was tone-deaf. So, in one deft stroke – since discounted – my voice was silenced. I pursued art and gained prizes, but it wasn't my voice and I rejected it for academia. I asked for a guitar to explore music, but this was beyond our family means and might have exposed me to singing again. So, creativity collectively went out of the window.

Yet the voice has never entirely gone away. It was a major tool of exploration in my therapeutic analysis, but was only ever considered that – a tool. I wrote books of poetry, then burnt them as a sacrifice after the death of a partner, possibly because I was fearful they may be worthless as art and be judgemental of me if I were to die soon after, which was then a possibility. I tried writing at various times, but this was negated too. Only of late have I recognised that much of this latter negation was personal and professional jealousy that instilled in me a sense of inadequacy and fear that, if exposed, I would have no voice.

Of late there are people who have come into my life who have stressed the opposite and continued to challenge me. I have come to see that no voice is concealment, hiding behind a fear of exposure. So, it is ironic I should pick the topic of sexuality for this voice! Yet a voice it is, I have found it. You may not like the voice or the style of its expression, there is much music and song I do not like. You are free, of course, to find what does suit you. I implore you not to reject this work simply because you may not like the voice – it is mine and I have grown to like it.

No, that's wrong: I have grown to love it. If you are a pornographic consumer, I hope this work will open your eyes to dimensions of your activities for psychological integration, overall health and your future enjoyment. If you are not, I trust it will be read with an open mind, as I believe some of the issues explored here are far bigger than pornography itself and even bigger than sexuality per se, as we are using them as a lens into a far deeper and more mysterious world.

1

"The Real Stuff"

"Do you want to come out to the back and see some 'real stuff?'"

It must have been one day around 1973 or 1974 on a bright afternoon when I try to recall and reconstruct the event. Although the date and time may be inaccurate, the memory is clear and solid. For some reason that I can't remember, I was walking home from the hospital where I was undertaking my training when my custom was to travel home by public transport. In a seedier part of town, I passed an innocuous-looking second-hand book and magazine shop. On impulse I decided to buy something soft to stimulate my sexual fancy, as hardcore pornography was not legal at the time. I was then twenty-three years old, but this was not an adjunct to my sex life; it was more to stimulate my imaginative life, which I was already beginning to see as distinct in the realm of sexuality, at least.

Inside were a variety of men's magazines of the Playboy variety and I was the only occupant. I was perusing these when the shop attendant – if you could call it a shop – issued his invitation. I was surprised as this had not been my intention, as I didn't know that this 'system' existed, yet I immediately knew what the invitation was about. I went through a door and there were racks of unfamiliar magazines on the right. The attendant stood silently on the left and I started casually leafing through, although surprised at the gold mine in front of me that seemed

23

regal in spite of their second-hand nature. The magazines were smaller than I was used to with the glossy men's magazines of the time and were European, mainly Danish and Swedish, where I knew pornography had been recently legalised.

Then I came across the picture of the Nordic Goddess. The photography throughout this particular magazine was tasteful and artistic; it was based on two colour picture stories as well as letters and articles, and was produced in Sweden. Enraptured, the Goddess had a beatific smile and sperm was ejaculating onto her face from the erect cock of an unseen man whilst a lesser Goddess, obviously her 'assistant' in the illustrated story, was to one side and also the recipient of some of the sperm. What was different from my experiences to date was that the sexual content was not flagrant and that the women were both natural and beautiful. I felt a depth open up within me that I had not experienced in this context before and was almost religious in its intensity: You could call it an epiphany. I was sold in more ways than one, although I had my wits enough about me to negotiate the price down and I left the shop. Thus began my journey through the world of pornography … Well, not entirely, as I wouldn't have come to this point without some prior experience, but I'll come to that shortly.

The above experience produced an indelible memory that challenged my previously held, rather confused, position and opened up a world of exploration, both in pornography and sexuality, that continues to this day. I made a conscious choice at this point to actively pursue the division within myself that I knew had occurred sometime prior to this point. The way I have described it above may give the impression of something base, inferior and instinctual. It is exactly premises and prejudices of this kind that we will need to face and challenge on our journey. So, let me re-word the exploration: Does eroticism and the imagination make it sound better; somehow more artistic? There are many levels to such questions, and, hopefully, we will be getting answers to most of them.

My adolescence and attendant sexual development carried the usual load of distortions, although there was no overt physical or mental abuse in my immediate personal background. These distortions are by no means unique; in fact, I have come to realise them as the societal norm, but at the time, I didn't know that. So, although my own experiences through this life transition – I will describe them shortly – may be somewhat personal, what was and is still relatively fairly uniform and common was the background of lack of preparation, denial and secrecy. Although these were personal experiences, with subsequent experience I consider them representative. The ultimate outcome of this background was that my sexual development, in those impressionable and formative years, began to take a parallel path to my overall psychological development: a psychic division had occurred.

My father was a farmer, and up to my adolescence, my entire life had been lived on the family farm. This farm was a mixed one: there was a herd of cows for milk and also mixed corn production. Other features were veritable tribes of cats, chickens, sheep, pigs and dogs. The cats were exclusively female to minimise the production of litters of kittens, although this didn't seem to stop the intrepid Tomcats from the neighbouring village and beyond: This alerted me very early to the power of the sexual drive. One of the childhood challenges was finding the missing cat when she didn't respond to the milk call, as she was obviously tending a new litter. The consequence of the discovery depended on the cat population at the time and a collective abundance meant giving them away was not an option. Like all the animals, there was work to be done, and that of the cats was to keep down the vermin that sought the stored corn.

This working aspect was also true of the dogs, which were pedigree and bred for commercial sale of the pups. The dog litters were born at home, usually in the back rooms of the farmhouse with my mother as midwife.

What this conveys is many-fold, but the most significant features I would like to outline are the exposure to birth and death: Oh yes, and sex. There was an abundance of this on the farm and, of course, my younger sister and I would track it down. Life was made considerably easier in this voyeuristic activity by a brief commercial venture in breeding exotic rabbits. They were kept in cages, like chickens, and the greatest of sports was to take the male (buck), put him in with the female (doe), then stand back and watch the action. He would mount the doe – not in the missionary position I might add – and after a few frenetic thrusts would utter a squeak and then fall on his side, seemingly exhausted. The doe was quite passive, sometimes continuing to eat. The show was over and we left sniggering after returning the buck to his cage to recover.

There are many stories, enough to fill a book I would imagine, and a significant proportion of these would have the birth, sex and death theme embedded within them. Collectively, what this exposure and these experiences provided me with was a level of normality to the Great Cycle of Existence – or birth, sex and death – and was to stand me in reasonably good stead for adolescence: In effect, I was able to fall back on this experience whenever I was faced with the distortions of such exposure at the human level.

There is one story that illustrates this point par excellence. It is recalled from memory and I am sure both my parents – both still alive at the time of writing – have differing recollections. However, this is my story, and, as you will discover as we move through this field, I hold great store on the subjectivity of memory. I was kicking a football around on our front lawn when my mother approached and invited me for a walk. The first alarm bell rang ... we never went for such walks. 'I'm playing ball,' I protested, but mother was insistent, so I followed. My intuition was working overtime; this is going to be the sex-talk; I just knew it! I wasn't looking forward to it though ...

Why? Because I felt it should not have been my mother. As we walked, I saw my father on a tractor in a neighbouring field; *it should be him doing this*, I thought. This is a significant point as there was, of course, no logical reason that it should be him. I later presumed, and as a result of a forthcoming event, that my parents had decided I needed the prescribed talk. Why it was my mother who picked the short straw I don't know, but I suspect my father would have had more difficulty here because of his own relatively inhibited background, whereas my mother was more 'worldly' in this respect. She had four older brothers and came from rural stock; my father did not. So, the 'reason' I felt this to be my father's responsibility was again intuitive and pointed to the issue of initiation, although I did not know this at the time. Let's pause there for a while and look at the place and value of initiation.

That I recognised that it 'should' be my father was, I believe, an intuition of something Carl Jung would describe as archetypal. Don't be too frightened of the word archetype, as you will become familiar with it as we cover this territory. Archetype describes patterns beyond the personal, common to all peoples and cultures, and often manifested in ritual and ceremony. I was recognising that it was Fathers who should instruct Sons in the ways of sexual education. Herewith the first distortion: Why was my instruction not like that?

My father was a product of an English background; need I say more? Well, yes, I do. Although his sort of background in England in the earlier part of the last century has been jocularly dismissed as "English", there are some deeper reasons for this relative failure of responsibility that need describing. My father's father spent many years of the Great War on the front line. My father was too young for the Second World War and spent his adolescence mainly in the company of those remaining, as the able-bodied men were at war. There was thus a considerable disruption in the normal father-son transmission of family, ritual and initiation functions during the century. It is my considered opinion that the effects are still with us.

Now the reason for the talk:

"Beverley is coming next week and there are some things you need to know." So, there it was: the reason for the talk. From there it became quite factual: Babies and sexually transmitted diseases could eventuate from such an encounter. Hold on, hold on! I was screaming inside … I haven't got that far yet! As it transpired, all Bev and I got up to was some relatively innocent kissing and cuddling. It was our first foray into a differing relationship with the opposite sex, and neither of us was ready or prepared for intercourse or even any genital exploration. Anyway, I knew about babies from the schoolyard, but the disease bit was relatively new.

Then the second hit: Those sorts of diseases occur when a man has sex with a lot of women, I was informed. Ye gods! No wonder I wanted my father to do this. I glanced to my left and in a neighbouring field was the ram with an appreciable number of female sheep (ewes), which he was meant to single-handedly "service". I would bet my bottom dollar he wouldn't get a disease, so I discounted that theory and knew I'd have to explore that one further … but elsewhere, because maybe my mother hadn't got it right either, or wasn't telling me the 'truth'. That was it … a relatively failed initiation and nowhere else to go for the present. After Bev's departure, I felt I was getting on the runway, but I was shortly to return to an English boarding school and that would provide a few more curly aspects to my development.

I have generally many things to be thankful for with my English Public-School education, but my sex education wasn't one of them. One alternative was to stifle sexual development altogether and channel the unfulfilled energies into study and 'higher' things – further academic achievement, arts or the choir, for example. I suspected this is an ingrained pattern developed in boarding schools, as with monasteries, and exactly for the reasons mentioned – 'higher' achievement. It was just that, by the time I went there, this method was becoming a little out of date.

The second choice was homosexuality, particularly during the impressionable and fluid stage of adolescence. I was fortunate as the 'crush' I developed was on somebody quite aware of the inherent dangers in this option and what was happening to me. He was some three years older, had successfully negotiated this territory, and was able to steer me appropriately away from that path. That was not the nature of the crush anyway: He was an idolised and idealised older boy and an example of what I aspired to become. In other words, he was a symbol and not a sex object, and he knew the difference.

The third option was what I ultimately chose: voyeurism. How did I manage this? Well, there was always the holidays, which were just long enough to maybe establish the beginnings of a relationship with a girl. The difficulty here was that my male contemporaries went to co-educational day schools with local girls attending. They were so far in front on the pursuit stakes and were constantly acquiring new tactics that I remained a relative newcomer for several years. I did manage to nurture the parallel path, however, which started as an accident.

I came across an American "men's magazine" and I even remember the name: Jem. I don't recall how I obtained it; I suspect it was a cast-off from a peer. It was not pornographic; there were no displays of sexuality or men, just women being portrayed in various stages of undress and acting provocatively. As an aside, I won't go down the track of the more popular glossy magazines such as Playboy, unless for comparison. Why? They may have been picturesque and exotic, but I rarely found them erotic. Maybe men do buy Playboy for the articles after all? Inside Jem was a picture series I can still recall. There was a blonde woman, attractive and well-endowed, performing a strip-tease. She was a 'castaway' on a 'raft' and the sequence was conducted as she struck poses around the 'mast' progressively discarding her 'rags': An early version of pole dancing, maybe? Of course, in the sixties, the panties mostly remained on and when off there was no clear view of the genitals, certainly no pubic hair, but what magnificent breasts! I didn't know it then, but I had found the forerunner of the Nordic Goddess.

I found a suitably safe and obscure place to hide Jem, and I would return to it — her — in the vacations if there was no available girl on the horizon; maybe even if there were … Little did I know it then, but this whole process was all significantly ritualised and served to enhance the experience. So much so that I don't recall whether I 'used' the story to masturbate or simply to worship her. I presume I did masturbate, but the memory — I did warn you of the subjectivity here — was of awe. It provoked me to look for more; was this the beginning of an obsession? I was to find other similar magazines, but never another Jem, both literally and metaphorically.

During those school years I was thrown back on the Playboy alternative, remained dissatisfied, and did not find a satisfactory alternative. Then came a change of direction: my parents emigrated to Australia. I spent the years from sixteen to eighteen in Australia and the whole voyeuristic pattern took a back seat as I had some urgent catching-up to do. I was now at a co-educational high school; the girls were tanned and gorgeous with the longest legs I had ever seen, the sun shone and my English accent was a winner.

Was this to be the end of the 'parallel pathway' in my psychosexual development? No, it wasn't. I now re-entered the boy meets girl arena with a different perspective. I had done my catching-up, discovered my sexuality and developed skills in relating to girls, who were rapidly becoming women. On a concealed level I had no difficulty with my experience as a neophyte consumer, as I was forming successful relationships and experimenting sexually. I presumed that, now this was occurring, the consumer would die and the experiences enjoyed there were but a precursor and preparation for external relationships. I rationalised that the consumer had been attempting to discover what my education had lacked and was, therefore, appropriate. I was also in Australia that, in the late nineteen-sixties, effectively precluded any pornographic pursuit. I was wrong on all counts.

In fact, I might not be writing this book at all if there hadn't been a twist or two in the tale. The first was that I gained a place at a very prestigious university – an opportunity not to be foregone – and to satisfy some of the university entrance requirements I returned to England and my old boarding school for a few months. It was at this stage that I viewed my first pornography of the hardcore variety. One of the other students had procured some material from abroad. He wasn't stupid enough to bring this into a boarding school, but he did have a brochure of products, which he gave to me to look at.

At first sight, the graphics in the brochure weren't all that attractive, but it was pictures of people having sex, plus doing a few other sexual things with a coke bottle, I recall. Now I had some graphics to educate and stimulate me as some of the practices in the pictures went beyond my experience to date. I do recall the pictures as being relatively vulgar and that was to remain the tenure of any sporadic exposure – which was usually in the possession of others – well into my university days. Yet, in spite of the relative vulgarity, there was something that remained attractive and, with the flowering of varied sexual experiences, I now found myself confused. There was something in all this very limited exposure that I felt went beyond my current sexual experiences. Of course, this found some pathological reflection: I must be somehow sexually sick, deviant or perverted. Don't be disappointed, I will be describing what these fantasies and actions were – and some still are – in due course.

If I was a sick puppy, there were presumably others like me, if the availability of such material and my school experience was anything to go by; although being "boys" we didn't discuss it. This was reinforced at university with my first exposure to a "blue movie". It was at a party when the word went around that there was to be a movie show, for anyone who was interested. I went into a reasonably crowded room, possibly all male, although I cannot be certain of this in hindsight. The host was a fellow student and obviously studious of the genre, as he circulated some pornographic magazines to look at whilst he set up the projector. The movies were 8mm and therefore silent: Basically, they enacted the sort of scenes that I had seen in picture form up until that time and I did not find them particularly attractive or stimulating, probably abetted by the poor production values.

One of the magazines had a picture series I do remember, however. It was simple: A man and a heavily made-up attractive woman having varied sex. There was a lot of oral contact and I saw my first anal penetration scene, which excited me and left me even more confused. There was also my first sight of a cumshot; the man was ejaculating into the woman's mouth, whilst she looked at the camera and continued to suck his still erect penis with semen dribbling from the corners of her mouth. It was of interest to me that the magazine rather than the actual film enactment of sex had a more sustaining effect on my memory.

I don't fully recall the pattern from here and there were several reasons for this. These could include that there wasn't any further significant exposure during this period and I was in a relationship. As you can note from the account to date, there is a clear recall of the pattern and distinct memories of the images that had a deep emotional impact on me. I now realise that emotion is a powerful factor in memory and crystallises the experience in a way that makes it easily available to recall. What the nature of the emotion was I could not readily determine, and it became easily submerged for reasons that I will come to shortly. The effect of this is that the memory stays and, if unexplored, will almost demand re-examination and re-experience, unless the will is strong enough to repress this avenue. Emotion is, therefore, a powerful driver of our experience and almost demands its full realisation by virtue of the literal or symbolic significance of the memory, in which it is contained.

You will note that this account has qualities of obsession and addiction about it. It will not be my main thrust to continue examining the experiences from this perspective, as the pathological route I find largely unrewarding, uncreative and not usually conducive to true healing. This is particularly so if it is the dominant or only route available, which I believe to be the case in modern society. It is more my contention that embedded in obsession and addiction are emotionally significant issues — and memories — that demand appreciation, understanding and psychological integration, not pathologising and judging.

You may also note embedded in my account features that pertain to the more modern issue of "repressed memory syndrome". In essence, my impression, such as with the memories in this account, is that emotionally significant experiences – either positive or negative – do exactly the opposite: it is almost as if they are 'burnt' into the memory. I think this is purposeful: to alert, guide and inform the experiencer into the future. I suppose there may be an argument that overwhelming and dark experiences could be repressed and only retrievable by techniques like hypnosis, but my professional experience is that they are not recorded or registered at all.

I think there is another aspect to repressed memory as a "syndrome" that is being ignored in our culture, and one this book will explore in some detail: The imagination is engaged by the emotion as at least a component of the recalled memory and that this is deeply significant, even fundamental to healing and personal evolution. With overwhelming experiences and no memory, the imagination may occupy the entirety of the so-called memory. It is unfortunate that such imaginative reconstruction is too often construed in a literal rather than a symbolic manner.

I did not understand the role of emotion, imagination and memory in the detail outlined above at the time of the described experiences. There will be considerably more reference to it as we progress to match my own developing insight and understanding, so please don't be surprised if the initial exploration of this vast and contentious field is not entirely clarified by the above foray. All that notwithstanding, at the time, I chose my willpower to avoid any further exploration as a consumer and this was assisted by my first extensive sexual relationship. My previous experiences had been casual and sometimes progressing to a relationship, but the difference in this one was the intensity and the exploration, which made the willpower option somewhat easier to maintain.

The relationship was extremely sexually intense. There was little common ground to it as a relationship otherwise, so it was sustained by the sex itself. This was frequent, mutually satisfying and relatively free of emotion, particularly that which could lead to expectation and entanglement. This did not stop the emotion creeping in, however, as I started to feel guilty about the sheer indulgence with a lack of any direction or commitment and presumed she did too. In hindsight, this guilt was obviously conditioned and strong enough to direct our behaviour. We attempted to define a relationship without intercourse and found ourselves in a vicious cycle when this failed. We tried alternatives, initially oral sex, but this drove us to a genital frenzy and accidental anal sex with the excess of fluids. This was mutually enjoyable and wordlessly repeated; I was surprised … and even more confused.

The specific sexual issues above I will explore in more detail as we progress, so I would like to take a detour into the emotional realms and their significance at this stage. Although, in passing, you will have noticed that I was beginning to integrate some of what is mainstream pornography into my active sexuality. The oral sex I could entertain, the anal left me confused as I was given to associate it with homosexuality … but I enjoyed it nonetheless.

It would be easy to see all this as derived from the lack of functionality of the relationship. Apart from any psychoanalytic viewpoint pertaining to repression, sublimation and reaction formation, there is the consideration of the pornographic elements being related to the dysfunctionality of the relationship itself. That is, from the conventional moral perspective, these activities were a product of the lack of respect and love. These are, in summary, all common criticisms to support what I will call the "censorship position" … a loose amalgamation of the moral majority: being the religious majority, elements of the psychological and sociological professions, the legal fraternity and the pro-censorship feminists.

I became overwhelmingly confused and guilty about my relationship. I was starting to experience a plethora of emotions, but in a chaotic and intense manner. I did not have the mechanisms to deal with them. I tried repression as, after all, this had worked for the earlier consumer – or had it? Was it now 'out of the box' and in the mainstream of my sexuality? Was I now a 'sick puppy', a pervert? I tried repression even harder as the emotions were so intense. I used alcohol as a medication and sport as a diversion. Then I realised I had some examinations on the horizon. A seeming nuisance, as up to this time I had never had trouble with exams.

I thought I had passed these satisfactorily and was devastated to be called for a follow-up interview to assess whether I should be passed in two of the four examinations. The interviews went well, however, and I was sure I had passed the other two, so maybe I had 'got away with it'. I hadn't: Not only did I fail one of the interviews and hence that exam, I had failed outright one of the two others. I was now faced with a summer of repeating those two, whilst my colleagues went punting on the river with their girlfriends and supped ales in the pubs that dotted the banks. I realised I had had a nervous breakdown and nobody, least of all myself, had noticed.

Appraisal time: I examined the emotional state I had been through and came to the conclusion that it was unacceptable at best and dangerous at worst. I felt threatened, insecure, frightened and … quite alone. I subsequently discovered that my ex-partner was in another relationship and seemed to have moved on comfortably without experiencing the difficulties that I had, which further confused me. Hadn't it brought up for her what it had for me? Maybe I was that sick puppy and maybe, just maybe, the pornography was to blame. Out came willpower and repression ... and alcohol.

I put my head down over the next few months, determined to pass the repeat exams. Maybe the so-called moral majority was right, I had taken a fork in the road marked "depravity" and "madness" and found they were right. I was back on track and passed. I also started a new relationship and I did not find the sexuality threatening in the way the previous one had been. It felt safe and I concluded that it was more conventionally normal and that there had been something amiss in the previous relationship, which I could not identify beyond guilt, except that it was characterised by intense sexual indulgence.

In this and subsequent encounters, any indulgence and experimentation would be contained in the relationship, which made it all right – at least that was my reasoning. I now had the experience of several differing, sometimes contrasting relationships, with the difference being primarily the sexual content and, from my perspective, my relationship to my own sexuality.

I have briefly identified at least two relationships, amongst others, to highlight my rather haphazard entry into adult life and a questionable sexual adjustment within it. There is more experience I could relate, but the main features I want to identify at this point in time are how my sexuality was 'informed' by pornography, the emotional confusion in adult sexuality and the partial resolution at a psychological level. I have done this by choosing symbolically contrasting relationships and my experiences of them.

I completed my degree studies at university and moved on to hospital training. All was well ... until I happened across that little book and magazine shop. Well, that isn't the entire truth. With the relaxing of legality and living in a large city, there was starting to be more of an open availability of sexual material, although difficult to access. I tried accessing it but was largely dissatisfied, as the material I received in response to advertisements in the glossy magazines were rarely what was portrayed; but whom could you complain to, as it was technically illegal? Also, if I was in a relationship, I made a point of declaring my consumption, although up to this point in time it was not a shared experience. It was a masturbatory tool, contained in the relationship along with varied sexual practice, so all was well. I had enough psychological maturity now to recognise that repression wasn't a good idea, so this seemed safe and healthier.

Then I found myself in the rear of the magazine shop and left in an excited fashion, keen to return home and explore the contents I had purchased (I had "seized the day" and brought two). It was the magazine with the Goddess that caught my imagination, which had been the case even in the shop. I wrote to the publisher and was able to buy direct, although the English customs, acting as de facto censors, received an approximately equal share – I still wonder if they destroyed them! By the time I had completed my medical studies, I had a small library of some twenty, exclusively of the same magazine. I considered myself a consumer, but justified as one of erotography rather than pornography. The whole issue had stabilised, the consumer was back and seemingly integrated. The only problem was that I would take up a medical position back in Australia. I would have to leave or destroy the magazines. How would the consumer cope?

We will return to him.

However, this book is not a simple "Confessions of a Pornographer", it is an attempt to use my personal experience to explore the pornographic phenomenon. In this respect, there is a perceived danger that it becomes seen as either a self-indulgent sexual autobiography or an attempt at further healing, therapy or psychological integration. It is, of course, possible to entertain all these possibilities and arguments. I will demonstrate a thread of arrogance though, as usually these are projections; that is, unresolved issues in the person making such a judgement. I don't hold my position as the exclusive truth and therefore right, but what I do hold is that it is authentically portrayed and such arguments and criticisms may be a defence against where my position might lead. It is always easier to shoot the messenger.

I would like to clarify my position: It is essential that I use my personal experience as this book is, after all, offered from the consumer's perspective. What has been written above goes into a fair amount of autobiographical detail but now, with the arrival of the Goddess, the autobiographical perspective can retreat somewhat as we explore the detailed inner and outer perspectives in a more collective sense, using my experience as a lens or window into these domains so that they have relevance to you, the reader.

First an interlude to explore some of the issues that have arisen to date: An analysis of the Goddess story would be a fitting place to start. The magazine was called "Private" and was the initiator of a huge business. Private remains European; is a publicly listed company, and one of the biggest producers of pornography in the world. At that early stage the editor, photographer and publisher – Berth Milton – had just emerged from having his magazine periodically confiscated by the police in Sweden. This was the era when pornography became legal, most notably in Denmark. The magazine, number seventeen, was produced in 1970 and had sixty-six pages. There were two photo stories, one of twelve and another of twenty-two pages. The magazine was otherwise full of articles, letters, stories and photographically illustrated reports, with only a handful of these other pages containing pornographic photography or art. The written languages were English, German and French, with Swedish additionally in the photo stories.

In fact, the publisher referred to the material as "erotographic" and the mission statement read: "We at Private wish to promote a more liberal attitude towards sex, and a better understanding of all sexual inclinations. We believe that sex is both natural and enjoyable, and therefore it is most definitely wrong to attempt to hide or feel ashamed about it. Furthermore, we know that good erotography has a positive and stimulating effect on human sexuality." (Quoted verbatim and in total.)

At this early stage of our exploration, you may agree or disagree with this statement. Maybe you might like to take note of your reactions and opinions regarding it and then compare when you re-read it, having finished this book. I certainly resonated with it; even if it only justified my position, it made me feel less psychically divided.

The first story was twelve pages, only six of which showed sexual contact between a man (face unseen) and a woman, who was voluptuous, natural and very attractive. The second was twenty-two pages and contained the Goddess. The story is actually entitled: "The Goddesses of Galaxia". Science fiction is a common pornographic theme that supports the 'escapism' and 'fantasy' elements, endorsing acceptability. The first six pages are of the Captain and First Officer, both women, in various non-pornographic poses. The Captain wears a brief 'uniform' and boots, whilst the Officer is dressed in a leather bikini and mask, indicating a light fetish theme, although the mask disappears after two pages. The next twelve pages are devoted to an increasing lesbian encounter; the contact includes digital contact, or fingering of the pussy, and some cunnilingus, or licking of it. The interaction is relatively light and playful from a sexual perspective.

In the last four pages the couple have 'captured' a man to test his libido on the pretext of seeing if the planet (Earth) would be suitable for respite for such female voyagers from Galaxia into the future. These comprise four pictures only. In the first we see an intercourse scene in the missionary position and from below; that is, back towards the genitals. Neither figure is identifiable, but the text and setting implicate the captain. In the next, the man (again, we never see his face) is astride the captain, who is holding his cock with some semen evident on her stomach. The last two are the ones that had such an effect on me and are both full-page.

In the first page, the Captain is gripping the man's cock and we see the glans (head) of his cock several inches away with an initial stream of semen heading toward and landing on the Captain's cheek. The First Officer is to one side and slightly behind the Captain; both have their mouths open and eyes closed. In the next, the cock has finished ejaculating and the Captain's hand obscures the glans, so we see just the base of his cock. She does not suck the cock at any stage. The Captain has sperm on her cheek with one shot across her closed eye, forehead and into her hair. It is also dribbling down her cheeks and is splattered across her throat and shoulder. The First Officer has sperm mainly around her mouth and chin and her expression is relatively unchanged, whilst the Captain has a seemingly natural and gratified smile.

Private also did, and still does, produce a centrefold in the manner of Playboy but of remarkably different content. There is an element of upstaging and unintentional satire here. There is even a page of the magazine devoted to selected quotes from an American report entitled: "The Illustrated Report of the Commission on Obscenity and Pornography". In addition to several quotes delivered to support Private's position, one makes reference to Playboy: "The unquestioned quality leader in porno magazines comes from Sweden. Private eclipses all other magazines, regardless of country of origin, in quality of photography and reproduction, not to mention aestics (sic) of design and layout, selection of models, etc. If (sic) features a 'gatefold' centerspread that Playboy would never dare try, and it is in a multi-language format." (Quoted verbatim and in total.)

In this particular issue, the Captain once again features in the centrefold and is part-reclining in an armchair, wearing her uniform and boots, with her thighs raised and spread. She is wearing no underwear and her pussy has sperm over it, although it is not clear where this has come from. My fantasy at the time – and still – is that it was the photographer Milton's ejaculate.

I have described my experience earlier and moved to a limited analysis of the magazine. There has been an amount of titillation in this; I am deliberately attempting to draw you into the experience in a safe manner so that you will be in a better position to appreciate the inner and outer perspectives I am about to embark upon.

Please excuse my rather Machiavellian tactics – although I do hope they have worked.

I am going to use the terms moral and ethical to mirror what I refer to as the inner and outer, or alternatively introverted and extraverted perspectives. This may not completely match the conventional or philosophical interpretations, or even your understanding of what these terms mean, as they are conventionally often used interchangeably and confusingly, so I will elaborate. The inner, or moral, perspective is one of depth and associated with values such as honesty, integrity, respect and beauty. In many respects these values are timeless and approach the term archetype we discussed earlier. Some, such as honesty, would more easily appear to be constant throughout time, whereas others, such as beauty, would seem more fluid and variable, although resting on timeless principles. I would like to think that, when individually constellated, such values constitute what I think of as the soul for that individual. We will have more to say of this later.

The outer, or ethical, perspective is the reflection of morality within our society and the external world. As such it would be expected that an ethical position would reflect and codify the moral one. However, the ethical position is subject to the fashion of the time and the dominant values a society may hold. It is also subject to manipulation and control. Ethics are commonly associated with religious institutions and the legal profession in the form of jurisprudence, although these institutions would seem to have a tenuous and ambiguous hold on the relationship between ethics and morality in our time.

I am going to make an initial examination of these perspectives to the point we have arrived at in my reflections. These themes will then continue throughout the book with the inner and moral perspective increasingly coming to the fore and commensurate with the position of examining pornography from the consumer's perspective. It is the inner or moral perspective that I believe needs examining and thus to restore the balance to the outer and ethical position that has dominated the arguments about pornography to date. What I will do here is briefly examine the inner perspective inasmuch as it refers to my account to this point and then do a similar analysis of the outer leading into a more detailed society and cultural one in the next chapter. After that we will be taking an increasingly inner and moral approach to my unravelling experiences and analysis, allowing it to reflect back into the outer only when relevant.

In colloquial language, the inner perspective left me wondering whether I was a "sick puppy". Up until the time I stumbled across the Goddess, this had been a serious consideration, notwithstanding some fleeting intimations of what was to emerge, such as with Jem. I had basically used pornography as a tool of sexual exploration in the absence of adequate preparation and ritual initiation into it, but didn't realise this until much later. As a consequence, I was undertaking an enquiry, drawn by my instincts and intuition, which was reflected in society as wrong. How did I cope with this? With great difficulty, as you have seen, up to and including a nervous breakdown of psychotic intensity. I had no detailed resources or instructions on how to negotiate what was happening to me; these would only come much later.

In essence, I had fluctuated between the poles of repression and indulgence, culminating in a partial integration. The indulgence was so at variance with the cultural "morality" – read ethics – that I was bound to question my psychological health. Even though I quickly learnt the intellectual tools to counter a lot of this, it did not appease my deeper emotional state and sometimes even added to the confusion, as I felt that I was justifying or rationalising my position. The rather tortuous outcome of this was a relatively contained situation in the context of a socially accepted institution: a stable relationship.

What of the features of the consumption? Did I explore these to qualify that if I was a sick puppy, then how sick was I? To some extent I did. I realised that in the scheme of things my tastes were – generally – reflected to some degree in my relationships and sexual practices, with a couple of notable exceptions. My consumption was generally of a heterosexual nature. I was drawn a little toward some extremes, fetishism, for example, but usually in a light manner. The First Officer's outfit, minus the mask, is an example, plus suspenders and stockings are always a hit. These aspects I was to find fairly common in consumption and reflected in the frequency that they are portrayed. I usually enjoyed partial clothing and outside settings as a variation. Lesbian contact was not significant yet enjoyable, but only if it was incorporated in a larger heterosexual context, somewhat like the Goddess story.

This last feature – lesbianism and a man – brought in an issue that theoretically could not be contained in a normal relationship, which was sexual activity involving more than two people. This was an extremely common feature in what I had been exposed to up till that time, most notably in what is called threesomes, although this did extend to more complex combinations. At first, and as reflected in the Goddess story, this revolved around a man – obviously me – and two women. This is commonly seen as the archetypal male fantasy and it certainly was for me, although it has changed importantly and significantly over time. Initially, I had to accept the fact that this would forever remain a fantasy in the boundaries I had set myself regarding sexual relationships. I presumed normal people did not indulge in acting out such fantasies, except in front of a camera or when money was involved.

I was and am wrong.

The difference between an extended focus on the women with men nondescript – even partially invisible – plus a significant focus on anal sex and the dominance of the external cumshot we will have cause to examine in detail. At this time, I simply accepted the relative invisibility of the male(s) as an invitation to 'step into' the fantasy. The cumshots I enjoyed, but could not explain why. Anal sex raised more than a few difficulties initially, as it was coupled with a personal enjoyment that was fundamentally different from vaginal sex. Of course, I examined the latent homosexual angle: was this the case? Well, I have never found men particularly sexually attractive and I had – and still have – no desire to have a cock in my arse. Maybe putting it in a woman's arse was something about power? I felt this was closer to the mark, but the fact that my limited experience informed me that women 'got off' on anal sex as well I found countered the straightforward power argument and confused me. Maybe I was stepping on the edge of sexual 'discipline' or sadomasochism ...

(A minor aside... I have introduced the word "arse" for reference to anal sex. The word "ass" is becoming increasingly popular, particularly in America, which I find amusing, as the ass is a member of the horse family and considered stupid! I actually find arse a more accurate term, as well as being spelt how I speak it. I will continue to use it, although you may wish to substitute ass. Out of interest, Australia lies somewhere between Europe and America on this point.)

All in all, and after appreciable emotional turmoil plus limited resources, I came to the conclusion that I was only a mildly sick puppy who appreciated a varied and intense sexual repertoire but who recognised that some, if not all, of the features I enjoyed in consumerism may be confined to my fantasy world.

In this respect, two issues helped greatly. The first was the breakdown. Whilst my solution to it was relatively incomplete, it did offer some release, respite and the attainment of a point of stability in the whole process. Up to that time, these issues emotionally racked me, and the breakdown allowed them to emerge and discharge so as to provide me with a – temporary – place of peace. The second was the Goddess. I stepped into a culture (Scandinavian), which had negotiated and examined this territory and found pornography acceptable in mainstream society. This gave me the perspective of the relativity of the cultural and associated ethical position, and that England may simply be slow on the issue of such social change. I was to find out it was more than just England.

Before I came back to Australia, I went to Denmark and Sweden and experienced that this impression was not just reflected in pornographic exports, it quietly permeated the culture. What the Goddess did was to open up the domain of nature and beauty and to incorporate sexuality into it in a seamless fashion. From my inner world perspective, I found nothing sick in this, I actually found it quite healthy and normal, but this left me with a mountain to climb. Some of this climb is hinted at in the medium that features most strongly in my memory: photography.

In Sweden, I had seen live sex – two couples in separate performances – and a large-screen film in Denmark. I also had access to 8mm films through a Publican employer whilst I was completing my studies. Further, I saw a range of photographic materials with the progressive decline of restrictions in England. So, what was it about photographic pornography that most attracted me? Strangely, I did not explore this question much at the time, as I presumed that it was simply that the medium that had featured the Goddess and Private contained the features of the pornographic that I found personally stimulating. I thought that once the cinema embraced the genre this avenue would lessen in significance. It hasn't, so it might be interesting to provide a limited retrospective analysis, as this will lead to one of the major themes of the book.

The photographic imagery in pornography engages the imagination in a way that other media do not. Film provides a reality that is attractive and is why it is often a shared experience. Photography can go beyond this artistically and is more often associated with solitary masturbation. I have indicated earlier, with the faceless men, how this might engage the male viewer as enacting the scenes portrayed. There are a lot of film productions that try and further this by having the woman look at the camera whilst performing. To my mind, this is not as effective as you might imagine it could be, and it begs the question as to why. One reason may be that when this is not the case the viewer actually has to step into the scene; the fantasy is more active than passive. It may also be that when the woman performer looks at the camera the picture loses its 'reality' or genuineness. The viewer can also 'fill in the gaps' with photography; that is, the shots that are 'missing' between frames, or even construct imaginatively some of his – or her – own. I argue that this engages the imagination in direct and varied ways, which go well beyond the simple act of viewing sex for masturbation.

Now let's move to the outer and ethical perspective, some of which is inevitably embedded in the above. This second perspective is reflected in the developmental, cultural and social dimensions of my experience. In essence, it is that viewing pornography was "wrong". By and large, my account to date reflects an initial dominance of this perspective, then a progressive moving away from it toward the inner moral one as my experiences and knowledge deepened. I am not going to entirely delude myself that the relationship between morality and ethics was seriously disrupted in my upbringing and that this explains my developmental difficulties with pornography as a substitute for a failure of adequate preparation and initiation into sexuality, but it does bear more than a little reflection.

With the vision of hindsight, which now encompasses approximately two generations and the advent of modern phenomena like the Internet that transgress the boundaries in which I grew up, I feel I can justifiably criticise the ethical standards I was raised in. Sexuality was simply not talked about. There was no sex education at school and my account of the "sex education lesson" I received at home has already been discussed. The media was limited and also subject to similar censorship principles.

In the so-called "Age of Enlightenment" – approximately the last three hundred years – we have seen the advent of reason and rationality and the flowering of science and their domination of our worldview. Religion previously held a dominant position, including over the State, whereas in my upbringing it had become relatively marginalised. Does that mean that it had lost its influence and control? Not at all, as it still held sway in the domain of ethical standards and the main tool of control was sexuality.

My general thesis is that medical science came to control birth and death, with religion retaining sexuality in the carve-up of the Great Cycle of Existence. It is this appropriation and use of it for means of social and individual control that I want to highlight. More specifically, with respect to sexuality, is that the concept of our individuality – our soul – has become diminished in Western religion and that it is only through formal religious contact and ceremony that we have contact with the spiritual world. In other words, control sexuality and you control the person. How do you do this? Guilt and shame: Of course, it is not as simple and clear as that, but it is worth stating my personal and reflected position in this regard before qualifying it, which I will now do in some detail.

The other more personal, recent and significant factor in any ethical distortion was that I was raised in the wake of the Second World War and my adolescence was overshadowed by this fact, even though it was during the so-called sexual revolution of the sixties. Well, I, for one, didn't experience much of the revolution. I have no doubt it occurred and foreshadowed the liberation I have subsequently experienced, but it was not a palpable movement for many others, including myself, at the time. More than a revolution, I believe the sixties marked a turning of the tide in the influences that hitherto had dominated the twentieth century and that these new influences have continued. I feel I have 'picked up' on these changes at various points in my development.

More critically, the wars and social changes of the early twentieth century, such as the Great Depression, had devastating effects on the world, the Western world in general and men in particular. Taking the most able and boldest of men and killing a significant number, as well as emotionally traumatising the remainder, would have significant and ongoing effects on the population as a whole. What I have alluded to earlier and want to highlight here is the effect it would have on the maturation of subsequent generations, particularly the males, due to the disruption of the initiatory process.

We are becoming increasingly aware of the importance of mentors and initiation in the developmental process, partly because of their absence in our own culture and partly also because of our windows into other cultures. Added to this is the previously held view that such practices and processes were primitive and that we had "outgrown" them. Although we could examine many social issues for the absence of initiation, I obviously want to focus on the sexual. In particular, I want to highlight that the absence of males as mentors, either by physical death or the psychological death of emotional trauma, has disrupted the psychosexual development of ongoing generations, particularly the males.

That this was my experience has already been stated. That the revolution of the sixties attempted to restore this balance – from a sexual perspective – is also apparent, although my experience was that it was marginal, associated with social groups uncommon to me and too drug-oriented. The changes of the sixties have had their creative effect and moved into the mainstream and, in this way, guided me in my own adult initiations through territory that might have been better explored in my adolescence.

These changes, combined with a distancing from the devastating effects of the early twentieth century, plus the mixed blessings of technology and the Internet, have all combined to bring pornography into the social position it now enjoys.

So, let's take a detour into exactly what that position is from an Australian perspective specifically, but applicable throughout the entire Western world.

2

The Who, How, What and Why of Modern Pornography

Who are they, these modern consumers? How do they get their porn? What are they actually watching? And why do they watch it? These are overlapping questions that I will attempt to answer as we take a journey through pornography in the early twenty-first century. After I initially planned this work, I was greatly assisted by the publication of a book called *The Porn Report*, compiled and written by three senior Australian academics and based on a research project funded by the Australian Research Council. Of interest is that it is written by two women and one man, the latter a self-acknowledged gay. I will be using their information and findings unless otherwise stated, as a backdrop to this chapter and then temper it with my own experience.

"We recognise that pornography is a subject on which people will always hold strong moral or political or religious views," and "Passionate debates about the cultural, social and moral effects of pornography have a long history" are two quotes that occur in the introduction. The tone is being set and the authors are on the outside looking in, feeling that informed debate is essential for a variety of reasons: Who consumes it, how it affects them, and the concern of exposure to children being the nominated ones. Already, as if you weren't aware, the tone is highly charged and emotional, which the authors themselves occasionally allow to affect their conclusions, as we shall discover. I would surmise that this is also the result of emotional challenges within themselves. However, overall, their approach is solid, informed and meets both my personal impressions and also experience, as well as providing a clear picture of the pornographic industry in Australia. This does not limit the conclusions that the authors draw, as their analysis inevitably extends to overseas (particularly with respect to porn products) and it would not be drawing a long bow to say these conclusions would be common to the Western world in general, which the evidence supports.

As I outlined earlier, my approach is generally restricted to mainstream porn, this being non-violent and sexually explicit material. As this is the category the authors are also dealing with, it is relatively safe to draw on their conclusions. The initial statistic is a broad-based one: "Three-quarters of Australians are comfortable with the idea of non-violent erotica being available to adults." I find the choice of the word erotica telling: Is this an attempt by the authors to define porn in a more acceptable way, thus supporting their position that it is part of the mainstream anyway, so let's sanitise it? Or does it indicate their collective emotional position with respect to porn? I suggest that both could be true. Add to this the fact that they found that one third of adult Australians are consumers – a figure also found in other Western countries – then a book such as theirs is long overdue. It is also time this silent consumer group, moving toward a majority, was heard against their vociferous, often prejudiced and inaccurate opponents, who are obviously becoming the minority.

This brings up an interesting issue: what exactly is pornography? An Oxford English Dictionary definition: "Explicit presentation of sexual activity in books, films etc. for erotic, not aesthetic, purpose." It derives from the Greek *porne* meaning a prostitute. Hmmm, makes you think a bit? Didn't

Private mention the word "aesthetic" – although miss-spelled – in its mission statement regarding the magazine? Does that make it or define it as a work of art rather than pornography? Was Private using the word "erotography" to get away from the sleazy image? Now erotic in the same Dictionary: "Of or arousing sexual passion or excitement", which derives from the Greek Eros. Incidentally, Eros is the god of love ... and we will be meeting him again. In the interim, doesn't this all sound a bit circular and confused?

The word pornography was used by historians to describe erotic art found by archaeologists in the Pompeii ruins, according to the authors of *The Porn Report*. Doesn't this further heighten the confusion and blur the boundaries? Why did they choose such an emotionally loaded and prejudicial term in the first place? No wonder there is a strong – and heated – current debate in Australia about art and pornography.

So, let's simplify the argument: Pornography derives from a word that means prostitute, the moral implication of which is obvious. However, what is erotic and not aesthetic? Is this in the eye of the beholder? Can the two be so readily distinguished? Is something that arouses sexual passion automatically not aesthetic?

I am not an ethicist, but let me offer a relatively simple way out of the dilemma. We are tending to look at the whole issue in a binary, or either-or perspective. What about being more inclusive and consider that erotic material can be both pornographic and aesthetic – they are simply at the two ends of a spectrum. Frankly, I find a great deal of porn relatively un-aesthetic, and this doesn't help its mainstream integration, a fact to which we will return. I am back to favouring the term erotography to cover the whole field and pornography to refer to the less aesthetic end of the spectrum, but for convenience, I will continue to primarily use the word pornography or porn.

Yes, you say, but you haven't yet actually said what porn is, have you? Well, I have, in a round-about sort of way. So, here goes: Pornography is sexually explicit material designed for erotic stimulation. To my mind, this is automatically non-violent and for sexually responsive people – adults – only. I do not consider the depiction of some extreme practices, currently considered as pornography, as primarily sexual and would thus exclude them from the definition. If I had my way, I'd strike the word pornography from history and memory and simply use erotography in its place as in the above definition; but porn it has become and is, so I will continue to refer to it as such.

I'm on a roll, so let's muddy the water even further: Why differentiate "hard" and "soft" porn? (I'm sure it's not the state of the male erection this refers to; then again, maybe it might be!) Surely according to the definition porn is porn. So, if "hardcore" is referring to sexually explicit material, why the need to define a "soft" version? Is it just the moral minority and its tool of censorship merely widening the net to include nudity? In doing this, does nude art become pornographic? In particular, does artwork – assuming it has an aesthetic value – that includes nude children become pornographic and hence paedophilic, when nude adult material is not considered pornographic? Is Playboy porn or art … or both? Does the depiction of sexual acts that don't include any genital views constitute porn?

My conclusion is that most in the moral minority have vivid imaginations and are projecting their own unseen prejudices – not to mention sexual proclivities by their choices – onto what they are judging. I would love to hear some of their secret fantasies and dreams. This is not to belittle the role and function of the imagination, about which I will have a lot more to say; in fact, it provides further support for its place, if my argument has any validity. Am I implying that there are members of the moral minority who are vicarious consumers? Yes, I am. Let me challenge you, the reader, by asking if any of the above questions has elicited an emotional response? Then I suggest this is an area of internal exploration rather than external projection.

After all, if the depiction of graphic sexuality creates mental disturbance if disclosed to the pre-adolescent, then how did the children of other and ancient cultures that do and have such material depicted on their temple walls not become depraved? You might argue that this could be the cause of Rome's demise, although I believe that was for other reasons, but that doesn't account for the rich and varied cultures like ancient India. This is not to say I am arguing for children to have the right to pornography on the Internet, so how do we explain this apparent anomaly?

Let me construct a likely explanation. I suggest that it is only with the advent of the Age of Reason and, in particular, the scientific era that things have become so separated. Science and religion are poles apart and the concept of soul has been left out to survive effectively rudderless. Sexuality is intimately connected with the soul and the Great Cycle of Existence, and I argue that exposure to it in a harmonious and ritual context is essential for our psychological well-being. How do we cope with sexual acts being portrayed on temple walls in times past in places such as India? Maybe because the sexual and the spiritual were not divided and the sexual was seen as an authentic pathway to spirituality. Maybe this depiction was an instruction to the adolescent and of disinterest to the child, until the hormones began to percolate. What I am effectively saying is that, at other times and in other present-day cultures, the sexual and spiritual had and have not become so separated. Where they have, as in our modern culture, I argue it is for religious, social or political control.

This is not a work that will cover the history of porn to any great extent, so I will restrict myself to a more recent sketch that is relevant to the current perspective. There are works that do this in great detail, such as Linda Williams in *Hard Core* (her spelling), which has become seminal in the field and spawned an academic basis for the study of pornography. The advent of porn as a category would seem to be relatively recent, quite prejudicial and would not seem to have been helped by the vocations and professions that might have re-established the role and place of the erotic, such as conventional religion, medicine and psychology.

My experience came in at the tail end of the twentieth century and for the sake of the main thrust of this book we will be excluding erotic art. For most of that time, photography and cinematography were the main media. Photography, in particular, and possibly because of some of the arguments I posed in the previous chapter, was more common than we are given to think and much has been retrieved from private collections and archives, even catalogued into modern books. Cinematography is obviously more recent and most characterised by the "stag movie". The stag contained many genital shots commonly called "beaver", if of the female genitals. As an aside, the choice of titles such as beaver shots and stag movies are interesting in and of themselves, lending them to symbolic enquiry. Sexual activity included the relatively unseen male, often with shoes and socks still on, but did not highlight what is now an indispensable part of modern porn: the cumshot.

This is where I came in, although the movies had progressed to the 8mm variety and usually from Europe. This meant they were not now usually watched in a collectively male setting, as with the stag movie, and could be used as a masturbatory aid; maybe that is why the cumshot started to predominate in the movies?

I was now in Australia and, lo and behold, times had changed. The seedy bookshop of downtown London had re-materialised in Perth, much like Dr Who's Tardis, and Private was back on the agenda. I also managed to get some 8mm films from Denmark through the customs, which were also performing a censorship function not unlike the one I had experienced in London. So, with contact re-established, life moved on at a gentle pace with the previously integrated position.

We are now in hyper-drive. Linda Lovelace strutted her stuff or, more specifically, her oral abilities in the now (in)famous "Deep Throat" (1972) and the big screen was in the picture. The VCR superseded this brief flowering and the remote control – along with the erect penis – was back in the solitary hand, rather than the 'dirty raincoat brigade' associated with the public arena. Then the videotape morphed into the DVD and the Internet arrived. Porn paradise had simultaneously emerged from the consumer's perspective. What had been a trickle is now a veritable flood. (Earlier I used the term 'explosion' synonymously with 'flood'. Fire and water, how Biblical!)

You might ask how my own interests and sexual development was going during this period? Before the floodgates opened in the years before the turn of the century and prior to obtaining a VCR, my pornographic interests remained predominantly with Private and I was in a relationship that reconciled much of the earlier ones I have described above. It was intimate at many levels and was intensely sexual. I had the opportunity of exploring my sexuality at a depth I had not experienced before. Although pornography was still not a shared experience, I felt that it substantially and creatively contributed to the sexual exploration and subsequently the relationship itself. What was not working for us, however, were other personal differences and our inability to negotiate them.

As a consequence, I went into therapeutic analysis, as these difficulties were making me depressed. What this process achieved was recognition of my own feminine nature and how this was entangled in the relationship. It also helped me to see these projective features in general in my life and in pornographic imagery, in particular. Although the intimacy and love continued, in spite of the demise of the relationship, I was able to see the illusory nature of such an intense and passionate union, which forms the basis of the "love at first sight" phenomenon and also identifiable as so-called chemistry, or more quasi-spiritually as a soul-mate connection. Whilst I recognise the soul-mate phenomenon to have wider and deeper implications I have seen it commonly, within the therapeutic perspective, to be a justification or excuse for indulgence of a mutual sexual passion.

Whilst the experience of analysis marked a turning point in both my personal life and professional career direction, it did not change my relationship to porn and I continued as a consumer. I didn't raise it specifically as an issue to be 'dealt with' in therapy, as I was not now experiencing it as a problem. Indeed, since I had come to Australia, I felt it had contributed to my sexual development and my appreciation of the feminine and relationships in general. The relationship between the two I viewed as pivotal in many of these changes and developments and it is something I have seen extensively in others. I was also now quite keen to step into a deeper and broader experience of the erotic.

As a consumer, this was and is not all good. In the last decades of the twentieth century and in addition to the existing availability of photographic porn across Australia, video movies became available from the two Australian Territories, which is where porn distribution companies began to establish themselves. There are some curious mixed standards here, in that movie porn can be purchased within the Territories or from outside by mail order, although movies cannot be sold in the States themselves. I have used Private to guide me through the vast ocean, but even that now has its limitations. Private itself has, of course, undergone many changes and reflects many of the changes that impact on the current position. I will use the development of Private from the consumer angle up to floodgate time and, from that basis, take an increasingly broader overview, although retaining Private as a point of comparison.

By the time I came to Australia in the mid-seventies, Private was well into its stride, numbering now in the thirties, with a new magazine published bi-monthly and a reasonably settled format still under Milton's lens and control. From inception in 1965, there was rapid progress such that the number seventeen (1970) I obtained demonstrated the format I have described earlier (in chapter one). An analysis of the earlier publications revealed some interesting trends. The very first Private magazine was entirely of young women with genitals exposed, but not actively stimulated in any manner. These could be compared to a progression of the beaver shots of the stag movie era. There is in subsequent early magazines a progressive opening of the vaginal lips and digital stimulation with some light girl-to-girl contact, although minimal sexual content. The contact between women then becomes more sexual and the genitals start to become more exposed and manually stimulated.

Men's genitals then appear, and number eight shows the first intercourse scene, not heavily exposed, although this does occur in the next issue and in the following one, we see the first cumshot – interestingly in a threesome involving two women. Toys then become introduced and the multiple partner theme becomes slightly more evident with number fifteen showing the first story involving a gang bang (defined as more than two men with one woman) featuring three men, various toys, the first anal and double penetration (a woman having her vagina and anus penetrated simultaneously) all in the one story. However, multiple partners do not become a dominant theme in this era, with threesomes being more the norm, if they are present at all.

There is a mixture of photographic themes: commonly a solo woman with or without stimulation and toys, lesbian encounters, couple sex and a more complex story. Intermingled with this are various articles on subjects of varied sexual interest such as prostitution, sex shows and transsexuality. There is usually a pornographic story, letters, a written article called the "moral" and a pornographic art painting, plus other varied offerings. These tend to support the earlier stated mission statement and actively promote a liberal and censor-free sexual attitude. It also highlights one of Private's success themes, often ignored, which is the use of narrative and the invitation to the consumer to enter the publication in a personal manner. This could be by correspondence, but also to literally become an active sexual participant or performer in the magazine.

Simultaneous with the floodgates around the late nineteen-eighties/early nineteen-nineties was Private number one hundred. The format was still similar, with the addition of an amateur photo story – usually mimicking Milton's photographic style – and containing many of the sexual themes explored more sporadically elsewhere. In the late seventies, Private launched the sibling Pirate in a similar format, but with supposedly stronger content. The sex was apparently harder and rougher, but lacked the finesse, place of nature and accent on beauty that characterised Private. There were more toys, fetish dress, complex numbers and the introduction of themes such as fisting (the closed hand in the – usually – vagina) and golden showers or pissing (urination, specifically on a partner). Pirate ceased after only eight issues, but resurfaced in the early nineties with the floodgates. I'm not sure of the reasons for this period of absence, but suspect internal issues rather than specifically the harder sexual content and any censorship.

From here Private and Pirate ran parallel courses with similar formats and content, but a differing accent. The themes explored in Pirate, specifically pissing, made occasional appearances in Private, but died out there shortly after number one hundred. I do not know if this was for internal or external censorship reasons, probably a combination plus a commercial judgement. I do know that now Private has released all its magazines on the Internet that there has been a progressive retrospective removal of these themes, plus any stories that may indicate a girl under eighteen years of age. In some early issues, this age factor was not as contentious, as the sexual liberalisation in Sweden included questions about the age of consent and Milton did explore this. I suspect the conformity with self-regulation is a result of a wider agreement regarding internal censorship and governed by America. It is interesting that other European publications continue to explore these themes significantly with the exception of the age limit, which is now universally of performers eighteen years or over. The laws governing paedophilia and the potential consequences are obviously more stringent.

With the floodgates, Private moves into movie production. There is the publication of an additional two magazines, so that four are now released bi-monthly; there is consequently a lot of repetition. Milton gradually disappears and the publications become progressively more professional and the performers are also increasingly professional porn stars. There is a loss of the experimentation, artistic accent, role and place of nature and the natural beauty that characterised the earlier publications. This is a theme not isolated to Private, but I, for one, regret the changes. Private remains European but bridges the divide between

Europe and America and is now enormous as a business. Although I continue to peruse Private electronically it has lost the romance, passion and enquiry that marked the period to the floodgates. I know I am not alone in this regret.

Is this just a justification? I obviously like to think not as, from the position of regular contact with Private photography, I saw many publications try to mimic it and periodically viewed others. In general, I found them to be lesser in quality and the characteristics I have described above. Also, before the floodgates, this consumer perspective seemed more erotic, exotic and – dare I say it – artistic. From this personal and idiosyncratic position, let us widen the net of the who, how and what as we move to the present day.

The era we are examining incorporates the last two generations and effectively stems from the sexual revolution of the sixties, with the challenging or overturning of many of the pre-existing values. Porn obviously rode in the slipstream of this changing time. Without examining the history in any detail, I would generally hold that porn is a relatively modern phenomenon that has been effectively created by the cultural forces that preceded it, and to which its formation remains a reaction at a fundamental level. What I am suggesting is that, in times where sexuality was more socially and culturally integrated, sexual depiction would not have attained the prejudicial definition that the term pornography creates and certainly not the emotional impetus. Born of the time when this integration broke down, porn is also intimately involved with the increasing dominance of censorship.

Effectively, it is the advent of the age of reason, the continuing control of the Church and the dominance of the patriarchy in the West that created porn. I have always held that one of the concealed tenets of the Church goes something like this: Control a person's sexuality and you control them as an individual. The Church effectively does this by driving a wedge between the individual's unique and personal relationship with the divine by being the only effective vehicle for that contact. We will have cause to examine this dynamic in more detail, but it also hints at the close relationship between sex and the soul. Guilt is a very effective weapon in this fight.

With the advent of the age of reason, this pattern and associated responsibility was undertaken by the patriarchy, with the implication that such control was necessary. This was under the guise of moral protection, so continues where the Church leaves off and further extends control to those not shackled by the Church's repressive morality. Caught in this net are those of lower socio-economic backgrounds and ... women. Control thus became social and political as well as moral. We have supposedly had a separation of Church and State in the West, but you would not think so if you examined the issue of censorship. One of the creative spin-offs of the depth psychology movement has been to give individuals the skill to negotiate this territory, which I know has been invaluable for me.

Interestingly, the subjugation of women under the patriarchy produced a split in the feminist position with respect to porn. Initially, this was pro-censorship, almost exclusively, as leaders in the movement – usually with an anti-male agenda – concluded that porn further portrayed and exemplified the male dominance and control of women. In its extreme position, this movement considered the act of sexual intercourse to be one of rape. I won't go into further detail here as this subject has, in my opinion, been done to death and is seriously flawed. The huge danger is that, taken to its extreme, women would be in an even worse position than they were before.

Thankfully an anti-censorship position emerged in the movement, which was and is altogether more wholesome. It believes that women have the right to express themselves sexually, both to liberate and empower them, which thus overturns the patriarchal dominance in a way that the pro-censorship lobby does not. This anti-censorship lobby has increased and has become more integrated into the cultural mainstream, because it is not as divisive as the pro-censorship position. It has also attained a significant voice in the porn industry, not only with porn stars, but also in porn production. I believe this position has been significant at many levels, restoring the balance between the sexes and the power of women, as well as encouraging relationships with increasing parity. As a male, I truly welcome it, as there are many men who feel as uncomfortable about the patriarchal position as this lobby does.

The net result of all these changes is that censorship has become far less a tool of social control and, rightly, is focussing on the more appropriate issues in its domain, such as child pornography. There are still some mixed messages in this regard, as evidenced by the situation between the Territories and States in Australia, but essentially the issues seem to be the ones that from an inner moral perspective do need highlighting and controlling. As a result of all these changes, the porn industry itself is starting to undertake its own self-regulation. I have indicated some of these developments with respect to Private. The danger is that it may be financial reasons that drive it and an association with governments that may limit what it can explore and express as a tool of social change. Obviously, this is a fluctuating and evolving situation, and history dictates that if there is too much restriction such exploration will emerge the other side of the legal barrier – and will be found by the consumer. Why? Because of the Internet.

Whilst the floodgates were already open prior to the wide adoption of the Internet, a veritable tide has now resulted. The

VCR allowed movies to go to the study or bedroom, as movies could be relatively easily obtained via sex shops and mail order. DVDs have made packaging and storage easier, yet the Internet transcends all of this. It is remarkably easy to access porn and we'd better get used to it, because the Internet is here to stay. There is also a vast – and I do mean vast – amount of material there and most of it is pulp that pushes the issues of censorship, workplace safety and self-regulation to the limits.

Irrespective of whether you agree with my arguments to date and my personal position with respect to porn, one lens I have always tried to use is the creative one: Is what I am looking at artistic and life-affirmative? When I do this then it is not so much what the actors are doing that might appeal to me – although I obviously have my preferences – it is more how. In this respect, I support the aesthetic view of pornography and is the reason I favour the word erotography. So also did Milton, and the reason I kept track with Private is because it did retain these values. Issues of beauty and goodness came into the picture (excuse the pun). So, it is not just that anal sex might appeal to me, it is whether the performers are enjoying it and the women are not being coerced.

There are many arguments to say that we can't determine issues like coercion and enjoyment from the product itself, but I beg to differ. It requires taste, education, experience and exposure to discern the value of an art product like a painting or sculpture. I argue that the same lens can be applied to porn products and is support for the aesthetic position of porn, not its exclusion as in the dictionary.

What are you saying, you might ask; you can actually tell from simply viewing? Yes, I can; added to that is my considerable exposure to and experience of depth psychology, and I reckon I'm a reasonable judge. Yet these are actors ... they could be faking it? They could, but that's where the psychology comes in.

When so naked, exposed and vulnerable the signs are usually detectable. Also, don't forget that even mainstream actors choose their roles. The arguments from the wider artistic and performance fields definitely should not be excluded from the porn industry. This sort of critical examination and wider community acceptance would do more to eliminate what is unfavourable in the industry than any censorship. It is also wholesome in a cultural way.

The wider issues that draw people to actually act in porn will not be detailed, as it is beyond the brief of this book and has been examined from many angles elsewhere. Issues of drug addiction and mental health should be examined in their own domains and not be used as an argument against pornography. We try and help an addicted sportsman with his addiction directly; we don't blame the sport he plays. One feature I would like to highlight is that I am sure that many – women in particular – are attracted to be in porn because of the uncomplicated sexual experimentation and freedom. I know if I'd had the opportunity I would probably have said yes.

Have I undertaken such experimentation in my personal life? This could be a bit revealing ... Yes, I have, though somewhat limited and not to the extent that I would have if I'd had the further opportunity such as the industry might have provided. I have had significant windows in my life when such exploration was possible. My first threesome was with a couple that invited me to join them for a drink after a social function. The invitation was via a practical demonstration on the coffee table in front of me whilst I was sipping my port. Declining would have been socially unacceptable, I reasoned. This created a fresh wave of emotional conflict, but brief and not to breakdown proportions, and I went to dinner when 'invited'. Since that induction, I have episodically been involved in other combinations, sometimes with a current partner, and have tried most things I have seen in the porn media with my sexual partners – and they with me.

Would I have done this exploration otherwise? Obviously, I can't say, and there are arguments either way. My honest belief is that with adolescence in the sixties and various interesting social groupings after, it was an inevitability that I should experiment in this way. It is strongly in my character make-up, and has not diminished over time, simply matured. Whilst the porn might have encouraged the experimentation, it is not a question of what caused what. I see that the sexuality I have been drawn to in porn is the kind that stimulates me in both my inner and outer lives. In other words, it is part of my imaginative structure and inclination and is mirrored in my experience in the world. In this respect, you could say that porn has helped me chart a territory I would have explored anyway with less information.

Porn has been an instruction manual of technique and alternatives and allowed me to negotiate the technical aspects of some of the sexuality in which I have indulged, but I have still had to negotiate the emotional planes. There is nothing like introducing different sexual practices, or partners, into a sexual relationship to confront the emotional dimensions and the deeper issues of needs, expectations and outcomes. The net result of these experiences is that I am vigorously exploring the nexus of sexuality, emotion, imagination and spirituality in an inner context extending to creative expression up to and including this very book. I also believe my spiritual maturity has been significantly encouraged, assisted and developed as a result of exposure, but it has also been an enormous challenge in this regard.

Am I like other consumers? Well, actually yes, and I have *The Porn Report* to support me. Today's consumer is remarkably average socially, politically and religiously. Men predominate –

they always have – although the percentage of women consumers is progressively rising. They also tend to be younger, possibly because of the historical reasons I have outlined, and of above-average education. Are you surprised? The negative arguments in the media such as porn leading to violence toward women and treating them as objects simply do not stack up.

I independently believe such negative arguments are psychologically flawed and match the distorted argument about the association of marijuana and hard drugs. As I have pointed out, the sexual outlets I have pursued are reflected in the porn I use. I suspect someone attracted to violent porn will also have a violent tendency in the same arena and prior to the porn. It may even be that the pursuit of such material protects a potential recipient somewhere and, although this may be difficult to actually prove, I find it psychologically compelling. All these issues around porn have also been extensively explored for causal relationships to sexual and other crimes by the moral minority: I assure you, if one were there it would have been found by now and they would be screaming from the rooftops.

In the political realm, consumers from the left and right are of approximately equal numbers, which superficially seems a surprise. It may say something about the duplicity of the political right and the issue of censorship. You may recall (in the Introduction) that I posed the question that many critics may be vicarious consumers; this fact may support that argument. There is a somewhat smaller than average admission of religious affiliation, but it is not large and is across the religious spectrum. So, and to repeat the above, the average consumer is remarkably average socially, politically and religiously. The gender preference is interesting. Men are proportionately higher consumers of visual material, whilst women prefer novels. Is this a surprise? Not really, even Carl Jung said that men were seduced by the image and women by the word. If we interpret seduction as a gateway into our imaginative lives, this makes sense and further matches my personal experience.

The authors of *The Porn Report* don't describe in significant detail what sort of porn people consume, although they do identify the media used. This is confined to issues about porn star authenticity, enthusiasm and whether the women are being used as sex objects. This is understandable, due to the nature of the study and that it otherwise would require a level of revelation that could be easily censored or distorted. What I have done, from a linear and personal position, is tried to provide some of that background. What I have concluded is that the sort of porn I enjoy is reflected in what I purchase, so collectively what is enjoyed is what is popular. Before we get to that question, I wonder if I have fully answered your question about what it actually is in the imagery that I enjoy?

Beyond a certain point this is difficult to describe, if not impossible, and could be considered pornographic in its own right and, as I am promoting the imaginative perspective, how about reconstructing it for yourself and see what you come up with? The general outline I have given as Private, so you could always research this for yourself. I gave a highly specific example from issue number seventeen in chapter one and that may indicate a predilection, although I will argue that has deeper significance as this work proceeds. Embedded in the content so far has been some of the activities and combinations I have been involved in and which are reflected in Private, although the extent is different. If I wanted more, maybe I should have rung them when younger and offered my services!

Let's return to *The Porn Report* and see how the authors assess what is collectively popular. They make some critical comments about the issue of violence, such as the fact that consensual spanking is not violent, nor is vulgar language, if mutually enjoyed. This is a clear, common-sense position, and does much to diminish many of the spurious conclusions that the pro-censorship position comes to; such as arguing that any apparent agreement represents coercion. The other side of this also needs to be stated: that apparent violence may be part of the narrative; it certainly is in mainstream cinema, after all. They do argue that, in the 1970s, and with the rise of the anti-pornography lobby, the issue of violence has diminished along with the male domination of the genre. This is not my experience, as I have found that the level of apparent violence has increased, most notably with a couple of female directors who explore the sadomasochistic aspect of sexuality. Maybe the authors have been selective, although they do conclude that the issue of violence may now be more about women's pleasure, an apparent and interesting anomaly.

Contrary to some of their conclusions, I would argue that the European porn I have been exposed to has taken the opposite perspective and supported women and their sexual liberation, although I suspect and accept this is simply one stream amongst many and one that I have preference for. Certainly, the issue of violence in porn is by no means simple and is supportive of a censorship political position, such as that taken by the anti-pornography lobby. It opens up the whole area of sadomasochism and the dynamics of power, which throws such simplistic arguments into relief and demonstrates how paradoxical the field can be. Maybe a resolution to the issue of violence in porn should rest on the issue of violence per se and not associate it with porn; otherwise, it can be used for political justification and – paradoxically – personal power.

With respect to the actors, now called porn stars, there are some distinguishing features. Men first: They tend to have bigger than average dicks and heighten this illusion by being shorter than average. The women are more varied and probably less stylised than other media genres. Of course, make-up and hair styling figures strongly and the breasts often attract a significant focus, which are frequently artificially enlarged; although there are significant segments of the industry where the opposite is actually promoted. In my experience, breast enlargements are a stronger feature of American porn and detract from the aesthetic position. Similarly, archetypal beauty is contrasted with the natural or girl-next-door approach and often exaggerated by the genre, such as fantasy porn as against non-professional, home-movie or couples porn. Clothing is very strongly emphasised and part of the majority of scenes, in both men and women. The women gravitate to lingerie, stockings and garters, distinctive shoes or boots, extending to leather and fetish clothing, and also take this further than the men. After all, they are usually the principal objects of the viewing and this is now reflected in the paycheque, which is certainly higher for female porn stars than their counterparts, the so-called "studs".

There is also a great levelling out of what used to be stereotypically based gender perspectives. This issue was touched on with violence in porn but it is across the board. That is, women are becoming more empowered and increasingly taking the initiative. There is also more focus on women's pleasure, and women are more involved in the industry. In this there is a reflection of community values and social change, which, in and of itself, indicates the level to which porn is becoming integrated into the mainstream.

There are some features of difference that do stand out. The focus on the male ejaculation remains strong and enduring, in spite of more reference to and portrayal of the female orgasm. There are some obvious elements to this, with male viewers predominating and the male orgasm being the focus and conclusion of much sexual activity. That it is usually external is also obvious and even paradigmatic. I will have more to say about why this should be so, apart from the simplistic argument that it 'confirms' the orgasm or is related to dominance. Where it is received is also very important and as to why it is very commonly the woman's face a significant issue. Supporting this position is the frequency of fellatio, or cock sucking, as opposed to cunnilingus, or pussy licking. I will be arguing that these differences mark a point of departure from the socialisation of porn and the attendant equality of the sexes. These differences point to challenges to the straightforward acceptance of porn and point to deeper issues, which we may only arrive at by exploring them imaginatively and emotionally. The so-called money shot exemplifies much of this and cannot be trivially dismissed as a 'male ego' thing.

Even the rather thin narrative that was often the context into which the sex was embedded is diminishing, and little pretence is seemingly given to getting to the 'real' reason the genre is being engaged with in the first place. Where the narrative genre has prevailed, it has also become more mainstream, with a more significant plot and acting requirement that supersedes the rather pathetic standards of the early days. Actually, in the past there was no attempt to act or perform in a more detailed narrative, with the film often being a take-off of mainstream movies or television and even appearing to gain satire status. I don't think anyone would call Linda Lovelace a gifted actress; her talents lay elsewhere ...

The Internet, in particular, promotes the "sex for sex's sake" position and does the industry as a whole no favour. There is so much that there is obviously a dilution of quality at all levels and a dulling of the senses and imagination. It is not a path I have explored too much, as it is unattractive, not erotically stimulating, degenerative and even life negating. There is also disturbing material readily available, which I would argue isn't pornography. It is something you would have to go deliberately looking for, and I have never seen them, which also says something about industry self-regulation even with something so vast as the Internet. The way I have negotiated all this is to keep control of what I access and the sites I choose, which are generally those of acceptable mainstream products, such as DVDs and magazines readily available and acceptable in Australia.

There are two trends that the Internet provides that are worth commenting on. I have a little insight from other people on this point too, although, as you might have guessed, the fear of exposure makes concealment a priority. The first follows from the comments above and leads into the questions that follow. The exploration does not usually go into areas that are different from personal preference, so if you like threesomes you don't tend to look for rape scenes, real or acted.

The second is quite significant from an imaginative point of view: if you like threesomes you'll explore lots of threesomes in differing settings and a range of activities. If you like facial cumshots, you'll look for that. Now this raises an interesting issue that varies a little from the threesome point and implied with the Goddess: how many people get involved? What about two men and a woman, or three men, or four ... or twenty ... and you will find this. What I am saying is that any theme that tweaks your imagination can be taken to the extreme and this in itself is a danger, as it – both the Internet and your exploration – move away from the imaginative faculty and also, I would argue, the aesthetic position.

The authors meet this issue, but unfortunately, from my perspective, handle it in a limited manner. For example: "We find this kind of pornography deeply offensive and abhorrent" when describing double anal penetration (as opposed to double penetration or double vaginal penetration), gaping arses (open anal views of women), extended multiple penetration scenes or when the semen is deliberately shot into a female's eye. Yet just a few pages prior: "We similarly do not believe that the alternate sexual practices popularly depicted in porn, such as anal sex or group sex, are in themselves dangerous or harmful to men and women." Or earlier still, when indirectly promoting the feminist position: "The film culminated with the (female) director Tristan being anally penetrated by all ten of her co-stars in what she described as 'the ultimate feminist gang bang'." Interesting that a feminist position such as this is from someone who has chosen a gender ambivalent name? Also, what does she mean by that statement? The authors provide no explanation or interpretation; it is left hanging.

Although a little tricky, let's go down this path a little further. Whilst the authors take a balanced feminist stance in their work, I wonder how they reconcile Tristan's position with their "deeply offensive and abhorrent" position later? Whilst the argument is that semen in the eye can transmit diseases, such as Chlamydia, surely this is a workplace issue and not a moral one? I feel they are at pains to support a feminist and couples-oriented position in their arguments, extending to family issues and particularly the rights and protection of children. I don't think that is at all wrong, particularly the children issues, and it does favour the acceptance of their work – it simply limits the enquiry. They are keen to establish a strong and ethical position based on the integration of porn into society and, in this, they have my undivided support, but in my personal opinion their comments restrict other avenues of exploration. So, rather than see my comments as criticism of their work, see my work as an extension into areas that their brief does not take them.

For example, with the quotes above, how does the issue of "anal gaping" meet with the obvious enjoyment of the parties concerned? What about the aesthetics of this, or the other practices they mention? Of course, there is much in this area that may be offensive, but I would argue that an aesthetic and pleasure perspective should be considered rather than simply a judgement of the content; an argument that I find holds for porn as a whole. Are they arguing that a double anal penetration must be painful? Are they contravening their own criteria of enjoyment? Maybe the issues of sadomasochism and mutual satisfaction have been ignored. The Tristan comment is from an earlier section in the book and is given with no further comment by the authors. To my mind, it begs for further exploration about issues of offensiveness, violence, feminism and power with which to look into the later issues regarding gaping anuses and the rest.

A brief look at the feminism question again would be appropriate here. Certainly, feminism has made big inroads in exploring the porn phenomenon and the industry itself, and about this I have no complaint. Although men predominate in my general book reading, in porn specifically, it is the reverse as I have read more woman commentators, so they have made an important and relevant contribution. However, as with the feminist movement as a whole, I think it is time for men to get beyond any sort of over-accommodation, which is often based on the guilt of their forefathers and a lack of instruction in their sexual development. Porn is probably a good place to start, as men predominate as consumers, and the imbalance with the commentators and critics is significant and needs addressing.

After that detour, back to some significant questions: All this porn ... does it make you addicted? Does it make you objectify and treat women badly? Do you watch it to avoid intimacy? These are relatively serious questions and ones I have had to ask of myself. Yet there are more: Are you more likely to be violent or commit a rape? Does it turn you into a pervert or paedophile? These latter questions I find of a different class, because it is arguable whether they are primarily sexual issues anyway. You may or may not be surprised, but the answer to all of them is "no", with a few qualifications as discussed by the authors of *The Porn Report*, but none that to my mind negate the "no". Also, as previously mentioned, I can assure you that if any study had come up with a definitive "yes" you'd be hearing it from every corner of the media, the pulpit and parliament house. It simply is not there to be found. Why?

I have already hinted at why this may be and compared it to the analogous marijuana and hard drugs, as well as drugs and mental health issues. We have a remarkable tendency in our society to allow the causal perspective to over-ride all others, particularly when not appropriate, and it is definitely not appropriate here. If we watch porn and it doesn't lead to any of the above, then we must be watching it for other reasons and it is this that has interested me during my life, and that exploration has been far more rewarding.

Before we get to that, let's have a look at the questions and start with the serious ones. Addiction? Easy ... if you're an addict you can become addicted to porn, not the other way round. Ditto with violence, rape and paedophilia. If you are a paedophile and you watch porn, you'll be looking for child porn, normal porn would not "do it" for you – although it might be part of a rehabilitation programme (joking, but with a grain of truth). Rape is violence and violence is ... violence; it's not sex. The argument that even if banning porn would prevent one rape then it is justified is quite pathetic. If you banned porn, you create more monstrous problems and I would argue that many crimes are actually not committed as a result of watching porn ... because it is ideal for discharging tension, and it is a tension build-up that stands behind many of these crimes.

Perversion? That's a little different, partly because the term needs differentiating and is often implied when the word fetishism should be used. Perversion, in a general sense, is an abnormal sexual practice, such as bestiality. We'll leave that with the rape and violence category, the latter being strongly implicated. Fetishism? Back to the dictionary: "Object abnormally serving as a stimulus to or object of sexual desire." I don't like the word "abnormally", it tends to pathologise and emotionally darken what would otherwise be an accurate definition. Garters and stockings, are these a fetish or a sexual aid? I suppose if you worship them and not the person wearing them, it may be a fetish; the boundary is obviously not clear and fetishism forms a significant pillar of the industry. Personally, I like clothes and toys, not routinely, but when in a light and playful mood. They bring out the "inner child" in me, so how therapeutic is that!

Let's go back to the two questions I've left: Does it make you objectify and treat women badly? Do you watch it to avoid intimacy? As well as the evidence not supporting these to be the cases, it is also my personal experience. In fact, my experience is quite the opposite. In simple terms, the first is not true because porn that is good and meets your constitutional nature will lead you to a deeper appreciation of your own femininity. (Yes, my male friend out there, you do have one!) This will lend more respect to the women in your life. The second is not true because the activity related to is more primarily masturbatory and imaginative, and, I would argue, that this is both a separate activity from sexual relationship and that imagination leads to emotion, soul and … intimacy. Don't despair; we're going to go a lot further with this discussion.

What did our authors find beyond the "no" to the questions? They found that whilst porn users did not have a negative attitude toward women, those with religious beliefs certainly did and that those with right-wing political beliefs probably do. Maybe we should ban religion? They found that the vast majority of people exposed to porn reported positive effects, including being more relaxed and comfortable about sex, more open-minded and willing to experiment, more tolerant of their partner's needs and the pleasure of others, and that it was a source of education and help in long-term relationship sexuality ... need they say more? The conclusion was that for many consumers pornography is a part of real relationships, not an alternative to them.

I want to highlight at this point that I will be taking a different line: Exploration with the assistance of erotic porn leads to an individual maturity that will assist you if you are in a relationship, and if not, it will assist you in a more spiritually-inclined way anyway. It's like the benefits to an existing relationship are secondary to where the exploration may lead you. In this, the authors are too inclined to emphasising the benefits in a relationship and you may argue that my position puts relationship in a secondary position, thus relativising it and that this is not a good consequence of viewing porn. You might, although I will contend the opposite as we go, so bear with me.

They also found that unrepresentative minority groups tend to drive the media debate. I agree, but I would also argue that this can be substantially negated by more consumers becoming public: Not to take a defensive or reactive position but, as I hope I am doing, to promote a positive, creative and instructive position. I have suffered the effects of the concealment of my consumerism, which were both unnecessary and unjustified, so I am more than happy now to be vocal about what I see as the creative and positive effects of my consumption.

Obviously the "why" of porn consumption is going to set the tone of the rest of the book. So, to complete this chapter I would like to discuss the reason most people consume porn: masturbation. Some personal history: nobody told or taught me about masturbation, although I was aware of it as an activity and other boys at school obliquely extolled its joys and benefits. I was also convinced I wouldn't go mad, blind or develop hairs on the palm of my hand. So, armed with a sturdy right fist I would hold my erect cock and rub in the manner intimated and waited ... and waited. Nothing happened, I was disappointed, but tried again ... and again. Now I was confused and distressed and, after many months, expressed to my mother (not my father, please note) that I didn't think I'd be able to have children. She didn't ask why I thought this, but arranged for me to see our local General Practitioner. I saw him at the end of one day, spent an hour with him and I don't remember a shred of the conversation, all I know is that after I felt better ... and continued my experiment.

Then one night it happened. There was a rapid build-up and eruption of energy throughout my body, a simultaneous eruption of semen and I instantly went into a blissful altered state of consciousness, for how long I don't know. I was ecstatic, literally, and when I regained normal consciousness, I cleaned up the mess and went to sleep – soundly. I was hooked and masturbation became at least a nightly activity, although one disappointment was that I never fully again – with masturbation – reached the ecstatic peak I had on the first occasion. I found that fantasy helped considerably and started getting aids to this, which I have already described. What I found helped in the actual porn I saw was an understanding of the mechanics of how to fuck – I was still a virgin – and that helped my imagination considerably until I started sexual relationships, which also became involved in my imagination.

I have been in that ecstatic state with sexual activity subsequently, but not with my first fuck, which was actually quite a messy affair – literally. There were elements of it with oral sex if I was allowed to ejaculate which, as you probably know, is the subject of much debate; some jocular, but usually related to the dynamics of power. I experienced it with my first anal orgasm, and this added a lot to my earlier confusion. However, the most significant time was with the partner I had the most intensive (though maybe not extensive) sexual relationship with. This was vaginal sex and, interestingly, followed a significant and threatening traumatic incident to her, as well as being in an isolated setting in the bush.

The quality of the ecstasy, both physically and mentally, was similar in most of these cases, although somewhat different with oral sex. This culminated in a unique, though repeated, experience once when I was being sucked off and allowed myself a complete physical let-go by lying on my back and allowing my partner do 'all the work'. This time there was not the intensity but subtle waves flowing through my body and a blissful state afterwards. When I shared this with her, she remarked on the similarity of my experience to a female orgasm.

I am now able to bring a range of these experiences into my sex life and am receptive to my partner's experience in this regard. I employ masturbation to explore this further, and use porn as a stimulant. I don't always masturbate when I look at porn ("I read Playboy for the articles"), though it is common and sometimes inevitable with the stimulation I am getting from viewing. I rarely orgasm, but I do take the experience to that point – sometimes frequently. I explore my physical and emotional responses and then often shut the porn down and continue imaginatively. I take my physical and emotional responses into my sexual relationships and I believe this to be healthy. I consider porn to have been a creative adjunct in this respect.

What about fantasy then? I have indicated that porn can stimulate fantasy and hence the imagination. One of the not so healthy aspects of the vastness of porn on the Internet is that the fantasy element can be taken over by the porn viewing itself, and that creates some dangers, such as the potential for addiction in the predisposed. But I hear you say, I bet you then 'substitute' what you see in porn into your sexual act with your partner and 'see' her as something – or someone else – that she is not. Well, some may, but generally I don't. I suspect this is because they don't see the role and value of the imagination in its own right and hence project this onto their partners, because it is unexplored. This can, of course, then engender guilt ... and be another path on the road to addiction.

Why don't I fantasise when sexually with a partner? Because it is, and I am, usually actively engaged. We may watch a porn movie together, or she may get dressed up in a provocative outfit. When having sex, I don't commonly fantasise; my attention is to the response of my partner, as well as my own. I see this as healthy and for porn to support and stimulate this process. I believe this divergence of potential response depends on the quality and aesthetics of the porn, as well as the active engagement of the imaginative faculty; points I think I have covered to date, although we will be paying far more attention to the imagination as we progress.

In summary: If an apple a day keeps the doctor away, does a wank a day keep the psychologist at bay?

3

Did Freud Get It Right?

Probably not, but we'll get to that.

What I am going to do in this chapter is provide a picture of sexuality that has emerged from the depth psychology of the last one hundred years and use it as a platform to continue a specific line of enquiry into pornography. This will retain the consumer's perspective as I, a consumer, have also had and have a significant involvement with depth psychology and used this to chart my own personal and spiritual progress. The previous chapters have this perspective embedded throughout, so I want to lift it out of that framework and use it to further explore the porn phenomenon.

There are many other views and perspectives I could take to achieve this, such as Karl Marx (socio-political), Michel Foucault (philosophical), various artists and their lives such as Anais Nin, and notable figures like Aleister Crowley. This could be an interesting perspective and the subject of a larger work, but I need to restrict the perspective and, as well as being my personal experience, I believe depth psychology has the most to offer in a re-visioning of sexuality in the post-modern world and porn's place in it.

First, there needs to be some words of explanation. I have used the title "Depth Psychology" as that best embraces the approaches of Freud, Jung, Reich and Hillman, the key figures to whom I shall refer, although there are many others. Depth psychology is possibly an unfortunate phrase, because in the modern era we have become accustomed to see psychology as clinical and academic and its thrust as cognitive and behavioural. For many varied reasons I find this a misrepresentation of the word psychology and some of the reasons will become apparent as we progress. Depth psychology is more about the experience of man beyond these limited domains and collectively the above men charted areas of the so-called unconscious, spirit, sex and soul, as well as their complex inter-relationship. That this hasn't significantly or appropriately informed modern psychology and psychiatry is a travesty, but it may yet do so and I, for one, will make attempts in this direction.

Sigmund Freud is, of course, most notable for his exploration of the role of sex in mental disturbance. The context is important: The repressive atmosphere of the late Victorian times and the higher echelons of Austrian society. Freud was a doctor and a Jew who initially came from a neurological or 'brain' perspective, as opposed to 'mind'. He is credited with the 'discovery' of the unconscious, the role of sex there and the mechanisms of its manifestation into illness, both physical and mental. His perspective is, therefore, pathological and medical. It is also biomechanical and objective. There is a lot of talk of and about sex from an observer perspective, but it is not one that will be very fruitful to us as we proceed.

One story about Freud is relevant and insightful, but for the direction he did not take. Freud's most notable model was the Oedipus complex, so incest and pathology rate a very high mention, as do the associated issues of guilt, punishment and death, from which he took a long bow to examine society at large. He further 'discovered' in the unconscious of many Viennese women an interesting fact; that they had all had sexual relations with their fathers. After a while, it dawned on Freud, with a little prompting, that it was highly unlikely that all Viennese women had been sexually involved with their fathers. He then appreciated that the imagination was involved and so these were fantasies rather than fact. Here the imagination makes an important entry, but is shown the exit door fairly smartly.

Jung was Freud's most significant and brilliant pupil, later to part with his master as he envisioned a much greater breadth and depth to the psyche than Freud had discovered or even conceived. Jung's psychology remains very influential and cross-disciplinary. But the most significant issue here is that he essentially left sex to the Freudians and it has, therefore, not been appreciably integrated into his psychology or therapy. How else could I spend so many years in Jungian analysis and not recall whether my porn habit was ever mentioned? Was I that good at concealment; was it buried in my 'unconscious', or was it that none of my analysts enquired? Jung was a good precedent, as he concealed his varied sex-life from the face of public scrutiny to avoid it being a vehicle for criticism of his psychology.

(A quick aside about terms used to date: I use the word "unconscious" because these pathfinders did, often very frequently. Apart from this historical implication, I am going to avoid using it, as I find it pejorative, and it can also be confusing. The unconscious together with consciousness, or ego-consciousness, comprises the "psyche" in the terms of these depth psychologists. I will be taking a more selective view of psyche and equate it with a revised Western concept of soul: This view also connects with more traditional terms in our culture.)

Anyway, I went into analysis because of the difficulties I was experiencing in an intense relationship, as I have already explained, and Jung did have a perspective on that which is important, as well as having a potential in the way of looking at sex – and porn – that is creative and instructive. Although he and his psychology have not fully taken that step, maybe along with others, that's my job, as it is my belief that sexuality needs reintegrating into the depth psychology movement in a more modern way and one that can help inform and reform our views of mental health. Porn thus has its place, even if indirectly, and maybe masturbation doesn't send you mad after all – in fact, quite the opposite!

In very simplistic terms, which will become much more elaborated as we progress, Jung's notion was that each man had an internal feminine part to his personality called the anima, and each woman a corresponding male aspect, called the animus. He saw these figures, or images of them, as having a personal component modelled on experience; that is, the mother and other significant female figures in a man's upbringing for the anima, and vice-versa for the animus. This is the level that Freud gets to with his emotionally-toned Oedipus complex, but Jung takes the idea further by saying the image is also archetypal, or pre-destined, and goes well beyond our limited personal experience.

Now this was what was mirroring my life and experience. My earlier relationships had explored many issues concerning my mother and other women in my life, but I was now in this intense "she's my soul-mate" relationship with someone who was socially and culturally so different from my upbringing, which wasn't working as a relationship and this model seemed to explain why. What the analysis did not explore to any depth, however, was the significance and importance of the intense sexual component, which made it very difficult for me to disentangle and so took the relationship well beyond its used-by date. In other words, I came to understand why I was in such a relationship, but the ongoing emotional and sexual intensity kept me in it when my head wanted out. I came to understand that neither Freud nor Jung had a real handle on emotion.

A little education – we will get back to the porn, I promise! For argument's sake let's take the man's position (another pun … please excuse my bent humour. Women are mirrored in this modelling process). The man's anima is his femininity. What this means is that the man has an inner femininity and this can be considered pure; that is, the man's anima is exclusively feminine. Of course, these are mixed in with the image of the man's masculinity and the combined result is the male. Male and masculinity are thus different, as the male (the man) has a mixture of masculine and feminine, which masculinity does not. Or, a man is both masculine and feminine and a woman is both feminine and masculine.

Of course, the masculine elements tend to dominate in a man and the feminine in a woman, particularly in early life. But, as life progresses, there appears to be a psychological demand to discover the opposite gender and this is the basic psychology behind the phenomenon of "falling in love" and other in-love states.

With me so far? The problem is that when a man does not have much contact with his anima – or feminine side – he sees it in a woman in his life who radiates the appropriate image of this feminine side back to him (this process is called projection in the trade) and he "falls in love", or "finds his soul-mate", or even "it's love at first sight" when the man mutually reflects the woman's masculine side back to her. Now the problem is that the relationship will only sustain as long as the woman plays the role of the man's anima or femininity and vice-versa. But – and it's a big but (that was the worst pun I've happened upon!) – a woman has her masculine side, the animus, so can't sustain the exclusive image of the anima for him and vice versa. There are now four in this relationship, as you can see, a porn director's delight! So, once these factors emerge, they will clash and fight; it's disaster time and difficult to untangle.

Another reflection of this is when a man is married and dissatisfied, then he will see what he perceives as the lack and limitations in his wife embodied in another woman. He has an affair, which is unsatisfactory for the aforementioned reasons and, when the pendulum swings back to the middle, he recognises the values in his wife. He then reasons that a combination of the two women would be his ideal. Heard this somewhere? I wouldn't be surprised. This also makes for a porn director's cut in the threesome, particularly when the two women 'get on' and symbolise the union of wife and mistress, or when from the man's imaginative perspective literally 'get it on'.

There are some interesting permutations and combinations of the above, such as when the 'falling in love' is one-sided. It also provides an interesting window into homosexuality as well as the image of cinema stars and their failed relationships. It can further provide a perspective on the power dynamics of relationships and even explore sadomasochism in further detail.

Am I implying that porn reflects these dynamics? Can porn have accidentally stumbled on something that has taxed great minds? Well, in a way, I am. Because sex is by and large repressed, porn can invert what is happening in daily reality. The dominant man can be submissive in sex, for example, and this is the basis of much of the sadomasochistic dynamic. Porn will pick up a lot of these denied patterns in our lives and relationships and reflect them back to us. If we can get beyond guilt and shame and explore porn in this light, we might find our predilections are reflecting back to us exactly what we need to integrate.

For example, and common to many men, my initial attraction

to porn was toward a threesome involving a man – obviously me – and two women. Remember my earlier response to the Goddess? She had a female assistant, and the man was effectively not seen as a sex object. How much is that reflected in the patterns I have drawn immediately above, and how much did the Goddess reflect my anima and anticipate years later what was now happening in my life? If I let you know that during the time that I was having the intense relationship described above, I never quite let go of a previous, more conservative and socially appropriate one, then does my fantasy make more sense? It was of interest to me that, after these relationships ended, then so did what I was attracted to in porn. With this integration I became attracted more to what gave the woman pleasure. ("How many men do you want to join us tonight, dear?")

I have predominantly taken the male perspective for all of the above. For the female – obviously – just reverse the roles, if I haven't already done so. Jung would be proud. But you may ask, this chapter is dedicated to Freud so what about his take on it all? Well, I may disappoint, but I'm not going to explore that stream too far, because I think Freud got it wrong. Well, not exactly wrong, but it is severely limited from our perspective and goes into paths and directions that I think are in serious need of revision. So let me explain why.

Freud, and others, effectively lifted the lid on the sexually repressive Victorian era and discovered in it mental disturbance and pathology as a – predictable – consequence. The fundamental limitation that I see in Freud is that he took a mechanical and intellectual approach to what is primarily instinctual and emotional territory; in other words, he did not tackle it on its own terms, but as a doctor, analyst and observer.

As an aside, that is a reason why I've taken a consumer's approach to the subject of porn, as I believe any other that doesn't include this will be subject to similar limitations. In the words of modern quantum physics, you can't entirely remove the observer from the observed as they form a fundamental unity. The more you do separate the observer from the observed, the more he or she affects and distorts the observed. When you are looking at repressed issues, such as sexuality generally and porn in particular, the distortions and conclusions can be gross indeed.

Freud's approach is biomechanical and limited to personal development. Also, with the Oedipus and corresponding Electra complexes, he painted a pathological picture of sexuality that is still with us. Specifically, it remains in medicine and our view of health. The simple conclusion of this, hand-in-hand with the Church, is that sex beyond certain norms is bad for you, which includes masturbation (it sends you mad) and porn (it makes you a pervert). Whilst Jung took a deeper and less personal view of mental illness, he was generally dismissive of sexuality, as he considered that to be covered by the Freudian camp. As Jung's view is fundamentally spiritual, he and Freud can be seen to characterise the division between religion and science.

An interesting inversion you may care to know is that Jung was a very sexually oriented man; he maintained an active relationship with his wife and another woman for many years. The details of this have been variously disguised and distorted by his followers.

Because Freud's view remains rational, biomechanical and scientific, it has remained in the intellectual and medical mainstreams. It provides a pole of the psychiatric model, because of the overlap in science and biomechanics. Although seemingly controversial in many ways, this may simply be an intellectual paper tiger and continue its inclusion as an acceptable and sanitised model of sexuality.

Another of Freud's pupils, Wilhelm Reich, appreciated this and explored sexuality in a more fundamental manner, promoting a health model that included the primacy of the orgasm. He also saw that the repressed sexual energies moved into bodily patterns and symptoms, ultimately leading to disease, and advocated a direct physical and therapeutic approach to deal with these "blockages". Reich was ahead of his time. He was persecuted in his later years in America and died in prison. His work has yet to be fully evaluated. One of the limitations was of his own doing, as he was dismissive of spirituality with which sex is fundamentally connected, as we shall see.

What we really need is a creative mix of these three giants of the field and I will be proposing such a mix inspired by a fourth analyst, James Hillman. Hillman is also the only non-medical practitioner in this group and, therefore, provides an approach that is not fundamentally pathological. It is from this wider perspective I shall approach sex and porn, as Hillman does not do this directly to any great extent. In this way, I hope to "close the circle" metaphorically and to use the outcome as a way of looking back to a medical model that is inclusive of sexuality – but on the latter's own terms.

Before we do this, it will be of interest to take the Jungian approach we have adopted above and apply it more directly to the sexual sphere, which I will do with a myth. At present, I am using Greek myths because they are commonly the most familiar to us. However, they may not be in our cultural background if we are of Northern European descent and I will look to redress this imbalance a little later. Irrespective, they are a storehouse of wisdom in their own right.

They say that Teiresias saw two snakes mating on Cithaeron and that, when he killed the female, he was changed into a woman, and again, when he killed the male, took again his own nature.

This same Teiresias was chosen by Zeus and Hera to decide the question whether the male or female has most pleasure in intercourse. And he said:

"Of ten parts a man enjoys one only; but a woman's sense enjoys all ten in full."

For this Hera was angry and blinded him, but Zeus gave him the Seer's power.

(From: Hesiod: *The Homeric Hymns and Homerica*)

Linda Williams also uses this myth in her book, *Hard Core: Power, Pleasure, and the Frenzy of the Visible*, which has become a classic study of porn and sexuality from the analysis of pornographic film. Although taking a feminist stance, she moves beyond the pro- and anti-porn perspectives and is a delight to read. Her arguments are well thought through and challenging, and it is strongly recommended, partly because it so complements my position. For this reason, I will not be referring to it in detail and, although she has much to say about the above myth, I will be providing my own analysis and interpretation. If it matches any of Williams' arguments, it is because we have arrived on common ground.

Before we start, I recommend you re-read the myth, watch your emotional responses, thoughts and feelings, and then sit with them a little before we move on. It may be personally instructive.

What I initially found intriguing is that, even though I have read this myth before, I did not find it in the two standard works of mythology I commonly use. I wondered why ... a subtle form of censorship, perhaps? I did find Mount Cithaeron and three interesting associations. The first harks back to Freud: It was on this mountain that Oedipus, as an infant, was put out to die. He didn't, and the whole tragedy unfolded as a result. It does have feeling-tone qualities that underlie a lot of Freud's work. The second is that it is one of the places in the myths where Zeus took Hera to and then de-flowered her. The third is even more interesting: It is where the Dionysian orgies were held.

Snakes reflect many things. From a Freudian orientation they are sexual and represent the penis. This shows some of the limitation of Freud's thought and his rather restrictive approach to symbols. Snakes are more fundamentally associated with healing; they shed their skin and symbolise the cycle of life, death and rebirth – with sex in the middle, of course, as in the Great Cycle. Entwined around a staff, or tree, they become the caduceus, which is the symbol par excellence of healing in the medical and allied professions. Sex, death and healing all mixed up together ... interesting.

We do have sex and death portrayed with the snakes in the myth, and the result of this interaction is that Teiresias becomes a blind Seer. The symbol of blindness or one-eyedness in myths is commonly associated with shamans, who are the medicine men, magicians and healers of antiquity. Blindness indicates an inner direction of sight toward the third-eye of the Eastern chakra system, the eye that sees in an intuitive and clairvoyant sense. So Teiresias doesn't die as a result of his apparent misdemeanour, he is actually and radically transformed. It would take us too far away from our theme to explore shamanism in any depth but it does indicate that Teiresias' role in all this is one of initiation through his actions, which make them deeply symbolic and not literal.

There is thus a rich and layered background to this tale. Like all myths, it overlaps others, and we have hinted at more than one. The Dionysus myth, in particular, warrants some exploration, because when myths overlap like this they inform and enrich each other. Dionysus is the son of Zeus, whose mortal mother was slain by Hera's jealousy. Zeus is given to having frequent sexual relationships with goddesses and mortals alike; Hera is routinely jealous and angry. These features also resonate with our myth involving Teiresias. Dionysus was also God of the vine and ecstasy. Ecstasy, literally being "outside of yourself", is a feature of shamanism (plus or minus hallucinogenic drugs) and you may recall my comments about ecstasy when I was discussing my experiences with masturbation.

We could stray further in an informative way, but I think the above associations expand the depth and feeling, so it's time to return to our myth. Teiresias has an experience of being both a man and a woman; he experiences both sides of his 'being' in a Jungian sense. The two snakes in Indian mythology entwine the spine, which is a feature of the caduceus, but also stand as a metaphor for our bipolar nature: masculine and feminine both. We must respectively die to one to experience the other. The death is symbolic and marks an initiation from one state of being to another, a transition.

Let's just dip into the Indian perspective a little further. The two snakes entwined around the spine start from the base of it and rise to the crown at the top of the head. There is a force, an energy called Kundalini, which lies dormant in the base of the spine. For spiritual growth and transformation, Kundalini must be awoken from her – she's a feminine energy – dormant state to rise like fire through the spine and chakras to arrive at the head, resulting in ecstasy and enlightenment. In brief, here is a condensed model of much that we have briefly explored previously and will be doing in greater detail throughout the book. So, what awakens Kundalini? There are a lot of spiritual techniques: breathing, fasting, yoga postures and the like;

although the most significant one from our point of view – and mirroring Dionysus – is Tantra, which is ... (dah dah!) sexual activity that is both literal and imaginative.

By literal it means that a man and women have sex together for the purpose of ecstasy and spiritual enlightenment ... and nothing else. No babies, promises of marriage or other personal entrapments. In fact, it is a requirement that the couple be specifically free of personal attachment. The sex is considered sacred. By imaginative it means that each is relating to their other and inner gender through the outer person. One of the requirements is the containment of semen on the male's behalf, and channelling of it up the spine in a symbolic manner as the vehicle of ecstasy. With the woman, this occurs with her orgasm. I may have cut a few corners in a far more complex issue here, but you get my point and all these features we will be exploring further.

I'll dip back into porn briefly here ... how much does this semen retention and channelling away from a vaginal deposit mirror coming onto the woman's body? How much is the attention to her orgasm the fantasy of a male beyond simply getting his own rocks off? How much is the setting and nature of the interaction mirrored in porn generally? If you bring the Dionysian element of orgy in here (and it is present in the Indian model also) then how many are attracted to porn, either as consumers or even performers, to get in touch with these neglected features in our modern Western society, for which we are being made to feel – inappropriately – guilty or shameful?

We've covered a huge amount of ground and in a quite condensed manner. I have done this to give a kind of summary of a lot of material that will follow and be further elaborated on, as well as to give you an initial sense of the inter-relationship of myth, shamanism and other spiritual disciplines. This is in anticipation of creating a perspective centred on a traditional spiritual discipline – alchemy – that will unite much of the varied discussion that has been undertaken to date.

Now we get to the sex in the myth, but never to forget that the features we explored above provide an integral background to what we will be discussing henceforth. Obviously, Zeus and Hera have been having a discussion – more likely a fight – about who enjoys sex more. From the outcome, it is obvious that Zeus thinks it is the woman.

"What do you mean, you randy old goat," is Hera's reply, "you fuck anyone and anything from Olympus to Greece and don't give a shit about me and my feelings!"

"That may be so," says Zeus. "It's hard work keeping up with and satisfying so many women's needs!"

He then ducks the right hook that comes his way, grabs her by the torso and throws her to the ground. They then have frantic and passionate sex with a fair bit of slapping and wrestling and reach a mutual orgasm. The question remains undecided, but Hera can't see beyond her anger and Teiresias is summoned. This is as close as I'll get to a pornographic reconstruction; please recognise this as my imaginative addition to the myth.

Hera displays anger in her response. Remember she killed Dionysus' mother out of jealousy? Interesting that she killed the lover and not her husband? Maybe another variation on the threesome dynamic and, as in life, you will find this reflected in porn too. But it is the anger I want to focus on. How much is Hera's anger an inversion of her sexuality; that is, is she angry exactly because she can't recognise her sexual enjoyment? How much of this is involved in power dynamics in normal relationships? At one level, the Greek myths are quite patriarchal, so mirroring modern times in the West. If this is the case, does Hera have to sacrifice sexual enjoyment for her own personal power? I would volunteer it stands behind a significant number of so-called normal marriages. Finally, how much do we see the seeds of sadomasochism and the dominance and submission themes here? And what about the profound connection between sex and violence that these questions intimate?

Of course, all these questions are rhetorical and don't have a clear-cut answer; pose it to a class and there will be as many answers as students. My feeling in Williams' analysis of the myth is that she tries too hard to get clear-cut responses to questions that simply can't be responded to in that way, although that is not to deny the validity and importance of the attempt. In spite of my reading her and going "nah", or "maybe, but not quite" to some of her analysis of this myth, I must accept that they are right for her. And this is the very nature of myth and symbolism, that such resolutions are layered and multi-faceted. So, consider my conclusions in that light too and explore your own as we move on.

I think we need to approach the resolution to the myth on the masculine-feminine level and not the male-female. Too often the myth has been approached in that manner and provides all sorts of unnecessary obfuscation. Also, too often in life we approach issues of sexuality and associated domains with the male-female polarity, when the masculine-feminine perspective would be much more creative and helpful. When we use the male-female polarity, we are in danger of getting into all sorts of gender-associated agendas, which have clouded the full integration of the feminist perspective … in my humble opinion.

If we take the masculine-feminine polarity, there is an analogue outer-inner. In the appropriate language masculine to feminine equals outer to inner, or masculine: feminine and outer: inner. With me so far? I think under the rational tools of the patriarchy and the associated age of reason we have lost sight of other ways of exploring issues like this. We have relied on a causal perspective of 'this goes to this', or means this type of mentality. Analogue thinking is more dynamic, fluid and magical, and it is in this manner that apparently irreconcilable opposites need to be approached, otherwise we never get beyond the divisions.

For example, one of the goals of feminism could be considered equality. I'm sorry, but I have news for you: Equality will never happen, it simply can't. Why? Because by looking at the solution logically in terms of equality we are dealing with the question in the wrong way as well as, ironically, from a masculine perspective. Why can't men and women be equal? The answer: Because they are not equal … never can be, no matter how much spanner-wielding women and baby-rearing men may do. So, the solution? Parity: being on a par or equivalent. Equal implies sameness, equivalence implies a balance such as man: woman, outside-labour: inside-labour, fatherhood: motherhood and so on. A balance leads to a creative relationship with unequal but equivalent contributions, which leads to creative outcomes; such as a child, if we consider sex at the biological level; or the birth of soul, if the psychological.

Zeus represents the outer aspect of sexuality and manifests it in his actions. It is single-focused, being on genitals and orgasm. It is all things masculine; linear like the erect cock, powerful like the jetting sperm, combative and challenging. Teiresias challenges Zeus with the inwardness by placing it in a differing order. Note: it is not one part of ten to man and the remaining nine to woman, but one to man and all ten to woman. Remember logarithms at school? Or 1:10 in analogue language … Teiresias is saying the sexuality of the feminine does not compete with the masculine; it is quite simply of a different order.

Woman's sexuality is internal. Her genital organs can be

considered an inversion of the man's. Her orgasm is more inward. Her substance is round: breast, vagina, womb and egg ... and belly, if impregnated. Man is obvious ... woman a mystery. Man's eroticism is genitally focused ... woman's is dispersed through her body. The challenge of sexual contact is to find the 'other' in each other and hence oneself; that is the wisdom of Tantra and in our own ritual past.

As a finale to the myth: Is Hera angry because Teiresias has explained the mystery to Zeus? (Who intuitively might have known it anyway?) Is that it ... the woman – or more specifically because we are dealing with archetypal principles here – the feminine that holds the secrets to sexuality? And thus truly has the power? Is it not surprising then that pornography would explore these themes and variances, nooks and crannies? Let's now turn to some of these themes.

If something is denied in our individual selves or society, it is pushed underground into what depth psychologists call "the unconscious". This is repression, and it has happened to sex. It then operates from this neglected position, inflicting trouble on us in the form of illness, such as hysteria (Freud) and bodily symptoms (Reich) leading to a plethora of potential diseases. The larger picture is archetypal (Jung) and is that sexuality itself has been repressed. When a collective, or archetypal, pattern is repressed it will seek a creative re-emergence, otherwise it will attract indirect attention and erupt disruptively and dangerously.

In a fundamental manner, porn represents this eruption. Sex becomes destructive when it has not been critically and consciously integrated, when it can inflict damage, such as with AIDs. From this repressed position, porn contains all the features that those who want to keep the lid on will look for to further justify a continued sexual repression, such as violence, abuse, coercion, dominance (of women) and the like. There is all of this and more in porn and I would argue at one level that it is an inevitable consequence of the severity of the repression. So, rather than try to keep the lid on and make it even more potentially violent and disruptive, we must at some level embrace and understand it. This is what I have attempted to do as a consumer.

Why? Because, at the core, sex is creative. It has been repressed and seeks reintegration, and this position is supported by mountains of evidence from other cultures and times and is further reflected in mythology, anthropology and archaeology. So, we need to go to the still place at the centre of the sexual cyclone and discover what is creative and transformative in porn. If we don't, the effects will not be simply individual and painful, they will be collectively so in the form of an epidemic.

I would further venture to say that the current supposed climate crisis represents more a denial of the associated feminine, if we see the Earth as Gaia, or mother, and our treatment of her being one of repression. In other words, the crisis is actually symbolic of the need for integration of the feminine, or mother. Whether there is literally a climate crisis remains a question, but if we don't appreciate the symbolic level of it, then we may actually be creating what we fear.

Before we look at the specific patterns in porn, let's examine the feminism movement from this perspective. Stripped of the recent political, legal, academic and social history, feminism has done a huge amount to restore the parity of the feminine in our society. This obviously has been women's doing primarily, but men also had and have their place. Their exploration of their own femininity has allowed a clearer perspective of masculinity in a balanced relationship with sexuality. From this dynamic perspective, my view is that the pro-censorship feminist position is regressive, repressive and in a deep way mimics what it is trying to escape from: the patriarchy.

Now we are faced with the challenge of the association of femininity and sexuality. The Teiresias myth would indicate that it is the feminine perspective, and hence women in general, who have the power in this respect. Instead of shooting the messenger, as Hera does, this should be directed toward a creative integration of sexuality. Where better to start than at the core of the return: pornography.

Women are doing this directly. They are significantly empowered in the workplace, dictating terms of engagement. They may enjoy anal sex, but they want either a condom or an AIDs test on the penetrator first. Many use it to explore their own sexuality and boundaries and, like prostitution, for most, it is a temporary stage in their personal, career and professional development. Some stay in for a career itself, the porn star, and command a wage significantly greater than their counterpart, the stud, who is no longer rewarded for his anonymity.

Women are acknowledging their sexual rights in the productions and their own expression. They are becoming directors, forming their own production companies and extending to other fields. Some are social advocates, others academics. Many maintain active relationships and can differentiate sex in the workplace from their personal life. Nor does this stop many enjoying their workplace sex; after all, we are encouraged to enjoy our work generally, aren't we?

Things are changing and women are being primarily responsible. I would argue it is at the aesthetic and erotic end of the pornographic spectrum that this is occurring, but why? Because here the mystery of feminine sexuality as an inner and mysterious process is most maintained. At the other end of the spectrum, we see the disruptive and dangerous aspects of the return of archetypal sexuality, and it needs to be seen in that light. In fact, bringing it out into the light is exactly what must happen, and then it will dissipate of its own momentum. At that level, the authors of *The Porn Report* may be right about what they were witnessing as "deeply offensive and abhorrent", I just think it could have been made clearer.

Sexuality is broad, varied and complex. As is porn, and as reflected in myth, history and anthropology. This further confirms the archetypal basis of porn; it is therefore not an isolated, distorted phenomenon. It is trying to tell us something about our sexuality and ourselves; we just have to use the right language to get a dialogue. I maintain that this is more symbolic and imaginative, rather than rational and intellectual. So, let's look at some patterns that occur with the sex in porn itself to see what they are telling us.

Let's hit the pause button and take a breath. I've covered an enormous amount of territory here, a bit like a jet passing over a large island. As I've indicated, we will be exploring a lot of this territory in more detail as we progress, so consider the chapter to date in many ways a summary that gives you a taste – a map – of the territory we will move through at a more leisurely pace.

I also had to hit the pause button. Distracted by other issues to attend to, the chapter was left at this point for several weeks when I would like to have completed it at that prior time. I had anticipated doing this by exploring the masculine: feminine, outer: inner and 1:10 analogues and their symbolism. But when I returned to this idea, I realised it was bigger than the chapter completion and needed to be explored further and integrated into the ensuing work as a whole. So, I thought about how I might go from here: I needed a bridge of sorts because I was now leaving the background territory of history (both personal and cultural), sociology and psychology, to move into a more detailed creative and imaginative perspective. How to make this transition became the question.

Then suddenly it became obvious. I could describe a representative pornographic film and analyse it. That seemed a good option, until I realised I was being seduced into a position I was trying not to undertake, that of the observer rather than the consumer. I then felt that I needed to describe the experience of consumption, even if it might be considered an act of pornography in its own right under the guise of creativity. Then again, by now you may have realised that I don't make these clear-cut distinctions and this could be an erotic narrative created to illustrate the points raised to date, which some may still interpret as pornography. I hope it has a creative aesthetic that renders such an accusation as marginal. But I suppose it depends on how you view what I've written to date, as well as your motive for reading the book at all.

What I have now decided to do is write an imaginative piece on the viewing of a porn movie. I have further decided to do little planning of this section, but to let it unravel as it will. As a product of my imagination, it will have my own biases and distortions but, as I hope I have illustrated by now, my consumption is relatively mainstream and therefore representative. As far as I can, I will not directly base it on any material I have actually witnessed, although I remain obviously informed by what I have seen. As an act of creation, I doubt if this position is much dissimilar to that of most artists anticipating a work to be undertaken. In this respect, porn is no different. I'll also wait in anticipation for the offers of porn movie directorship from the major producers ...

It's now 5 p.m. on Friday afternoon, and I have set the next few days after the weekend aside from professional duties to focus on this book, after this absence of several weeks. Now the creative possibilities start to dance in front of me and draw me in, but I am initially overwhelmed. I can see that my intention to this point had been fairly straightforward: Having first thought to finish this chapter with some further reflections from the depth psychology perspective, but then realising that wasn't the way to go, because the themes that have been raised are going to be woven into the ongoing enquiry throughout the entirety of the remainder of the book. So, then it occurred to me to write a short fictional piece to bring in the "Who, How, What and Why" issues from the previous chapters in a direct and illustrated way, by describing the viewing experience and content. This represents what the alchemist might call the "prima materia", or raw material from which the gold will be elaborated.

I then realised this is a formula I have used elsewhere, although in a slightly different order. Does that invalidate what I had proposed to do? I ponder: No, it doesn't, but maybe it won't explore the issue to the creative depth that I feel I want to achieve. A simple few pages of viewing a couple of pornographic scenes may be illustrative, personally cathartic and even titillating, but may not fully integrate the pornographic phenomenon into the more psychospiritual study that will follow. I would therefore be committing the sin of perpetuating a division – between porn and sexuality – that I am also actively trying to heal.

I look out over the lake from my study window and the still close of the day; it suddenly all seems too much. Somehow, I have to use the viewing experience as an integrated springboard into the remainder of this study and I won't be able to give it justice in a few pages. So where will that place this act of creativity, as it will now stand out and be of greater proportion than originally envisaged?

I started to further examine what I am proposing to do. If a porn producer read it, he (or she) may like some of the themes, but would they be any different from what has already been directed and produced? Probably not, and there are some dangers that the industry itself has readily fallen into. It could become comic by using names like "Rod" and "Dick" for the men and "Cherry" or "Fanny" for the women. (Maybe that was in the mind of the author of "Fanny Hill", John Cleland?) I'm amused at myself, but it has already been done – to death. While comic and self-referential, it doesn't lift the genre out of its potentially demeaned position, and thankfully, the industry doesn't largely engage the viewer in this manner currently.

There is a significant trend that doesn't 'pretend' about porn, so that the delivery is built around the sexual viewing experience and particular themes, usually expressed in the title such as *The Voyeur*, *Ass Traffic* or *Blowjob Mania*. In a film, there are several scenes, commonly about six and usually about ten to fifteen minutes each in length (although there is a tendency in successful series to lengthen both the scenes and the movie). These are built around a connecting theme, such as a commentator, or even with no theme at all. The scenes are action-packed and quite formulaic around whatever your fancy is. They are quite masturbatory in intent and divorced from any emotional expression beyond the instinctual. My impression is that they tend to reinforce the stereotypes within the industry and make it particularly easy for criticism. Why is this? Because the themes are generally derogatory, with overt hostility, conflict and competition. Terms like "slut", "whore" and "stud" abound, with directions like, "suck my cock, bitch" or "fuck my gaping arse". These can then be elaborated into "come on my face, you motherfucker" ... I think you get the point. The scenes themselves are of similar appeal; direct, sexual and often multiple. Almost invariably a cumshot, or more than one, finishes the shoot with a ravished and seemingly (self?) satisfied female face before the lens.

This is what I would classify as "porn" from my exploration of definitions in chapter two; it is hardly aesthetic and only erotic in a base and fundamentally instinctual sense. It does satisfy predilections, however, and may have a place for diffusing psychic tension, but it is not where we want to go. Too many commentators and critics have judged all pornographic sexual depiction from this perspective. Certainly, it serves to reinforce stereotypes, such as sexism, exploitation, dominance and other power issues. For this the industry – or the branch that produces this type of porn – makes no apology. In fact, I would suggest they play on it significantly to attract the market they are looking for (and knows exists) with any alienation in a larger forum probably good advertising. We won't be going any further down this route.

I also don't want to explore the "reality" theme or the material directed to the "couples market". Whilst these have a valid place and are a direct challenge to the smuttier end of the spectrum from, at least, a sexist perspective, they tend to remind me of reality TV shows and soap operas. Which is interesting, because the pattern of a lot of porn production for the screen mimics other genres, which shouldn't be surprising. It is symbolic, reflecting the degree to which the erotic has become integrated into the mainstream and is a long way from the stag or subsequent blue movie eras.

There has been a distinct attempt to make overt sexual depiction part of the broader movie mainstream and to have it judged from other perspectives, such as acting ability and production quality. The industry has furthered this with its equivalent of the "Oscars" and other awards. In my opinion, it is still a long way from achieving this unification, although there are some moves in the right direction. If such unification had occurred there would be no need to write this book, as it would symbolise the reintegration of sexuality in our culture.

The above minor – but significant – detour came as a result of my late afternoon reflections and the challenge of how I would present to you a written piece of pornographically-inspired erotic writing that would integrate into the book as a whole. What I was describing above are some of the avenues that porn has taken that perpetuate the divisions between it and the broader culture, and done this in a brief and cursory manner to illustrate how they are divisive; sometimes deliberately so. There seems to be a firm wedge driven between the instinctual level of sexuality and its creative unification in our whole psychological state. This is the fundamental problem this work is trying to redress, and I came to see that any creative writing I were to do would have to both have roots in the porn genre, yet also contain the issues that can effect a reunification of our sexual divisions at a cultural level.

After looking at the above themes, I realised that what was to come must include the issues that I have raised and wanted to continue to explore. The only way to effectively do this is by a drama, I reasoned. Of course, that is not true; I could use a fantasy structure or a satire, for example. Well, I could, but fantasy has been well and truly employed and serves to reinforce the escapism aspect of porn consumption. Satire is attractive and does exist in the industry, usually inadvertently. Drama, of course, has been extensively employed but usually lapses by comparison to the mainstream movie industry on all counts: acting, production, direction and the like. But drama can reflect life without lapsing into the "reality" or "couple next door" mode and can explore themes such as comedy, sexism and power in a more integrated manner.

So, it will be drama. I feel settled and the light is beginning to dim. I open a bottle of white wine, pour a glass and settle back in my chair. The computer stays on, but I realise the writing has finished and reflect on what I propose to do. Initially, I feel entirely inadequate and not up to the task, and briefly, I despair ... maybe even this work and the book will go no further? A sip of wine and the despair abates. What setting shall I use? I do a brief scanning of movies I have seen and there doesn't appear any that haven't been used. I also want to avoid ones that blur ethical issues and might add to the confusion.

I pause to reconsider. Why not choose a medical setting, or even a therapeutic one? After all, this work is essentially one of healing the divisions in our sexuality, so why not use a theme that directly pertains to this? I am attracted ... but dismiss the possibility. It does re-ignite my thoughts of a satirical work, however, maybe with Freud as the central character? No, all jokes aside, the reason I dismiss this setting is because I believe it is part of the problem in that our medicalised and psychiatric orientation toward sexuality is divisive and pathologised. Also, satire has become something of a lost art. I further believe that the healing comes from a broader creative and spiritual basis and that any contribution I might make be from that foundation.

I also realise that the impasse is because I want to depart from the writing formulae I have used to date and which the latter part of this chapter was in danger of leading into. I feel like I am facing unknown territory and that the last few pages are a direct reflection of this creative process and its attendant difficulties and confusions.

Ducks settle on the lake and the sun is disappearing. I look around at the magnificent setting I am writing in ... and realise something like this can also be the setting for the drama. People coming to a retreat... for a conference? The images start dancing ... two men in a drawing room after a dinner, smoking and sipping port. The 'wife' of one enters the room and ... the fun starts! I leave the computer and sketch some notes.

They are so alive! The figures in the drawing room are moving around in differing potential interactions: I am fascinated. I jump to other scenes and further characters emerge into the theatre of my mind. The relationships between the various characters start to take shape; secrets, innuendo, power and games all start to play. The initial scenes and their psychological activity play out fairly quickly, then the complexity sets in and the further scenes are in danger of losing the plot, so I withdraw from the imaginative route I have gone down, realising I can and will pick it up again later.

So, it's another wine, dinner and the end of the day. Then I realise something fascinating and perplexing; I haven't yet actually pictured any sexual activity in my imaginings. I have no doubt this will emerge, but the creative emphasis seems to be on the creation of the characters and the drama itself. I know this is significant and is something I will reflect on as I continue. Initially, however, it does point to something interesting: Whilst the sexuality will be overt and clearly illustrated, it is in the context of life and its wider ramifications – not the other way round. I realise this is a huge mistake that the industry is making and the manner in which we are trying to reintegrate the erotic.

And that is where I am now. It's the next morning and a beautiful day. I have penned the experiences of last evening and feel settled. I have family activities in front of me, and a relaxing weekend ... although I know the characters will dance and play in my imagination before I return to my study on Monday.

So, did Freud get it right? No, not at all. In fact, he has done us a disservice. The remainder of the book may explain why.

4

The Weekend Retreat

Now I'm going to take a step back from the discussion and introduce you to a fictional consumer friend of mine, who is going to narrate an account of exposure to a pornographic movie and the experiences it raises. I won't be far away though, as my comments will be interspersed with his reflections and we will be flowing freely between the two as the story continues … so, now I would like to introduce you to Brian.

I'm driving home and will be on my own tonight, as Val is working away and has taken the kids with her for a break from the usual routine, leaving me to finish off some overdue business tasks. At the Post Office, I pick up a parcel from Canberra; it's the porn DVDs I'd ordered online and I'm keen – even anxious – to have a look at them. It'll also allow me to scan them to see which ones Val might like for our next "viewing evening". At home, after tea, I decide to use the convenience of a quiet viewing in my study and go upstairs with a bottle of wine.

As usual, I find them to be a somewhat varied catch. I've found this is often the way when I stray from what I know and, on this occasion, I was trying to find some material with a little more edge in the kind of areas I enjoy. I also tried to select something that overlaps Val's tastes. She's not as keen on viewing and only watches this material when with me, although she knows I enjoy solo viewing as well. However, there are a couple of discs that do appeal, partly because I've selected from established production houses whose style and tastes I am familiar with, as well as porn stars I find attractive, sexually stimulating and whose preferences largely match my own. Things like style, elegance, beauty and sexual grace are important, as well as performing at the edge of my range of preference and even extending to avenues that I have not – as yet maybe – personally explored.

I effectively discard a couple that have themes I want to explore because they have what I call a degenerative feeling about them. The themes themselves seemed to lose any artistic quality; probably not the time to analyse this, but they seemed to degenerate by going too far into the theme itself with camera shots that were too genital, as well as a loss of glamour and perspective. Also, the performers seemed like they were just doing a job and did not present their most attractive features. Basically, they're material for a good wank, but very primal and instinctual and not what I was looking for. Shame, as they had been advertised in a more promising light, but there is only so much that can be gleaned from a disc cover shot on a website and a description that plays on all the porn clichés. There is a fair bit of trial and error and in many ways, it is similar to mainstream movies. There is an awful amount of pulp out there and, like the mainstream, I have learnt to appreciate and follow the porn stars, directors and publishing houses I have got to know and trust over the years.

One called *The Weekend Retreat* sounds promising, exploring themes I like and made by a producer I knew, although a director I did not. Some of the porn stars are familiar as well, so I took a minor risk with the director. What I was really looking for was a movie that contained themes and action delivered in an erotic, artistic and – dare I say it – aesthetic manner. The most enjoyable porn movie is one that engages me from beginning to end without recourse to the fast-forward button. To do this, there has to be some sort of narrative that isn't simply one to link action scenes together. I put the DVD into the player and decide to risk it and play the movie from whoa to go ... often I'd go to scene selection first and do a brief scanning of the content.

While Brian pours himself that promised glass of wine, we'll hit the pause button and discuss what this outline hopes to achieve.

The first point is what has been written immediately above. In a condensed manner, we have moved through several of the issues that I raised toward the end of the previous chapter and brought them into a summary of sorts. Why have I done this? Because I effectively want to part company with the more pornographic end of the erotic spectrum for the remainder of the book. At the risk of repeating myself, let me point out why I am doing this, whilst Brian has a sip of his wine.

I do see an argument that there is a considered place for this sort of basic porn material. One is that it may serve to diffuse sexual – and hence psychic – tension, which may not be able to be achieved otherwise. This build-up of tension may lead to undesired, even criminal consequences. It has been frequently argued that the opposite is the case; that such material incites such acts. Whilst there is absolutely no clear evidence that this is the case, it also does not make psychological sense to me that it would be so. On the other hand, it does pose some difficulties in that the material is primarily instinctual, devoid of emotional content or even access to it, and could be considered "degenerative". By degenerative I do not mean in either the moral or psychoanalytic sense, but that it remains locked in a vicious cycle and cannot become generative or even regenerative; that is, creatively stimulating and spiritually inductive. These are all points to which we will return in a cyclical manner, but here I simply want to point out that such a cycle as the one I describe will be repetitive and potentially addictive to the vulnerable.

Obviously, from a marketing and profit perspective, this would seem to be an ideal position to hold and many in the industry have taken advantage of it since the floodgates opened. Also, in general, this is the sort of porn that critics and detractors have chosen to focus on, as if it is all that the industry is. I hope I have made it clear by now that this is not the case, in spite of perceptions and media reports to the contrary. Were porn seen in the same light as other cultural phenomena, we would see the full spectrum. We do not, and it is a fundamental argument of this work that this is a feature indicating how poorly integrated the subject matter of porn – sexuality – is in our Western culture.

The second point raised by the opening outline is that we are going to be taking a rather unusual perspective. We are going to be looking through Brian's eyes at a porn movie and describing it from both an objective and a subjective position. We are also going to be taking periodic steps back to look at Brian's position and responses. We may also take a step back from my responses to all of this as they emerge. This may create a sense of abruptness on occasion, even frustration, but I think it may provide an approach that can move around the subject matter in a creative and insightful manner.

This is the point I struggled with at the end of the last chapter. In an earlier book, I had introduced a fictional segment as a way of illustrating the points I wanted to convey to the reader. I found this successful and was a part of the enterprise that I really enjoyed. Yet there was something that I found dissatisfying about that process. Although it was a useful mechanism to get several points across and to introduce some autobiographical material, it did create a discomfort about the depth of the characters and, hence, their authenticity.

I had been in danger of simply repeating this style here. I then realised that the concerns that I had about my previous attempt at fiction was that it was useful in style, but lacked a depth of content and hence deeper meaning. In that work, this was entirely appropriate, as further characterisation would have taken away from the points I wanted to illustrate. In this work, however, this would have been a regressive step, I felt. Why? Because one of the criticisms I have about the industry as a whole is that it doesn't employ depth of character and other creative mechanisms that are employed in other artistic media. The almost over-emphasis on sex and its portrayal makes this a secondary consideration.

I wanted to rectify this and present an erotic piece in a way that did explore more depth and hence be more commensurate with other creative output, and from this platform examine in more detail where sexuality – following this initial integration – may take us. So, I have chosen two ways of doing this. The first is to attempt to give a little more depth to the personnel in the movie than is usually given in the porn I have seen. The second is to expand on some of the creative angles I have employed before, such as bringing in autobiographical content and moving from subjective to objective stances in a fluid and cyclical way.

The last point is that I would like you to step into the narrative. More significantly, I would also like you to explore your responses in a bit more detail than you might usually, so let me explain how. To do this successfully, I would ask you not only to read the story in a rational and/or intellectual manner but also to watch your physical and emotional responses. This shouldn't surprise you, as these sorts of responses are exactly what the industry wants to achieve. In a simplistic manner, it is not a very good movie if it doesn't turn you on sexually. We won't be exploring the subtleties of these physical and emotional responses for a while, so at this stage, it may be simplest to recognise repulsion and attraction, both physical and emotional.

Repulsion is the more obvious one. It is socially conditioned and culturally sanctioned in this domain. It is easy to identify, but is it honest? Is it what you think about when you are reading or watching, when your emotions or physical responses may be quite different? Be careful, as it is easy from the rational perspective to then get into value judgments, such as; what sort of "sicko" is writing this? You might notice the conflict, rational repulsion with physical and/or emotional attraction. Attraction is more difficult to deal with, although it may be more creative and enlightening. Again, it is the physical and/or emotional attractions that are more informative and instructive, although sometimes difficult to admit to. Just try to be honest ...

Back to Brian, wine in one hand and the remote in the other.

There are four people in the car, two men and two women. It's a bright, clear day and, whilst the introductions and credits pass across the screen, the vehicle moves from motorway to road, then to a lane and finally to a driveway leading up to a large country house. At various times we see the occupants from camera shots inside the car. The two men are in the front; one is more extroverted and boisterous, and he is driving. A quieter man sits next to him and we will discover his name is Paul, whilst Graham is the driver. Graham's wife, Carole, sits behind Paul with Emily, Paul's partner, sitting next to her and behind Graham. Emily is quiet and demure, Carole more forthright and often seemingly at odds with her husband. There is little interaction between Paul and Emily.

Mick and Helen, who run the country house as a "Weekend Getaway" from the city, greet this foursome at the door. What we learn from the discussion at the ensuing evening meal, which the four attend and are waited on by Mick and Helen, is that they work together running a small advertising agency. Graham is the manager, Paul the graphics expert. Carole administers the business and Emily has only recently become involved in the marketing of the products. The weekend away has been organised as a "bonding exercise" and to deal with some personality issues that have emerged. There are some undercurrents that become apparent as the meal progresses. The first and most obvious is that Emily is attracted to Graham, who doesn't recognise this. Carole does, although Paul is also quite oblivious to the fact.

The business and their roles in it rapidly disappear in content and importance as the personalities and their inter-relationships emerge. This is a relatively common manoeuvre in porn, a story that serves the purpose of providing a narrative background in which *The Weekend Retreat* is no exception. Brian does wonder whether this may also be a technique to leave other narrative possibilities open, should there be a sequel. It is a passing thought; he is intrigued by some of the performers and their interactions. The acting is not bad, he concludes. He knows several of the main performers from other productions.

Carole has long dark hair contoured around her attractive and seductive face. She is strongly made up, possibly because she has been around a while and – in porn terms – getting on a bit. She is well endowed and Brian knows from other performances that her breasts are natural. She is also dressed blatantly and glamorously in an overtly sexual manner, which is, of course, no surprise to Brian, who finds her sexually attractive and is one of the main reasons he got this movie. Carole is the sort of woman he would have no difficulty fucking, because she displays intelligence, wit and a more than passing acting ability; she also appears to really enjoy her sexuality. Brian also likes this easy-going sexuality and although she has done some lesbian scenes, these are obviously not her preference.

Brian deplores the tendency to focus on youth alone. It is not that he is exclusively drawn to the ageing end of the porn star spectrum, but he feels maturity makes the acting more authentic and multi-dimensional. Val has sometimes commented on the age factor in porn actresses and questioned whether Brian's porn attraction is compensation to her own ageing. He assures her this is not, and knows it to be, the case, yet it continues as an undercurrent in their relationship, even though women like Carole seem testament to his position. Because Val doesn't use porn for masturbation, he wonders whether this perception is because she doesn't appreciate the differing sexual functions that porn fulfils; not only for Brian, but also for many others.

Mick is a participant in many porn movies and is an experienced and enthusiastic stud. A big strong and silent type with rough good looks, he is known for the size of his erect cock and his ability to wield it. Brian is comfortable with Mick, mainly because he is relatively unobtrusive as a personality – a lot of male porn stars seem quite narcissistic in his opinion – although his sexual presence is strong. Brian wonders whether this makes it easier for him to identify with Mick and his sexual activities. His 'wife', Helen, is of a similar vintage to Carole with long blonde hair often elaborately styled and, although also well endowed, her physique is a little more Amazonian. Brian knows she has a varied sexual repertoire, which usually includes lesbian roles. He knows she also acts in exclusively lesbian movies.

In passing, the impact of homosexuality on the genre has some interesting features, which may be better understood when we explore the gender perspectives in the coming chapters. In general, lesbianism is acceptable in mainstream porn, whereas male homosexual – gay – activity is not. The lesbianism takes two forms: it can be part of a mainstream movie, as it will be here; this is usually in a mixed scene involving heterosexual activity, although it can also extend to an entire scene on its own. Exclusively lesbian movies seem to have a niche place with mainline porn consumers and are often part of the range advertised.

This is not so with gay movies. Although multiple male presence in threesomes involving two men, gang bangs (one woman with three or more men) and orgies (a varied number of men and women together) is common, the contact between them gets only as close as sharing the same orifice or receiving an accidental sperm spillage, which has usually been destined for some part of the female anatomy, but erratically or poorly aimed. This is not the sort of thing that you can easily do another "take" on, so you usually only get one chance and must accept any inadvertent consequences. There is the occasional "bi" movie, that contains two men who do have sexual contact as well as with the same woman, but this is not common. In general, gay movies form a separate genre.

When there are two or more men present in a scene, Brian has noticed two distinct patterns. The first, his preference, is when the attention of the men is toward the woman, or women, often in a co-ordinated and choreographed manner. He feels this enhances the sexual intensity, particularly from the feminine perspective. The opposite seems the case when the men seem to reinforce and attend to or compete for each other's performance. Here, the woman/women become more objectified and even demeaned, as there are undercurrents of misogyny and, I suspect, latent homosexuality.

Brian recognises Graham as a regular performer, usually as the archetypal alpha-male businessman, entrepreneur or the like. The roles he takes often portray affluence and are matched by his use of jewellery and his thinning hairline. He is an extravert, but reaching the end of his porn life, surmises Brian, with his diminishing role frequency. Like Carole, he has begun to dabble in other aspects of the genre, such as direction and production. Brian senses that, unlike Carole, Graham will quietly disappear from the adult industry, as he appears to be a frustrated role actor. By contrast, Mick, whose genital focus is strong and not inclined to look to a role in mainstream acting, is the stereotypical 'stud'.

The other two, Paul and Emily, he doesn't know. This intrigues him, as Paul is obviously seasoned and he wonders why he is now acting in porn if, indeed, he hasn't before. He briefly wonders, because of his soft and retiring nature, whether he has moved across from the gay movie seen, as he wouldn't have heard of him if that were the case. He thinks it more likely that he has crossed over from mainstream as the movie progresses, however, wondering whether this is a ploy by the director to 'inject' a stronger acting focus. Emily is younger with long brown hair and she may or may not have acted in porn before. Was she to stimulate Brian more sexually, he may investigate online to see what else she has done, but as this is not the case, he may well not, unless her sexual activities in the movie engage him. She is attractive, with average-sized breasts and a virginal figure, and her role is initially quiet. Other actors and actresses will appear in some of the scenes. Brian recognises most of these extras, usually by their face, breasts or even penises, although not their names.

The meal is over and Emily excuses herself. She tells her companions that she is tired and wants to have a bath and retire early. Graham and Paul leave Carole chatting with Helen and retire to the drawing room. Here they smoke (a continuing feature in porn, by contrast to mainstream) with a glass of cognac and settle into facing lounge suites to talk a little business. There is a brief interjected scene of Emily undressing and getting into a bubble bath, and then a switch to Carole and Helen talking, whilst Mick is tidying up after the dinner. Carole excuses herself and goes to join the men. When she arrives, she finds Paul alone, as Graham has gone to get a file from his room.

Carole, from her position in the dining room, had actually seen Graham exit, which is why she excused herself from Helen and went to the drawing room. Inside the room, there is a very brief flirtation initiated by Carole and to which Paul is initially hesitant. However, when she moves her fondling and kissing of him to opening his fly, Brian can see from Paul's developing erection that there is a definite response and that his endowment may have contributed to his selection for the role. Carole has taken off her dress revealing the standard porn attire of jewellery and lingerie with revealing bra, garters and dark stockings, plus a G-string. She then demurely goes down on her knees between Paul's thighs and starts to suck him whilst he remains seated.

It has taken nearly ten minutes to get to this point, the first sexual depiction. Now, in porn, this is quite a time and the director would have to balance the 'getting to the action' with the development of the plot and narrative. I suspect as the industry currently stands, still relatively divided from the mainstream, that this could present quite a challenge to a director trying to bridge the gap. You may recall this is a new director to Brian's knowledge and he has recognised from the complexity of the plot to date that this is a more ambitious work and the director is asking to be taken seriously. Brian has also enjoyed the build-up. He has noted some sacrifice, such as the lack of attention and detail to the workplace issues that envelop the foursome, but realises the obvious reason for and easily accepts this. He also has noted the interesting mix of the porn stars themselves and that some of those he knows in this production are at interesting points in their respective careers.

Meanwhile, Carole continues to suck Paul's cock and he is increasingly responsive, as recognised by his breathing, hip movements and some guttural sounds that occasionally emerge into words, such as: "Yes!" "More ... " and "Babe, you suck so well!" These utterances are quite soft though, and don't jar the senses or continuity of the scene, because we don't see much of Paul's face. Commonly, this can be used as a fill-in in porn scenes, with longer than-average camera shots of the expressive faces of the male actors. When Brian sees this in a movie, he surmises that the guy may be having trouble with his erection, the porn star is not actually involved in her work, or the director is padding out the scene. There is a distinct lack of such evasiveness in this movie already, which pleases Brain. The eye contact is also good and this remains a constant throughout the whole movie. The focus in this scene is almost entirely on Carole going about her work, with Paul – and his reactions – as a relative background. She starts off teasingly and slowly, with occasional looks up to Paul, responding to his physical and verbal cues. Brian admires her; she's a real professional. The sucking becomes quicker, deeper and, on occasion, she engulfs Paul's now quite erect penis in its entirety.

Then Graham comes back into the room, looking at the file he has retrieved and talking about the contents at the same time. Of course, he drops the file – and his jaw – when he sees what's going on and is met with an equally compromised look from Paul. Yet Carole, bless her heart, doesn't miss a beat and seems to know what's happening even though her back is toward the door. What she does instead is direct her right arm backward toward Graham, whilst the left continues with its grip on Paul's cock, and invites Graham forward with a wiggle of her index finger. Graham obliges, and Paul's look is something like "I bet this isn't the first time you've done this!" The scene now takes off in Brian's opinion. He feels his own erection straining against his trousers, so he decides to remove them, whilst still watching the movie.

Graham fingers Carole's pussy, moves the crotch of her G-string to the side, licks her from behind, then kneels and penetrates her whilst she all the time continues her uninterrupted rhythm with her mouth up and down Paul's cock. Brian is quietly stroking his own erection whilst watching. Then there's a change in scene:

We are watching Emily reclining in her bubble bath and stroking her open pussy lightly with the assistance of a slender shampoo bottle being used in an innovative way not on the label description. She has her eyes closed and the camera pans in onto her face in a way that makes the viewer realise the next scene is her imagination. She is seeing Graham in varying scenes that we have already witnessed in the car and at dinner; none of these are sexual, they are simply memories. Meanwhile, back in the drawing room, there are several rapid scenes that build up a bit of frenzy, both in the scene and in Brian's body. Carole sucks both men together alternating from one to the other. Then at other times, she is being penetrated by one whilst sucking the other in a kaleidoscope of changing positions over the lounge suites and deeply carpeted floor.

Upstairs, Emily is startled by a lightly night-gowned Helen coming into the bathroom, ostensibly to give her a towel. Emily gets out of the bath, and Helen doesn't offer her the towel. Instead, she starts to dry her, with the action silently but progressively becoming more erotic and sexual. Helen is always the instigator of her actions, notes Brian, which is true to the casting. Helen then begins to kiss Emily on various bodily areas, progressing toward her mouth. Initially, Emily remains quite passive and even unresponsive to the kissing but gradually responds, as Brian can tell from her jaw movement and then closing her eyes. Helen leads Emily to the bed, lays her on her back and then progresses to kissing her breasts. Finally, she parts Emily's thighs and begins to lick her open pussy with long practised strokes of her tongue.

In the drawing room, Carole is riding Paul, who is now lying back on the carpet naked, although she is still wearing her lingerie but with breasts exposed. Initially, Graham is not seen, and Brian recognises that this is building up to a double penetration; that is, when the woman is penetrated simultaneously in the arse and pussy. Graham comes back in the scene with his cock in hand; Carole stops her rhythmic activity without looking back, maybe in response to a cue from Paul. Graham is able to easily insert his cock into her arse and then they start gyrating almost in unison.

Then a brief interlude of Helen eating Emily's pussy with increasing vigour, moans from above, and resulting in Emily having an orgasm. Then there is a return to the threesome with this time Paul doing the arse fucking in another double penetration. The activity is now frenetic, with Carole thrusting back on the cocks that penetrate her in unison. The camera shows fluids dribbling down from the occupied arse onto the pussy, the cock below and beyond, whilst Carole shrieks her orgasm with, "I'm coming, god I'm coming!" The camera then pans to her enraptured face.

Brian is very involved now and wanking in response to the images that move in front of him; he almost feels part of the action. Now he knows why he likes Carole; she's totally immersed in what she's doing and the two men almost dance around her in response to any initiative she makes. Too often, he briefly reflects, the men control these sorts of threesomes and gang bangs. When this happens, it makes him feel a little uncomfortable, almost to the point that it seems to be becoming abusive. This is definitely not the case here and if Carole is just acting, she's doing a damn good job, he thinks.

Carole then moves to a kneeling position facing the camera, although she never looks at it. The men position themselves standing on either side, and Carole masturbates them simultaneously whilst alternatively looking up at each man in turn. Finally, the men ejaculate and Carole keeps her mouth open a few inches distant from each successive erupting manhood, so that some sperm goes into her mouth and the remainder around it, over her cheeks and falls down over her exposed breasts with some dripping onto the carpet. She finally gives each cock a loving suck then gets up and, with a broad smile, asks who is going to get her a drink.

Back upstairs, Emily, who to this point has been quite passive, opens her eyes and looks down at Helen with a fixed glare. Helen meets her gaze and briefly stops her licking, which has gently subsided after the orgasm. When she resumes, their eyes remain locked and Emily raises herself from the bed by her elbows. Helen stops again, she is non-plussed: What has happened to this demure little creature that she thought would be such a sexual pushover? Emily disengages herself and grabs Helen by the hair, pulling her onto the bed and pushing her to lie flat on her stomach. Emily then begins to smack Helen on her buttocks. Helen squeals in response to each slap, but whether in pain or pleasure – or both – Brian finds it difficult to determine. He is a little on edge here with the spanking, particularly as Helen's cheeks start to redden. She is making no attempt to move away though; is that part of the acting? Has this crossed a boundary?

As Brian has these thoughts the camera pans to Mick, who is watching this all from the slightly ajar bathroom door. He has a smile on his face, and his erection is being gently stroked through his dressing gown as he watches the scene unfold in front of him.

"My lady didn't pick this one ... or maybe she did!" he mutters to himself as Emily inserts fingers into Helen's pussy and then one from the same hand into her anus. Helen is beginning to writhe a little now as Emily continues the occasional smack accompanied with "Bitch!"

Back in the drawing room, the sated threesome is having a post-coital drink. Contrary to Paul's surmising, Graham and Carole confess this is the first time this has happened, but it does come in the wake of each discovering the other's infidelities and that the relationship is on notice. They imply that this was a make-or-break weekend for their marriage and hint to Paul that what has just happened will certainly decide one way or the other.

Of the two, Graham appears the more confused. Carole is more assured, and Paul starts to reflect on her initiation of what has just transpired. Where does that put him? His relationship with Emily was and still is drifting, although he had not been unfaithful – until this evening. He wondered what Emily was thinking.

The answer is: Not a lot. Emily is fingering Helen quite vigorously, occasionally ducking her head to provide a tongue to the penetrative mix. This is time for Mick to enter, Brian thought. He quietly moves up behind Emily, intending to penetrate her but, to his surprise, she simply turns and grasps his cock and then begins to devour it whilst continuing to simultaneously finger Helen with her other hand. Mick appeared equally surprised.

As was Brian, but he was really enjoying this! The fact that the feelings and responses were with voice-overs on the film didn't take away the dramatic intensity too much, as the technique was utilised subtly with the voices of the actual performers, not substitutes. Also, the director had managed to match this with the facial expressions very well and thus provided a more detailed emotional perspective – and a more integrated one – than Brian was used to. This, he knew, was generally not well done in porn, so this introduction of emotion and the complexity of the issues being raised was very stimulating. He knew, for these reasons alone, that Val would enjoy this movie.

Back in the bedroom, Emily has turned Helen over and is literally devouring her pussy whilst Mick, on his knees, fucks Emily vaginally with long deep thrusts ... after all, that is what he and his cock are renowned for, chuckles Brian! Then Emily directs Mick's cock – followed by Mick – from her pussy to his wife's, where he seems to continue thrusting almost without breaking rhythm. Emily moves to the side with her head over Helen's stomach and eventually Mick pulls out his dick and Emily sucks and masturbates him to orgasm: his cum is directed over his wife's open pussy and Emily gives his dick a long suck, almost as if she is cleaning it, then leans down to lap up the sperm from Helen's pussy; the last of which she keeps on her tongue and moves up to share with Helen by a deep kiss. The scene fades ...

Brian pauses the movie and refills his glass. The last scene hasn't been as erotically stimulating for him, but he found himself intrigued and challenged in other ways. Whilst Carole's threesome was overtly sexually stimulating and emotionally engaging, he found the one involving Emily to leave him a little up in the air. He was being analytical: it actually wasn't that clear; even though the reversal of roles and the sadomasochistic undercurrents were not overpowering, they did dampen his erotic response somewhat. He was challenged by the whole complex of events and his erection had subsided from its previous intensity, although not entirely.

Where am I left writing this? There are a range of emotions I have been experiencing. At a sexual level, I have felt some 'stirring in my loins', but not to the point of getting an erection. What has been most noticeable is how the characters have taken a life of their own and this has been as a result of engaging the emotional level, the personalities themselves and their inter-relationships. I can honestly say it is unlike anything I have actually seen and the characters are also unique. In this respect, and emerging creatively from the genre itself, it feels quite genuine. I am challenged in another way. It is so overtly erotic that I wonder whether it will achieve the unification process I had anticipated, or simply degenerate into a piece of erotic fiction. Would it get overwhelmingly judged that way, even if I felt it had achieved more? At this point, I am feeling more than a little nervous about where this venture is headed.

There seems little choice but to press on.

Brian restarts the disc: it has been going some forty minutes and the movie is about two hours long, which is slightly longer than a standard porn movie. It is still relatively early and he is certainly enjoying what has happened so far – at many levels – and is keen to continue.

It is a relatively silent breakfast table the following morning at the Retreat. The viewer is given no indication of what – if anything – transpired after the various activities of the previous evening. Mick and Helen, however, seem unaffected. Maybe of all of them, thinks Brian, for these two this might represent business as usual. Some retreat!

Graham leaves the table; he is palpably disturbed and has lost his usual exuberance. He walks outside and passes to the side of a lake where he sits on a bench looking at the water. Emily notices him leave; something also observed by Carole. In her own mind, Carole feels her marriage is over, but her flagrancy had reached a peak the previous night and she doesn't know where to take it from here. She felt that her natural personality had moved powerfully into a sexual domain that she had not explored before yet, almost as a contradiction, she felt a softness and vulnerability that was new. She looked up to find Paul looking at her, seemingly expressionless yet quite intent. She was confused and left to go to the toilet, where she wept for nobody in particular, maybe her marriage, maybe herself.

Of all of them, Paul felt the clearest. He now knew that his relationship with Emily was going nowhere, but his intuition told him that he didn't have to rush into any action and to watch events unfold. He picked up the paper and started reading when Emily announced she was going for a walk. She wasn't; she was going to look for Graham. Paul both knew and was also accepting of this. He continued to read the paper whilst Brian had a pensive sip of wine.

An Emily brimming with self-confidence found Graham relatively easily and they initially walk silently together. Emily then starts talking and outlines her vision and plan for the advertising business. Graham listens silently, astounded at what is happening. He also recognises that there is no place in her vision for either Paul or Carole and he confronts her on this. Emily responds by talking about the two of them and what she sees they can achieve, and then moves into a discussion of the erotic potential between them.

In all of this, Graham remains strangely quiet. Is he still disturbed about the previous night, or has something changed within him emotionally as a result of what happened? It is difficult to know and is something he doesn't pursue; he simply listens to Emily. Brian is also a little jarred and reflects a little whilst these two continue their walk around the lake to the wood beyond. There was something about the relationship with Val in all this, he thought, not specifically because of what was occurring now between Emily and Graham, it was the whole complex of issues and inter-relationships that were challenging him more. He recalled the age difference between Val and he, and that this had presented some distortions for a while. Brian remained the father and Val the child, and this continued even with the children's arrival.

What had changed this pattern? It certainly hadn't been the pop-psychology of parent-child patterns in relationships; it had been something else. It had been when Val found a confidence in her work, with a corresponding creativity and self-assurance that surprised him. He recalled that this gave him the freedom to withdraw from some of his professional pursuits and explore his musical career from the writing perspective. What had been a part-time interest since his days in university now became more centre-field and he loved this development.

What had happened to bring about this change? Had Val had an affair that she had not told him about? He doubted it, as that kind of secrecy was not now a part of their relationship; in fact, the opposite: they were open to voicing their attractions, and fidelity was certainly not a given, as we will discover. He sensed that the movie was reflecting a similar pattern to the one that had taken Val and he to a new position and understanding in their relationship. In front of him, he was impressed by the psychological wisdom that was present in the movie and, hence, the skill of the director and his (or her) screenplay. He simultaneously suspected that it was Carole and Paul who were more reflecting the questions that he and Val were currently facing. So, it was unlikely to be regressive fantasies of 'lost opportunities'; more likely that he and Val were in a no man's land beyond this, and maybe he was jarred because of the lost romance.

Brian further realised that, at this level, the changes that had occurred in the movie to date were symbolic with respect to his marriage. Of course, he didn't require other sexual alternatives and his relationship didn't require a partnership change. Then again, it wouldn't have been a porn movie without such alternatives and changes on the screen! He laughed. Yet he was intrigued at another level. He could see that Graham and Emily were going to 'get it on', yet the movie was barely halfway through. Whilst Val and he had negotiated the changes that Graham and Emily were going through, they were currently dealing with another ill-defined impasse, which was one of the reasons for her being away at the time he was watching the movie. Did the second half of the movie contain some information about how they, as a couple, could proceed from here?

Emily starts stroking Graham's hair whilst their eyes engage. They are on the edge of a wood and they silently move into it without a word being said, both aware of what was happening and possibly going to unfold. Emily leads, holding Graham's hand. Graham is happy to follow and he now feels his loins begin to stir. I'm also starting to feel a bit more comfortable, mainly because the narrative has moved to a more psychological perspective, but I remain aware that the director may challenge me significantly in the remainder of the movie.

Whilst Graham and Emily disappear into the wood there are four people in differing emotional positions back in the Retreat. Paul is reading the paper, but contemplating on where to go from here. He was aware that this may well have happened to Emily at some stage, although he wasn't clear about what could have been the trigger for the eruption and presumed she had just gained the confidence to express her feelings to Graham. The relationship had never gained the strength that would support the changes Emily was going to go through, Paul also realised that was because there may be another and different stage in his development that he was moving toward. Frankly, he had had enough of working with Graham and not having his creativity fully valued, and further, with what was happening between Graham and Emily, it was unlikely the business venture would continue to sustain him either financially or creatively.

Paul was also intrigued about what had happened with Carole and could impute all sorts of motives to her actions, but maybe she didn't fully understand them. Seated on the toilet, bent over and weeping, you'd be inclined to think so, thought Brian, but there was something intriguing about her that was now blossoming beyond the erotic attraction. He was aware, of course, that this was simply a psychological projection and a result of the director's motives and planning, yet he could not see where it would lead. He was doubly intrigued in that it somehow mirrored what was happening in his own life.

Meanwhile, in the kitchen, there is an abrupt scene of Mick vigorously arse fucking Helen over the table; he is dressed like a waiter or barman, and she is a waitress. Helen's eyes are closed, and her face is expressionless; she is also making little in the way of any verbal or physical response. Is she being punished, thinks Brian? The scene is brief, wordless and unexplained. It seems to contrast and even be out of place with what is happening elsewhere in and around the Retreat. Without any conclusion, the scene shifts back to the wood.

It's a sunny day and some of the light is filtering through the trees onto the leaf-scattered ground that will become the bed of Graham and Emily's consummation. Now, this is a nice touch, thinks Brian, soft and romantic even down to the music, although he does remind himself it's less than halfway through the movie and that this sort of scene is usually reserved for the endings. In fact, from my observation, it often is even if the movie is not actively representative of a "couple's movie" and has witnessed some intense hardcore scenes before the closure. I wonder why I feel disappointed when this happens. Shouldn't I also be content that it all ends "happily ever after" when my fantasy is a flagrant orgy?

After some initial kissing, the couple sink to their bed in the woods and silently undress each other. Emily is wearing light erotic underwear with no garters or stockings, most of which are gradually discarded throughout the scene. Graham initially licks her pussy around the panties and then silently removes them to continue his oral pursuit. Emily remains framed by the sunlight as she gazes up toward the sky. She then takes Graham's head in her hands and lifts him toward her for further kissing. There then follows various scenes of intercourse, but always vaginal. The lovemaking is increasingly intense and in varied positions, yet retains a gentle aspect that is reinforced by the scenery. Finally, Emily gets Graham to stand, whilst she kneels in front of him and he masturbates onto her upheld exposed breasts. She rubs the semen into her breasts after he has finished and licks the last drop from his cock with the tip of her tongue, with a look up to him like it's honey that she's eating. She stands, they kiss again and are last seen fully dressed walking from the wood toward a car parked conveniently some short distance away. And they leave.

Then, just as he is left to bask in the tenderness of the scene, Brian is catapulted back to Mick and Helen. He is still arse fucking her and the impression is given that he has been doing this throughout the whole time that Graham and Emily have been together in the woods. He then abruptly pulls his dick from her arse and sprays a significant amount of semen over her buttocks and lower back. Brian recalls that Mick is also renowned for the volume of sperm he produces and the intensity of the ejaculation as, unaware to his viewing; some was also deposited just inside her arse before he withdrew and now slowly leaks out. Brian wonders whether this is something that Emily would recall at some later time, having witnessed it so closely and finding it more than a mouthful to digest from his wife's pussy lips. This also reminds Brian that he is now quite involved in the complexities of the movie and, whilst he remains aroused; he is not now so genitally focussed.

As he is having these thoughts, the scene then switches to the early evening when Paul and Carole have met at the bar and are being served by Mick. Both Paul and Carole have received a text message from their partners announcing the end of their respective relationships and their joint business association. What a weekend, says Paul, and it's only Saturday night! Yes, it is, responds Carole, so where to from here? Both of them feel and act more settled, eyeing each other with a mixture of respect and amusement, even a hint of eroticism. Mick takes all this in as he pours a drink for them. Helen then emerges from the kitchen, still dressed in her uniform and gives Mick a kiss on the cheek with an accompanying smile. She then proposes that the four of them enjoy the evening with a visit to a club of which she and Mick are members. She says this with a glint in her eye.

We will pause there and add some reflections from my perspective. The literary style is interesting because it adds levels of complexity to the story that may be implied but are then creatively elaborated. By contrast, if this story had been written as a literary piece only, it would have been quite different. Does that make it valid as a description of watching a porn movie, or are there other ways of approaching the question? Certainly, the literary reflections of the performers' thoughts and feelings, under the thin guise of them being present in the movie as voice-overs, are an embellishment. Rather than see this as a criticism and that without them this would simply be another porn movie, let us examine the technique a little further.

In effect, the narrative, as I have written it above, is literary fiction that describes the watching of a porn movie rather than the description of the visual content of the porn movie alone. This is further elaborated by including first Brian and his reactions and responses, then myself and even ourselves. What I have done is deliberately left the movie in a format that, with some minor exceptions, any seasoned consumer would recognise up to this point. We're about halfway through, there have been three or four scenes, and these have been put in the context of a plot and narrative that holds the scenes together. We have gained the impression, however, that the director is attempting to achieve something more than a routine skin flick (an alternative name for a porn movie).

I have done this on his (or her) behalf by introducing the voice-over as a connection to my more emotional and psychological elucidation of the story. I have also implied acting abilities in the performers to reflect this in a way that may stretch your credibility at present, but which is not beyond the bounds of future possibility. What I am implying is both these aspects reflect the director's intent to make a more comprehensive porn movie that links more to and integrates with the cinematic mainstream. I would argue that maybe the "six scenes in ninety minutes" formula itself needs revising and some aspects of this movie reflect attempts in that direction; by mixing the scenes, adding memory in the story and bringing in a brief scene (Mick's arse fuck with Helen) as a screenplay device to add contrast to the unfolding plot. There is still a way to go, however, in this regard and I think the extent of my literary interpolation may reflect this, as well as my active creative involvement in the story.

With more to go, Brian, now a seasoned critic of the genre will certainly be keeping his eye on this director and publishing house into the future.

Where the porn stars are positioned with all the above may be of interest. From the beginnings of amateurs and casuals, and disregarding the 'those that are doing it for drugs' argument (because it may apply equally to anything an addict would do to obtain money for drugs), there has been an increasing trend toward an organised porn-acting industry. This is increasingly also reflecting mainstream acting and movie production in general, so it is feasible this unity is on the horizon. This may demand not just better acting ability and training on the part of porn stars, but mainstream actors and directors introducing sexually explicit erotic scenes into the mainstream. The perceptive amongst you will notice that this is likely to be the case when we have fully reintegrated sexuality into our Western culture, which pornography at the erotic end of the spectrum may assist with. This is precisely my argument and what this book is designed to creatively assist. The role of the director we'll have cause to return to.

The sex itself presents many challenges. The most fundamental is the actual reality of the sex itself ... real people just don't get up to this sort of stuff ... do they? Well, no, they don't in general. Isn't that one of the functions of porn though, to display sexual activity that is impossible in 'real life'? Certainly, that is one argument and one we will continue to explore. The industry itself promotes such a position, by and large, telling us that because it is impossible that their performers are "doing it for us". I find this argument self-referential and a good marketing tool, but is it true?

It could be argued that porn is also educational and instructive, this being the angle taken by couples or reality styles of porn. If so, the margins become a little blurred, don't they? Maybe the answer to the question is not either/or, but both/and. If this is the case, it can integrate at both the literal level of sexual conduct and also the imaginary or creative expression. Brian is at an interesting point in his development here; his consumption has been largely masturbatory and imaginative and has helped him explore his sexual relationship with Val. There has been the introduction of porn into their occasional evening viewing and they have explored some sexual variations in their private lives, which the porn has helped instruct, although maybe just at the physical and erotic levels to date. You may be left with the impression there is a little tension in the air here. Indeed, there is, as also exists with some of the remaining characters at the Retreat.

It has always been an argument that the actors, the female porn stars in particular, represent a particular class of women who undertake a range of sexual activity that is not available to the rest of us. This is reinforced by the word pornography itself, which, as we discovered earlier is derived from the term for a prostitute. The equation then is that only bad girls perform in pornography. You might easily get that impression from the female porn stars at the Retreat, Carole and Helen, in particular.

To examine this perspective, we may need to begin an exploration of it by using other disciplines. The psychological one being an extension of the feminist one, with women exploring their sexuality and thus integrating the 'whore' with the 'cook' and 'lady'. (From the old – somewhat sexist – adage that a good wife should be a cook in the kitchen, a lady in public, yet a whore in the bedroom.) There is much truth here, which is abetted by women's increasing involvement both in the industry and as consumers. This could extend to historical and cross-cultural studies that indicate that sexual activity may be much more varied than we have been accustomed to seeing in the West and which phenomena like pornography are expressing and further exploring.

What about the wider sexual arguments? The quality of the production minimises any perceived coercion and the descriptions to date don't incline to objectification: If they do, they could be applied to both the male and female stars. You will notice that I am increasingly moving away from any feminist, sexist-based arguments and criticisms here, and may ask why I am doing that? I would like to return to the discussion of the last chapter, where an initial exploration of gender issues was undertaken.

This, in my opinion, forms a psychological platform that can transcend many of the male-female dichotomy, sexist and –

negative – feminist arguments. It will take time to build further on this position, which is embedded deeply in the book as a whole, as it represents not only a transition of our culture at a sexual level but also a transition of our culture as a whole. I further argue that sexuality is spearheading these changes, which is why they are denied, feared and judged, because they represent at least a metaphoric death of the established order, something that is deeply resisted by that order.

What about some of the more marginal themes in the movie to date? There are issues of dominance and submission between Emily and Helen, as well as some play – spanking – that borders on violence. There is also the arse fucking scene with Mick and Helen that both serves to contrast the anal sex Carole indulges in as well as the implied tenderness – even emerging love – in the scene with Emily and Graham.

The anal sex is interesting, as it indicates that it is not the activity itself that is necessarily dominant or even violent. Carole appears to enjoy it, yet does Helen not, or is she undertaking a submissive role? Does the absence of anal sex in the scene between Graham and Emily equate to an emergence of love, or just the inability to confront these issues at this early stage of their relationship?

Is the absence of a blowjob an acknowledgement of the act being a dominant one, or an indication that the role-play between Graham and Emily has some subtle psychology involved? Could this be considered his submission to her newfound dominance or the discovery of a more feminine perspective within himself (and vice versa for Emily)?

There are all these questions and more, we will continue to explore them and invite more as we proceed. We remain left with two contrasting and – seemingly – opposing positions. Graham and Emily have each had psychological changes that reflect the discovery of their individual contra-sexuality. In simple terms, Graham has started to experience his femininity and Emily her masculinity. This more balanced psychological perspective allows them, it would seem, to wander off into the sunset. This seems a step up from the classic role-played love match that we challenged in the previous chapter, but is it the final statement in the relationship?

The contrast is more nebulous at this stage. Paul and Carole are now a little lost and in limbo, yet there are elements of the contra-sexual recognition that Graham and Emily may be experiencing already somewhat mutually recognised, such that they can display these contra-sexual tendencies without – necessarily – losing their primary gender identity. At this time, Carole seems to manifest this more strongly. Mick and Helen are a little enigmatic at this stage and appear to be acting as catalysts, even mentors, in this unfolding drama. The main question that I would like you to bear in mind as we proceed, and as Brian is doing, is whether the sexuality (as here portrayed) is a creative agent in this process. And, if it is, where will it lead?

We move to the "Club".

5

At The Club

Brian pours himself a second glass of wine and sets the chair in a more reclined position. He is drawn in and now experiencing low-grade anxiety in his body. Some of this is sexual tension, and although he knows that if he were to masturbate, it would disperse, he feels to maintain the tension and just soften it a little with the second glass. He is simultaneously reflective of his relationship with Val as the movie progresses, as it seems strangely connected and even synchronous. He suspends further reflection and gets back to viewing.

I am equally curious. I have just sketched out a rough outline of the remainder of the movie and the details of the scenes in broad-brush strokes. Yet I also know that I cannot see the completion in at least two of the scenes, so I realise I will simply have to start writing and trust the creative process. Without going into detail, I am also curious how issues in my personal life might be at least symbolically reflected in what I am trying to achieve.

Mick and Paul are dressed in comfortable suits, whilst the girls steal the show. Carole wears a simple yet elegant low-cut light gown that demonstrates her boobs, yet contrasts with her flowing dark locks. Helen's dress suit borders on the severe, and her long blonde hair is gathered up onto her head. She also begins the evening wearing her glasses. Both are wearing stockings and high-heeled shoes. The jewellery is ornate and abundant. There is absolutely no doubt as to where this evening is going to go, chuckles Brian to himself!

They are seated in two, facing leather couches, with drinks and some light food refreshments on the coffee table between them. The music is a light techno, the lighting is low and there are several other people in the room. Some at the bar are watching Carole and Paul with a certain amount of intrigue. After questioning Mick, they understand it is because they are guests in the private section of the Club and that this always raises a little interest – for reasons that will become apparent but for now only obliquely hinted at. The establishment is quite large and extends to a public section of the bar with a restaurant in between. The restaurant is accessible from both the public and private bars but also serves to provide a boundary between the two. This effectively makes the bar they were now in and its associated function areas not only private but also relatively unknown to the casual public.

Brian does a brief stock-take. Carole has had sex with Paul, but neither Mick nor Helen. Paul has fucked Carole, but has also not been with Helen. Do you notice the indirect homosexual etiquette the genre employs here and that Brian has adopted? I could have said, "Paul has fucked Carole, but not Mick or Helen." I don't think Mick will feel offended! Similarly, Mick and Helen are not overtly aware of Paul and Carole's sexual activities to date, though Brian guesses that they might have some idea. So, although the atmosphere is sexually laden, there are elements of the unknown – even some mystery – about where things may go from here. There is thus the obvious duplicity; it is obvious that it will proceed in a sexual manner (it is porn after all, and that's what it was bought for, right?), yet it is duplicitous in that there would seem to be no fact or experience from which Mick and Helen would be taking Paul and Carole to the Club. I mention this, maybe as a flaw in the director's script ... or maybe he (or she) is implying more wisdom in the experience of some, if not of all of the participants: all that notwithstanding, the evening is about to take off.

At Mick's instigation, they leave the table to adjourn downstairs, with the twinkle in Helen's bespectacled eye promising the nature of the adjournment. Carole recognises this and excuses herself with a reassuring hint that she is aware of the nature of the invite and that she will join them when she has had a little time for repose; she is still a little shaken by what has happened as well as the nature of her emotional response. Paul is surprised by this and is disappointed, although, now being in the mood for a good evening, he follows Helen, whilst Mick shows Carole to a dark corner with a drink and a reclining chair before he, too, goes downstairs.

Mick joins Helen as she is showing Paul a range of fetish clothing in a change room. Without a visual, the extent and nature of this clothing would be difficult to describe, so maybe you can drop into your local sex shop to get an idea. There is a range of mainly women's though also some men's clothing, generally in latex (rubber) and leather. There are also boots and masks, some whips and dildos. Paul is impressed and puts on some leather jocks, boots and a light mask; the latter he is encouraged to do by Mick, who indicates there is an initial "play" anonymity, as he selects one for himself and suggests another to Helen. Helen wears a black leather bikini with a lace-up panty crotch and thigh-high boots. A cat mask provides an alternative intrigue to the spectacles, now discarded. Lastly, she takes a whip from the wall.

Once dressed, they move through a door into a much larger room, which Paul recognises as a "dungeon", as the apparatus there is patently for sexual purposes with a sadomasochistic edge. There are ropes and cuffs, chains and swings, as well as other tools of suspension and restraint. Helen moves to the centre of a large deep leather couch accompanied by several sex toys, mainly dildos, which she begins to handle separately, as if she is shopping and deciding which one to choose or use. The whip remains at her side. There is a beamed light focussed on the couch whilst the surroundings fade into darkness.

At the same time, Carole is reclining in her upstairs armchair, removes a dildo from her bag and begins to play with it. She lifts her dress, parts her legs and with one hand moves the panties to one side, as the other hand moves the dildo over the vaginal lips and clitoris before beginning a progressively deeper penetration of her pussy. Whilst this is occurring, Carole is muttering: "I just love my cunt full!"

Brian is a little taken aback: this is the first time the word "cunt" has been used in the movie; it is not as commonly used in porn movies as you might think. There is something a little enigmatic in this, he ponders, because of the common perception that cunt is a demeaning term used by men toward women, which indeed it sometimes is. Yet other terms are used in a more demeaning and sexist manner, such as slut, bitch or whore. A further irony is that it is a woman – Carole – who first uses the term here and she is referring to her own vagina, or cunt. He reflects a little further; there seems more to this than meets the eye. He also notices that, in general, it is the term most avoided in all walks of life where sexual or swear words are employed. There seems to be something a little uncomfortable about it that goes beyond the simple sexist explanation.

As indeed there is. Contrary to it being a word that can be used in a sexist and demeaning manner toward women, I suggest that it is exactly the opposite; it empowers women. Let the outrage settle … How can I possibly imply that? Well, some of my argument stems from the comments above and the apparent anomalies in them, so I thought I'd do a little research of my own when I came across these issues some years back. What I found was that in the Northern Mystery Tradition one of the runes, Kenaz, Cen or Kaun, has a link with the feminine mysteries: "Freya teaches Odin seidr, which is a form of witchcraft and includes 'sex magic.' ... The Middle English word 'cunt' relates to cunning ... Cen is described as having a shape similar to that of the female genitals." (From Freya Aswynn: *Northern Mysteries and Magick*).

Maybe there are other dimensions to this. Does cunt, in fact, refer to a woman's power, as the term "I love my cunt" has been used as a feminist catchphrase? Is this because it was associated with the Northern Traditions, hence witchcraft, and suppressed by the Church and, subsequently, the patriarchy? Has it become a derogatory term to take away any power and reference to it that may exist in the folk and magical undercurrents of Northern Europe? Do you still find it a difficult word to express publicly? Is this because of the reaction of others, but could it also be due to the power of the word itself? Maybe the answer to all of these questions is yes, so we will continue to explore this.

Opening the lace at the front of her leather panties, Helen begins a simultaneous tour of her cunt with a similar but darker dildo, with the images briefly flitting between Carole and Helen and then finally settling on Helen when she also inserts a slightly thinner pink dildo into her arse. She continues to move both in and out, sometimes in contrasting and sometimes simultaneous motions. Paul and Mick watch expressionlessly, with arms folded across their bare chests and with their masks still on. Helen closes her eyes as the tempo hastens and gives silent powerful verbal and facial expressions to her rising pleasure that transcend the restrictions of the mask. Gradually, the men approach Helen and start to touch, fondle and kiss her whilst she continues to play with the dildos.

At the fringes of the room are two other couples in various acts of sexual play, mainly manual and oral, whilst watching the highlighted scene in front of them. As Paul and Mick increasingly engage Helen, the two women come and join the more central play, whilst their partners stay in the shadows watching and manually maintaining their erections. When Mick gently removes the dildos from his wife's cunt and arse and then starts to eat her pussy, the two women each take one of Paul's hands and raise him to his feet from the kneeling position from where he has been sucking Helen's ample breasts. The two women are also lightly masked, and their physical attributes become a blur to Brian as he is watching: a brunette and redhead maybe?

The lighting is dim and the scenes are moving rapidly with a slightly stronger background techno music beat. The clothing disguises, teases and stimulates. They are on their knees sharing Paul's cock, now he is fucking one, then the other, sometimes licking one, whilst simultaneously fucking the other. Then the women engage in a "sixty-nine" (simultaneous oral sex), and Paul fucks the kneeling brunette in the arse from behind whilst the redhead simultaneously eats her cunt with an occasional lick of Paul's shaft. Then the women change places (dizzy yet?) ... all the time Mick is lasciviously eating Helen's cunt whilst she becomes progressively more animated and vocal. The women then disengage from Paul and alternatively or simultaneously take over Mick's duties whilst he and Paul offer their cocks for Helen's mouth after removing her mask, in which she achieves feats comparable to Carole's efforts with Paul the previous evening.

The two other women then move back a little, and Mick sits on the couch getting Helen to sit astride and facing him so that he penetrates her vaginally, whilst Paul gently moves his cock into her arse from behind. The two women assume a role like servants, continuing to touch, fondle and mildly stimulate this gyrating threesome. The climax is reached as Helen comes to orgasm and we immediately move upstairs to see Carole quietly and more gently reaching her own climax. Back to the dungeon where Mick and Paul are ejaculating over Helen's offered breasts and available mouth in an alternating fashion, whilst the two assistants move in to lick and suck extensively and simultaneously on Helen's proffered tits and their creamy topping.

The women kiss Helen, then each other and return to their partners in the shadows where their sexual play continues with the men. Paul sits on the couch beside Helen; he removes his mask and gently holds her hand. Mick smiles, retreats into the shadows and decides to go upstairs to see how Carole is faring. Helen gives Paul a kiss, as he is looking somewhat bemused about what has happened. They then begin to share a little of the experience, when Helen also reveals the Club and its inner workings behind its more public persona.

To Brian there is little of interest in this latter discussion, but it may be informative to viewers who are unaccustomed to dungeons and fetishism. He also guesses that this may be the director's intention because, apart from the clothing and dildos, there was no use made of the other props and equipment, which were thus simply used to set the scene for what followed. As he is reflecting on this, he notices that Helen and Paul are now dressed and have decided to catch a cab back to the Retreat. They retire to a large bed in a dimly lit room, where there is a little further gentle intercourse before they fall asleep. The tone of this is quite different with little overt sexual activity available to the viewer. The feeling to Brian is that Helen is somehow gently comforting Paul after what is something of an initiation for him, and which she doesn't want him to lose track of. Paul hasn't lost track; he feels awake and vibrantly alive. He is also thinking of Carole and then begins to drift into sleep.

Let me offer a different slant on some of the features above, and particularly the topic of fetishism. Personally, I find the topic has been well covered and even exhausted by various psychoanalytic perspectives, so I would like to use it as a window into something different and commensurate with the direction of this work.

Psychoanalytic theory is essentially mechanistic and reductionistic; its depth is confined to the material realms of the rational intellect. This means that an issue is looked at in a mechanical way by breaking it down into its component pieces. In very simple terms, for example, problems of femininity in a man are due to his relationship with his mother and hence unresolved psychological issues and traumas leading to interrupted and even impaired development. These are seen, par excellence, in the sexual domain and are well illustrated in fetishism and perversions.

A contrasting, more holistic, and spiritual perspective would be that a man opening up to his femininity means that he is developing beyond his personal history, exploring the feminine as soul and leading to spirit. Sexuality is then a valid tool of this exploration, as seen in other cultures, and other modes of sexual expression explore the ritual and ceremonial context of that development.

What this means is that any situation that contains these psychological and sexual issues can be read in two entirely differing yet complementary ways. In general, the more holistic and spiritual perspective is inclusive of the personal, mechanistic and reductionistic, but the reverse is not usually true. Certainly, all the above actions to date, plus what is to follow, could lend itself to a psychoanalytic analysis, and this is commonly the way that the various commentators and critics have approached sexuality in general and pornography in particular. I have tended to avoid this as it is not the thrust and direction of this enquiry. It would also exclude the imaginative and creative dimensions, which I see as the activity of the soul. You can see one of my conclusions here: Sexuality is a pathway to the soul, and pornography is a modern medium or tool of enquiry, even induction and initiation on that pathway.

I have given hints that Paul's journey in the Club may have inductive and initiatory perspectives, which I believe is the director's intention. Often, such ritualised and complex sexual activity achieves this and is reflected in the mystery traditions of many cultures, both ancient and modern. A broad perspective says that embedded in the repressed sexual – as symbolised by pornography – will be found features of such ritual, myth and initiation. I believe this to be the case, and is yet another theme that we will be taking from this tale and exploring in more detail.

Ritual has a high degree of ceremonial involvement, in that there is much "acting" or performance. There is also an emphasis on roles and role changing, which can be seen occurring in the movie as well. Throw in the theatrical props of setting and clothing and we have all the elements of ritual and ceremony at hand. Exactly what are these rituals, though? For this, we will have to dig a little deeper.

Brian is doing likewise and he is still aroused, but he is also deeply contemplative – such as asking questions like: What is this all telling me about the current challenges that are presenting themselves to Val and I? I have tried to understand them at a personal and psychological level, but do we need to do more?

That sounds risky! It is, but then again, there's no change without such risk-taking; that is one of life's unfortunate rules, and Brian may now be getting to appreciate it.

Brian has the feeling that these initiatory features are contained in the movie. Maybe Graham and Emily achieved an appropriate level of initiation for their personal development and that's why they left? Paul seems to be undergoing a slightly more rigorous 'examination', although there is an aura of enigma that he retains through it all that seems to reduce any overt anxiety. By contrast, Carole has moved from a self-confident position at the beginning of the movie to one of vulnerability, so it is her to whom we shall now return.

Carole has straightened her panties to cover her pussy and dropped her dress; she licks and sucks her dildo clean then replaces it in her bag, whilst bringing her chair to an upright position, followed by a sip of her drink. She is wondering what Paul was up to? Not in a jealous sense, but after last night's exploration she felt she wanted to spend more time with him. Maybe the feeling wasn't mutual and that was why he went off with Mick and Helen. Although she did now question whether his last fleeting enigmatic glance was an invitation for her to ask him to stay. Maybe it was better he hadn't, she thought, as they'd both been through a lot in the last twenty-four hours and there's nothing like good sex to clear the air!

Talking about good sex, she looks at Mick approaching her and reckons he'd be a good fuck and might be able to clear her head. She briefly wonders what – and who – he's been up to in the last hour or so, but decides that might throw some damp water on the possibilities. So, she takes his silently offered hand and walks with him to an upstairs bedroom, which is elegantly decorated and dimly lit. There's even some music playing; it's modern and she doesn't recognise it, but it's quite subtly challenging. On the two right-angled sofas two couples are seated ... are they the same couples as in the dungeon? Brian can't be sure because they are now dressed casually and informally and, of course, there are now no masks. He thinks they may be the same, but as they seem to be providing a supportive, even ritualistic and symbolic function he doesn't pay that enquiry any further attention ... although he does find the brunette cute!

Carole has a brief shower, becoming excited at the possibilities and returns to find Mick in a silk gown and an array of lingerie – her size, of course – lying out on the bed. The colours are mainly black and red with a little blue. There is also a pair of long gloves and a choker with a jewel in the middle. The items are quite challenging as they are overtly sexual and indicate the intent in no uncertain manner. Carole puts the lingerie on and then turns to see Mick now seated between the two men on the facing sofa, whilst the women come to the edge of the bed and start lightly kissing and fondling each other. She notices they've slipped out of their clothes and are wearing a similar style of lingerie to her own. The garters, suspenders and stockings contrast in colour and style and they are wearing heeled shoes, so Carole puts hers on and faces the sofa.

On impulse she gets down on her hands and knees, then crawls across the carpet toward the sofa and the men, who are eagerly eyeing her every movement. She moves to each in turn, undoing the zipper and sucking each dick to full hardness, then circuiting and moving progressively further down the shafts of their cocks with each cycle. Satisfied, she rises, removes her now sodden panties and sits astride Mick on the sofa, taking his cock vaginally, whilst the other two men take alternate turns in fucking her arse and then her mouth.

Seemingly on cue, the two women move from the edge of the

bed and extract Carole from the grips of the three men and lead her back to it. Here they indulge her jointly, and it seems to Brian there isn't an inch of Carole's body that is not paid attention to. A camera angle shows the men watching from the sofa and playing with their erections, although the women seem oblivious to their voyeuristic activities. Each woman takes a turn to eat Carole's cunt, whilst the other either kisses her breasts or mouth. Eventually, Carole becomes more animated as, up to date, she has been less active than in her earlier performance with the men.

This is clever, thinks Brian. He knows Carole, the porn star, isn't inclined to lesbian scenes as a routine. So, her role fits her personality, as she is being inducted into a lesbian scene and activity of which (from her role in the film's perspective) she has little previous experience. This is either very good acting, or she really is getting into it! This is what Brian thinks as he, somewhat surprisingly because of his own preferences, finds his erection resuming and he begins to gently masturbate to the evolving scene on the screen.

The activity on the bed becomes more vigorous but remains confined to tongues and fingers, and there's not a dildo in sight. There is a mixture of fingers in pussies and arses, tongues lapping the increasingly moist cunts and engaging, even challenging eye contact between the three women. Eventually, with one woman eating her and another attending to her breasts, Carole is seen to have a quiet yet intense orgasm that leaves her body shuddering. What's happening to Brian? He's surprised by his reaction, too, and feels shaky in a way that seems to mimic Carole. He puts the movie on pause and gets up, pacing the room with his wine in hand.

Brian is troubled. There is something very deep, emotional and significant happening to him. He pictures Val and finds the image warm and tender; tears come to his eyes. He feels, deep in his being, that their relationship has to move in another direction. He doesn't know how or in what way this will be, he only knows that it has to change. The irony is that there doesn't seem anything particularly wrong with their relationship. They have been together some ten years now and negotiated the age difference and the challenges that bringing their contra-sexual personalities to the fore promotes. This had been done with some domestic and parenting role reversals and their sexuality had accompanied it all.

Fidelity is also not now an issue. They had engaged with others in sexual activity but had always been honest about this, realising that other sexual partners didn't offer an alternative to their core relationship, which they were both prepared to work hard on. The porn involvement had mapped much of this, even informed it, as of latter years, if there was any extraneous sexual attraction or potential involvement, then they brought it into the relationship in varying threesomes. Usually, these didn't last long, as the third party often found it difficult to sustain, but it was also Val's choice on one occasion when the dynamics of sexual challenge and enquiry had ceased to be present. Simple indulgence wasn't an option. They had allowed the porn to offer some instruction in negotiating this territory and found they were almost invariably more comfortable with the exploration than the third party. Sex with another couple presented an even more complex challenge, and for an extended period they had such a mutual relationship with one particular couple, although this was no recent engagement, so it may now be over.

As both Val and Brian both enjoyed the challenge of sexuality and their relationship within it, they wondered how they could take it further. Val had raised the possibility of a club or advertising, because the emotional closeness of some of their contacts made them want to be more discrete. This was difficult territory, as they knew few who had been there before and they were left to explore it on their own. In the last couple of years, there had been an increasing hiatus, occasionally filled by porn, but not by a third or other parties as both sensed the difficulty and that such an action would muddy the waters, unless the other party or parties was similarly experienced. Brian felt that his current emotional state had a lot to do with all these issues and questions. He returned to the movie.

The women were leading Carole from the bed back to the three men. They stand her in front of Mick, turn her around and then slowly lower her onto his stiff cock, which he guides into her cunt recesses with practised ease and a single stroke. With a hint from his hands that are gripped on the top of her pelvis, she slowly starts to move up and down. God, I'm juicy; it's pouring out over his balls! With an experienced hand, Mick helps Carole to a pause at the top of her up-and-down cycle and slowly moves his cock into her arse. Carole feels somewhere on a knife-edge between pain and pleasure, and voices this as she continues the same rhythmic activity with Mick's cock in its alternative position.

Carole doesn't come again; that didn't seem to be the purpose of this segment. Yet she seemed transported into another state accompanied or even directed by the music. The two women are on their knees in front of her alternatively licking and fingering her pussy whilst Mick continues to work her arse. The two men then come up behind their respective partners, simultaneously penetrate them vaginally and continue to pump in a loose union. Then, just as Carole feels she might pass out, Mick lets his dick come out of her arse to spray his seed over her pussy, pubes and belly. She looks down and fingers the warm white sticky fluid, and the two other women do likewise, cleaning up the offering with their tongues as their men simultaneously spray their seed across their backs. Carole then does pass out.

Paul wakes up and rises to find Helen making a light breakfast. Mick is with her and lets Paul know that Carole is still asleep, as she had a big night! Brian is wondering how the remainder of the movie is going to pan out; he suspects there will be some sort of resolution and reconciliation but is not sure what this will be and how it will proceed. Paul is now the shakiest of the group; with Helen and Mick acting like everything that has happened is quite normal. He feels a slightly nervous hold on his emotional state and he is feeling very drawn to Carole. Should he wake her? He decides not to, as it would be more to satisfy his own need and as he is thinking this, he notices that Helen has already gone to raise her.

Do you feel an air of tension? Are you asking how this might resolve? Do you wonder whether I am asking myself the same question? Well, exactly at the time of writing I am. It would be easy now to head off into a discussion of what happened, particularly to Carole in the last scene at the Club, but I sense that would be a diversion. I could also take Brian's responses elsewhere, but feel I may get too closely identified with him. I'll get back to the action and let the creative process unravel.

Over breakfast, everyone is in gowns, with the women wearing some underwear and with Helen and Mick entirely at ease. Carole is also starting to fully wake up and seems to have a still confidence in their company, even eating a little, whereas all Paul can do is drink some coffee. Helen feels the tension and decides to take a hand, but just as she is about to do so, it seems that Carole has read her mind and jumps in first by inviting the others back into the lounge.

Carole allows her gown to drop open whilst she alone remains standing. There is some light dance music in the background, which she proceeds to move to and slowly, ever so slowly she moves the dance into an erotic performance without any overt sexual stimulation. Paul is entranced; he need not be concerned, everybody is. After what seems an age Carole slowly moves over to Helen and invites her onto the circular carpet between the various seats. Carole dances with Helen, who slowly gathers the rhythm and responds to Carole's advances. Carole starts to kiss Helen, who slowly responds. They seem oblivious to all around as Carole gently moves Helen down onto the carpet onto which an astute Mick has thrown some cushions in anticipation of what may happen.

Carole eats Helen's pussy like a seasoned lesbian, and in Brian's opinion, Helen's response is entirely spontaneous and natural, as may be her very rapid orgasm. Carole then disengages, leaving Helen gently panting with eyes closed amongst the cushions, and gets up to lead Paul into the centre. She commences a similar dance routine with him leading to kissing and then guides him toward Helen's pussy, which he patiently revives. Meanwhile, Carole continues moving around the couple, paying particular attention to stroking Paul's erogenous regions, yet temporarily leaving his burgeoning erection.

The expressions on Paul's face begin to change. He senses his anxiety fall and a quiet confidence and strength pass through his body. He lifts his face from Helen's pussy and finds everyone looking back at him. A tear wells in his eye, and a smile of gratitude and love comes to him, which is conveyed to the others in silent communication. He looks at Carole intently and she suddenly seems demure and coy. As an observer, Brian is going through every emotion in the book and is entranced. Paul moves to Carole and kisses her, then drops his head to her breasts and as he kisses, or more correctly devours them, she lets her head drop back with an almost silent gasp. He takes her hand and guides her next to join the now kneeling Helen, where both engage his manhood in skilled and shared delight. He drops his gaze to the two women below him and then looks up to see Mick watching him with a gaze that could only be construed as pride.

From there it is a blur, made more so by the camera movements and angles. In Brian's opinion, these pick up on the entrancing atmosphere present in Carole's engagement of the previous evening with Mick and friends. The three of them, Paul, Carole and Helen, engage in all manner of sexual activity, which would almost be repetitious of me to recite and detract from the emotional intensity. Suffice it to say that, from this twisting and twining ménage, Paul gradually engages Carole in a way that is novel for the movie, yet does not lose its sexual intensity. In fact, there is the impression that Paul becomes even more entranced and poetic in the way he engages the two women sexually and invites a similar response. Yet, in the tableau, there is a sense that they are all perfectly aware of where they are and what they are doing. Together, Paul and Helen take Carole toward the precipice on which she is held as she is laid down gently on some cushions with her eyes closed.

Mick stands up from his seated position and walks toward the other three, who now come into view. Helen is seated cross-legged on a cushion and is gently stroking Carole's hair and head, which is immediately below and seemingly nestled at the crossing of her legs. Mick now stands behind Helen and gently massages her head, neck and shoulders. Helen shows no surprise. Paul is on his knees between Carole's thighs, her buttocks slightly raised on the cushions, and is slowly and rhythmically penetrating her, such that his cock moves almost out and then returns to become fully engulfed by Carole's glistening womanhood. Apart from Paul's slow and deep penetrations into Carole's body, there seems to be little movement from the grouping apart from Carole's breasts gently shaking with each thrust; her eyes remain closed throughout.

Paul gently disengages himself and sits astride Carole's torso, still facing her. After gently massaging her breasts, he takes his cock in his hand and slowly strokes himself to the point of orgasm as some clear liquid drips from the tip of his cock onto Carole's upper belly. Then he stops and directs his cock a little more upwards. With the next stroke, a jet of semen erupts from his cock and lands in Carole's slightly agape mouth, with the continuing stream landing like the flow of a new-born river across her nose, with the main portion finishing in rivulets between her eyes and onto her forehead.

Carole savours the nectar in her mouth, licks some from her lips with her tongue and then smiles, opening her eyes and looking up to Paul, who has temporarily stopped, but now again begins his slow rhythmic stroking with a highly focussed demeanour and visual intent. The second stream is directed to her throat where the droplets ripple slowly on and around her neck. Carole's eyes now remain open, vulnerable and fixed on his. The remaining streams now come in rapid succession and are directed over her now upheld breasts, as a painter would a modern canvas. As the eruptions stop and the spasms in his dick settle Carole takes hold of his reclining erection and uses the tip to massage the glazing on her breasts deep into her skin. She then places it in between her cleavage and presses her breasts over so that it cannot be seen. After only a short number of gentle thrusts from Paul, she releases her breasts, once more takes his manhood in hand and gently encourages him toward her so that she can suck off the remaining fluids and kiss him deeply. Not once do her warmly lit eyes disengage from his.

As the cock is slowly withdrawn from her mouth, Carole's face is all that is seen. Out of sight, Paul has obviously re-entered her as her gaze moves a little down towards him, and her head and shoulders start to gently rock. Her eyes become a little glazed like the glistening sperm upon her body, whilst they slowly gain a distant, tearful look beyond and above where Paul's head would be. Slowly, her face seems to lose some colour and a soft sweat comes to her forehead and upper lip, adding another radiant fluid to the mix. Her eyes slowly roll upward, and her mouth opens more as little pants emerge, culminating in a soft gentle scream; then her eyes close, followed by her mouth, and her face begins a gentle flush, and the scene slowly fades as the radiant smile returns.

I think I might have crossed the divide and got pornographic there. No, I didn't. It was utterly erotic writing this and I must thank the director. Please excuse me; I was enraptured too. Maybe the loop with the Nordic Goddess is now closed, or maybe it is opening to another level ...

Brian is lying back in his reclining chair staring at the ceiling, raising himself to see the final credits and acknowledgements pass across the screen with images of the four clothed and having coffee together, then Paul and Carole being escorted to their car. The final scene is from inside the car; Paul is driving. He and Carole look at each other, smile, and then, in unison, break out into laughter.

Brian sleeps well and wakes to a dream. He is watching a man emerge from a misty background. Although he hasn't met the man, he knows his wife and son; they are the 'original man and woman'. The man is dressed in a dark suit of the indeterminable period over a white polo-neck sweater that makes him look a little like a priest. He appears tired and worn out. Brian goes to a fridge, which is opened by one of his secretaries and inside is a jar with an unknown content. He knows that he must give the contents to the man to revive and rejuvenate him, but the top is tight and he can't open it. He realises, as he wakes, that he will need something strong, like a vice, to achieve this.

Val is driving back home with two squabbling children. She packed the car the previous night, and after an early light breakfast, she decided to set off to beat any likely traffic, as it was the beginning of a long weekend. She was keen to see Brian. She hadn't missed him, in fact, after how he had been for the last few weeks, she was pleased to have a break. She also assumed he may have exactly the same thoughts and feelings about her, so maybe it had been good for both of them. The marriage was in a transition stage, some would say crisis, but neither party was treating it as such; they were both endeavouring to negotiate some difficult and challenging terrain.

As Brian has coffee, he reflects on the dream. It seems important and won't leave him. Obviously, the man was himself, and the suit could well be his work attire. Although he never wears polo necks and a white one at that, so maybe the priest aspect is something 'underneath' or 'emerging'? The jar is intriguing, as is the secretary. He has not had a sexual relationship with Stephanie, but they were mutually attracted. The play on the word 'vice' amused him and, combined with Steph's presence, he surmised that a light Freudian view would be appropriate! However, it seemed deeper than this, like a precious liquid rather than simply sexual juices, or maybe it was both. It was also simply telling him he would need all his strength to deal with the transition, which had some distinctly spiritual connotations. He finished his coffee, laid the dream to rest for the time being and started on his weekend agenda.

Strangely, Brian gave little attention or reflection to the movie that had had such a strong emotional impact on him. Maybe the dream was the consequence of the experience and that is why he is looking at that. We will part company with Brian at this point. I had originally intended to simply have Val and Brian as characters experiencing porn and how it affects their lives. As I am using porn as a springboard and integration into the wider sexual domain, and beyond, I have decided we may continue with their marital journey as we progress and not simply leave it here. Like the movie, their relationship may help to inform us as we progress deeper into the sexual domain.

Before I continue with a further discussion of the movie, I would like to point out what was not included in it, as well as maybe why I made such exclusions. Also, what may have been included, but which I chose not to put in the main body of the text.

The director was obviously attentive to not putting in scenes that many people might find offensive, such as the gaping anuses and double anal penetrations that raised the ire of *The Porn Report* authors. This introduces another perspective on this issue, as one reason these are not included is that they would be out of context and so push the production toward the degenerative end of the spectrum. That they are not necessary for inclusion does not necessarily indicate inoffensiveness, though, it is simply that they would not augment the narrative.

That he (or she) does include facial cumshots and other "money shots" is, therefore, significant. They, of course, are seen to routinely almost define a porn production in modern times (they were commonly not present in stag movies, as we found out) and the average consumer expects their inclusion. I will be arguing that the significance goes beyond the identification factor, and point to other deeper issues of a creative and even spiritual nature. I suspect this is the motive of the director as he (or she) often includes them in a ritual context. We will have a similar cause to look at anal sex in more detail and it is extensively used in the movie, along with several double penetrations. At this stage, I would simply like to group the anal sex with the money shots until we explore them in more detail.

Of course, the inclusion of other controversial material, such as pissing, would define the movie in a different way according to the promotion of porn. If it were to have a place, the director would find it difficult and it would seem to me that there are many money shots that serve a similar function, such as when Emily laps up Mick's sperm from Helen's pussy. Predictably, none of the material has questionable sexual relevance or violence, the spanking being excluded on the grounds of mutual acceptance and possible enjoyment. The paradoxical relationship of pain and pleasure in issues such as spanking is reinforced by Mick's anal penetration of Helen. Not only would unacceptable practices alienate many and support the critics, it would also stop many consumers: it would me.

I have tried to give a general atmospheric with respect to clothing. At one level (stockings, revealing bras and G-strings), it is simply representative of the genre, often abetted with heavier than usual make-up, as with the earlier description of Carole. At another, it serves a ritual function, as in the dungeon, and has symbolic significance. Jewellery is usually abundant and I have mentioned it almost in passing at the risk of becoming repetitive. Your imagination may incline to see a necklace on Carole in the very first scene, but maybe not on Emily or Helen in the second. I have chosen not to describe the genitalia in any detail. I could have described him "penetrating her exquisitely manicured pussy mound with hairs that reached to the edge of the lips, gracing but absent around them, as the pink of her lips blossomed to the touch of the tip of his glistening manhood", couldn't I? Well, I haven't, as my impression is that the narrative then does truly become a pornographic work, even with all the eloquence. Mind you, after that sentence above, I am tempted ... so I will supply a general description. The women usually have pubic hair styled and maybe trimmed, with hair around the vagina and anus commonly removed. In this work, all retain most of their pubic hair, as it is felt this endorses the acceptability of the narrative. Similarly, the men do not engage in the depilating practices that are becoming common in some porn. This trend breeds its opposite; you will not be surprised that there is a trend for movies with "full and natural hairy bushes" will you?

Lastly, I have not included condoms. This is obviously a vexed issue and my opinions here are certainly personal and available to all sorts of criticism. I find the use of condoms in porn mixed and strange. Of course, the argument is a workplace one about sexually transmitted diseases and that is why condoms are – sometimes – used. This argument could extend to it being a marketing tool, which I suspect for some in the business it is. When they are used, there are some strange paradoxes. Commonly they are not present for blowjobs, then appear for vaginal or anal penetration, then disappear again for the money shot. So, they are absent in half the domains of routine sexual contact that can also be the source of disease transmission, so what is going on here?

To be quite frank, I'm not entirely sure myself beyond the comments I made about marketing. I would have thought adequate screening and contracts would obviate the need for their usage beyond a certain point. Certainly, in a movie like the one described, routine use of condoms would detract from much of the narrative and symbolic intent, unless their use would support it. The dungeon scene could possibly incorporate condoms, but for ritual and symbolic purposes only, I would suggest. Surely the issue is workplace and hygiene? There is not an AIDs epidemic in the industry, in spite of comments and criticism. Were there to be so, it would provide more than enough fuel to shut it down. Nor is syphilis and gonorrhoea rife. Both, like AIDs, can be easily screened. More problematic are infections like chlamydia, which we have already discussed.

One further issue you may have picked up is what the industry calls 'arse to mouth', with the varying interactions between the participants and their respective involvees in the Club. This could be the source of other hygiene and disease issues, so I can only presume this is dealt with by inner cleansing such as enemas, when such activity is anticipated. Let's assume this is what occurred to Carole, Helen and the two supporting women at the Club in the narrative.

It is becoming increasingly the norm to use body piercing and tattoos. Obviously, many performers are inclined to either or both. Beyond a certain point, I feel it is overdone, and in a movie such as this, there needs to be about as much – or maybe a little more – of what would be in the general population. In this work, there is the occasional earring on the men, and similarly, the women have an occasional belly stud. Also, the sight of a tattoo can reinforce the imagery and even the symbolism of a scene and would not exclude any performer in a movie such as this. Extensive tattooing and use of studs and other body piercings would tend to define a production toward the degenerative end of the spectrum, which is a fact rather than a moral judgment on my behalf.

What you may have noticed in the movie is the contrast between the first and second halves. The first half seemed to have a love match as its completion, and, as we saw, this could well have been the ultimate finale depending on the audience for whom the movie was intended. If this had been the case, there would have been additional scenes to reach the 'complement' of around six and these would have involved pairings and combinations that had not occurred up to that point to fulfil the standard porn movie formula, prior to the final coming together (now that pun is awful!) of Emily and Graham. As it happens, after Emily's initiation and Graham's movement away from Carole, these two make a premature exit by porn standards.

What does this achieve? It provides a contrast to the second half of the movie and also provides a more detailed psychological study of the performers. The contrast is in several ways. The most obvious is that the second half mirrors the first, with the final pairing of Carole and Paul. This mirroring effect is more like a resonance, in that although Carole and Paul do unite, like Emily and Graham, there are some significant differences. There is not the same sense of "boy meets girl" that is achieved by Emily and Graham's union: Indeed, it seems these two must leave before they become exposed to anything that might threaten their pairing. The pairing of Carole and Paul includes further, deeper and more ritualistic experiences. Their relationship is thus more mature in a psychological sense and may be of a higher spiritual order.

So, there is a sense that Graham and Emily 'discover' each other as a result of some mixed self-discovery, whilst Carole and Paul 'discover' significantly more about themselves and then each other as a result. We will have more to say about these issues in the next chapter, so don't despair if all is not immediately clear. It has taxed the great minds of many a poet and artist, let alone the man or woman on the street. It is also something that sexuality can achieve in personal growth and spiritual development, which porn can inform and serve further as an educational tool.

By contrast, Helen and Mick remain relatively unchanged. The implication, reinforced by the Club, is that they are "seasoned campaigners" in the terrain the others are moving through. This may be the case, but it could also be that they are performing a specific role as catalysts, instructors and initiators. If this is so, then they provide a kind of backdrop to the characters moving around them and need to retain a stability and consistency for contrast, comparison and reference.

This is one of the reasons why their personalities in the movie are not significant, beyond any criticism of their acting ability as porn stars. For example, the more the actor has an archetypal function, says Mick, as a male initiator of people through various sexual and, hence, personal transitions, the less will a personality shine through and be relevant; indeed, it could detract from the archetypal role. By contrast, the personalities of most of the others are more formed and so more readily related to by the viewer.

The first half of the movie is also more literal, as reinforced by the settings and style. It explores the more personal issues of the four visitors and the corresponding levels of their evolution. By contrast, and as stressed by the change of setting, the second half becomes more ritualised and symbolic. There may even be a progression of this dynamic throughout the whole movie, such that there are cycles of development throughout.

This analysis is tentative and early. It is based on a straightforward analysis from the pornographic perspective of the industry, as well as the knowledge and experience of a consumer. Actually, there are two, Brian and myself. Although there are some points of overlap, it would be grossly stretching the truth to say that Brian is simply autobiographical and, beyond this point, it is actually untrue. He certainly started out that way, but as the movie progressed, he began to evolve his own character with some differing perspectives and experiences emerging. This is probably why I have decided not to "write him out of the script" at this time and use him as a significant observer in the book as it unfolds, maybe beyond my personal experience, but of validity from the creative and imaginative perspectives.

What the development of the theme requires from here is the introduction of other disciplines and perspectives. To some extent, one has been significantly involved already: depth psychology. This is hardly surprising; given my background and that it has been a major tool in my exploration to date. It also gives me the ability to explore porn and sexuality from differing perspectives to those of my background and conditioning.

What I think this branch of psychology has done already is to expose the flaws and distortions in the common public arguments about porn as an industry and a genre of creative expression. From this, the step has been to reconnect porn with sexuality by indicating it represents the return of sexuality from a position of relative denial and repression in our modern Western culture. Depth psychology will continue to be used as the scaffold that keeps porn and sexuality united, but as more approaches and dimensions are incorporated this will become less necessary.

Sexuality contains and is inclusive of pornography; it is not the other way around.

The Director's Cut

Part 1

The set is being dismantled and packed away, and it is getting late in the day. Carole, Paul, Helen and Mick are seated comfortably in fold-up chairs on the garden in front of the Retreat and chatting idly. There is a sense of completion in the air, along with a satisfied sense of a job well done.

The director goes to a cool box in the boot of a car and takes out a bottle of French champagne. The bottle is demonstratively corked, which gains the attention of the seated foursome. Five similarly chilled glasses accompany the open bottle on a tray to the table set up in front of a vacant fifth chair amongst the group. The director pours some bubbly into the glasses, handing one to each of the porn stars and then picks the last up.

"Cheers and to a job well done!"

They all respond, take a sip, offer some vocal appreciation of quality, and then sit for a while in silence.

"We were just talking about the potential of a sequel, which we'd presume you're considering?" Carole asks the director but with a firm look.

"I'm planning a series called 'Voluptas'."

"What or who is…?" chimes in Paul.

"Voluptas is the goddess daughter of Cupid and Psyche in Roman mythology. She represents pleasure or bliss, and the name has a beautiful ring about it, don't you think?"

The question was rhetorical, and he continued, "I usually

incline to Greek myth, where Cupid is Eros, but Voluptas is Hedone and this seems to incline to 'hedonistic'. As a title, it doesn't quite suit the tone of what I would like to achieve.

"Voluptas will be about some of the themes we've explored here, although taken further and deeper. The plans are very much on the drawing board, particularly with what we have delivered here."

Carole looks interested. "Would you care to join us for dinner tonight to share the ideas and explore the possibilities?"

"Yes, I would like that. I have had some ideas whilst doing this shoot. I think all of you have come on immensely in this production, the pun intended, of course, and really tuned in to what I was trying to achieve, and I believe we got there. Voluptas could stretch your limits … and I'm not just talking physically!"

There is a collective chuckle and a pause follows.

Carole drops her gaze, looking unusually coy and slowly traces an index finger around the rim of her glass. "We thought we might go to the Club … only for a drink, of course!" She pauses and takes a deep breath before continuing, "I believe you acted in mainstream before you got into this business and directing, so why the change, I wonder?"

6

Gender Bender

Let us start with a little recap from the earlier chapters and use them as a lens in our appreciation of *The Weekend Retreat.* From there, we will broaden our exploration from a mainly depth psychological perspective or rather, as I shall often and increasingly refer to it from now on, the psychosexual perspective. I am doing this renaming so that we don't get into any confusion with the term "psychological" for the reasons we have already discussed, but also because by using the prefix 'psych' in psychosexual, in its more authentic meaning as 'soul', I am making a definitive connection between sex and soul.

Maybe this is more than a connection; the concept of soul is actually inclusive of sexuality in a fundamental way. One way to view this connection is by the denial and negation both soul and sexuality have suffered in recent eras as a result of parallel religious – as opposed to spiritual – and scientific mechanisms. How valid all that is will, I trust, become apparent as we proceed.

Earlier we attempted to lift sexuality specifically from the rational, mechanistic and reductive grips of such movements as modern scientific psychology and some forms of feminism. Such 'grips' would confine sexuality to the instinctual level, personal psychology and sexist politics. In fact, it is difficult to find any study today that doesn't see these psychological, sociological, academic and political tools as defining porn and hence, though indirectly, sexuality.

As I indicated earlier, this reductive and mechanistic

approach to life and experience is but one pole of the two that are possible, the problem being that the first does not include the second (science sees no place for spirituality), whereas the second more holistic and even emotional position does recognise and include the first (spirituality, though not necessarily religion, does see a place for science), but in a relative manner. Having clarified the position we are going to take, let us proceed to this psychosexual exploration knowing it will include other established arguments and positions occasionally but will not be defined by them and will hopefully transcend them.

I'm going to reintroduce our analogue perspective for some re-familiarisation, as we are going to employ it in more detail as we progress: Jung: Freud as Holism: Reductionism or even Spirituality: Science.

The Freudian approach is governed by our personal biography and remains confined between conception and death.

Jung's approach includes this but extends beyond, to the spiritual realms of existence, then turns the directional arrow around and sees our personal existence as a kind of consequence of a greater and fundamentally mysterious reality. Jung found it necessary to step out from the confines of his medical upbringing (scientific, mechanistic and analytical) and explore other disciplines in his search. Most significant of these was alchemy and the study of the mystical aspects of religion, which I have and will continue to term "spiritual".

Jung obviously found Freud's approach restrictive and did not sit well with his inherent personality, so he parted company from his master and forged ahead. My impression is Jung's genius is yet to be fully appreciated, with the academic and medical mainstreams tending to incline to Freud when a depth psychology is called for, rather than Jung, who is more problematical. He is often described as "mystical", but as a derogatory term that, as we will see, is quite an irony.

The aspect of Jung's psychology that marked his literal and symbolic departure from Freud was his identification of the contra-sexual element within the personality, which, he considered, had one step in the personal and one beyond in the transpersonal or spiritual realms. Such an 'element' or principle he was to identify as an archetype, meaning the original model or a sort of prototype. The contra-sexual archetypes in man and woman he called the anima (feminine) and animus (masculine), respectively.

Jung does not deny the personal; he includes it. To take a man as an example; his feminine features are, at a personal level, determined by the principal women in his life and, most significantly, his mother. Freud had a lot to say about this relationship and, because sexuality was the cornerstone of his appreciation of the psychoanalytic view of depth psychology, his view has remained dominant and is sometimes held to exclusively by academics, commentators and critics when they explore sexuality. This can lead to conclusions that are reductive and regressive, which may be suitable in some cases, as with sexual pathology and the more degenerative end of the porn spectrum. It is just that it is not the only lens we can use to view the psychosexual picture.

Jung did a disservice by not fully integrating the sexual dimension into his psychology, partly because of the evolving nature of depth psychology in the twentieth century and his relationship with Freud. I have also indicated that I believe issues about his personal life and a desire to have his work taken seriously also influenced this lack of integration. So, we here are going to restore some of the balance.

You may recall that Jung's psychology implies that a man (and a woman) is actually a mixture of masculine and feminine genders. There are personal elements to this, in that at a basic psychological and genetic level, his father and mother (given a 'normal' family and upbringing) provide the images of his masculinity and femininity respectively. In the first half of life and engagement with the world, Jung saw that the dominant feature would 'win out' – in this example, masculinity – such that a man would see himself as exclusively masculine. As his life progressed and the immediate demands of survival, success in the world and family rearing became complete, then the other principal would come increasingly to the fore as he looked more 'inward'. Before this time, the feminine is seen largely in projection, usually as a figure of the opposite sex in the world. If the man is naive then this could be a marriage modelled on his mother (either her like or the opposite), but increasingly different from her the more psychologically mature he becomes. Simply reverse all the above for the woman's position.

As a man gets older, this development shows as his creativity and feeling states, as well as a greater trust in the irrational and his intuition, although initially, it can be appreciated as emotionality and moodiness. There are obviously all sorts of ways that this can get tangled up with women in his life and any developmental distortions play a significant role. You may see the patterns that could be explored in homosexuality, for example. When the distortions are significant and traumatic in the upbringing, subsequent development may have problems with sexual development and lead to particular fetishes, deviations, perversions and other sexual problems.

In general, these are not going to be explored by us as I will also leave this to the Freudians, but in a genuinely acknowledged manner. What I further indicate is that these traumatic distortions then became seen in a pathological manner, and unfortunately, this is then the exclusive lens with which particular sexual arenas, such as pornography, are viewed. And make no mistake, porn is full of psychopathology, but not exclusively so, as I have been at pains to demonstrate.

It seems a relatively trivial step to move to seeing each of us as masculine and feminine; but make no mistake, it is of cosmic proportions – quite literally. I believe, and will be later expounding, that the current movement from the age of Pisces to that of Aquarius is having a significant determining effect on us individually and witnessed in our psychology. You may not believe in astrology, but it is hard not to argue that the way out of the patriarchal, overly-masculinised, war-mongering trap of the last aeon (two thousand years; since the time of Jesus) is not now becoming an over-reaction into the feminine (as initially espoused by the feminist movement), but by a balanced masculinity-femininity. It was this that Jung's psychology was to indicate and anticipate what was to come; he was a genuine prophet.

We start off with ourselves. We are – men and women both – sexual creatures. We each have masculinity and femininity in our being and we are striving for a balance, equivalence or parity with this and not a strict equality as such. It is in this manner that we must approach our sexuality, as well as pornography. Which means: If a woman is being demeaned in a porn movie, then we take insult because we see the feminine as demeaned, man and woman both. I am fully aware this sounds like an exalted position to take and even be in, but all the signs are that this is how we are developing, not only as a culture but also as a species; I think it is all that big. We are not going to appreciate a lot of our sexuality – or pornography as a guide to its development – until we start to move beyond the sexist position. In modern lingo, it is the time of "both/and" rather than "either/or". So, in each of us, there are really two (actually, more than that, we are truly multiple personalities, but I won't go into that here) and in any relationship, there are actually four. No wonder it sometimes feels crowded!

This was Jung's first step beyond the confines of the personal and he was to go a lot further, but we have enough fuel for our journey from where he has taken us thus far. One further connection he made was to see the contra-sexual elements within each of us to comprise the image of the soul. I find this a little simplistic, but it isn't a bad first step into depth psychology to see it this way for the time being and it provides another facet in the linking of sexuality and soul. This means when I see a woman demeaned in porn, I am seeing the demeaning of my soul. When a woman denigrates the man doing the demeaning – even if she is vicariously attracted to it for academic or politic reasons – she is seeing her own potential for demeaning. Challenging stuff.

So, let's be expansive and creative. If it's written in the stars and the cosmic wheel is turning in that direction, how about a balance of the elements in ourselves, particularly as seen in one of their core expressions: sexuality? And the area that's spearheading the return of our repressed sexuality: pornography? It is my contention that it is in such a re-visioned perspective of the sexual that we will enhance and creatively undertake the changes that are demanded, not only just in our personal lives but also in our culture and even our species. Let's see if sexuality, in general, and porn, in particular, answers this challenge.

At one level I had made a deliberate choice to write a porn movie that would reflect the issues that I am going to explore throughout the remainder of the book. But you may find this a little paradoxical: because if I have, and they are so to be explored and found in the book, then how can it still be a porn movie, which I believe it is? Or, looked at alternatively, if it "turned you on" (or, depending on your orientation, disgusted you), how can it also contain the creative and spiritual dimensions? But isn't this precisely my argument from the both/and perspective, that a piece that does "turn you on" is indicative of the reach of sexuality and is a doorway into the other dimensions I mention, and even beyond?

Of course, most porn is not written, produced, acted and delivered with this in mind. An awful amount doesn't get beyond the Freudian and sexist limits. Some do, though, and this may be deliberate on the part of the writer, director and performers who tap into this force with their respective creative abilities. But some may also do so not deliberately but inadvertently because the return of healthy sexuality will contain or even demand these other dimensions if my thesis is correct. It is just that when anything returns from a repressed position it inherently contains a lot of frustration, even anger, and there is an initial overcompensation until things settle down and a more balanced perspective is achieved. This is one reason I think the pro-censorship, anti-pornography feminists are shooting themselves in the foot.

Let's step right back to the beginning of the book and use Private as an example. I doubt if there was anything so deliberate in what Milton may have achieved, as his proclivities and personal issues are well-known and discussed in the trade. But he did use a creative tool – his camera – plus his innate creative skill to photograph sexuality between people and in settings – commonly nature – that resulted in photographs that are very aesthetically pleasing and erotically arousing. In the right hands and with the right tools, maybe, just maybe, sexuality as an archetype will do this all on its own and use us as a creative vehicle for that expression. Maybe sexuality has chosen my creative abilities to write this book. You might chuckle at that conclusion: coincidentally two kookaburras just did so on a tree outside my study.

It might be valuable to examine some of the characters in "Retreat" to explore the psychosexual areas and perspectives discussed. Before I do, may I alert you to another interesting embedded issue that only came to me after I finished writing "Retreat". Jung has often said that a man is seduced by the image and a woman by the word, and this may explain the porn preferences as discussed in an earlier chapter (Chapter Two). I have chosen to write about a porn movie by installing a viewer – Brian – as a go-between or commentator. I have further chosen to write about the images and use that means to conjure further images in your own mind, which I'm sure it would have. In other words, I have been using a combination of word and image, or masculine and feminine functions, to achieve this result. It wasn't something I was aware of at the time; it seemed the only way I could combine my writing (a creative tool) with my enjoyment of images from the sexual perspective. My impression is that it has given the work a balance it may not otherwise have achieved.

If that is the case, has the creative act in some way chosen this pattern to get the message across? As I indicated immediately above, has sexuality determined its own means of expression? Or, somewhat jocularly but with deeper intent, has the director whom I thought was only in my creative mind come from a dimension beyond ... and is now 'really' directing the whole show? Please don't worry about my sanity – just yet.

I won't describe all the characters at this juncture, as you may like to explore the psychosexuality of the ones I don't. (It gives you a chance to re-read the narrative, after all!) I will also be increasingly focusing on Carole and Paul as the book progresses. I found Carole the most enjoyable character to write about. She is also very, if not the most libidinous. You may be tempted to conclude that she represents my feminine side … it bears more than a little reflection. She has sex with everyone, except Emily, even devouring all the acting extras in the Club. It would be tempting to get into her straightaway from a psychosexual perspective (that's two bad puns in a row!) and then balance that against the developing relationship with Paul. So, first, a brief look at the others.

Graham and Emily represent studies in the development of the psychosexual aspects to the emergence of the contra-sexual stage. Graham follows Carole's manipulations into the threesome with Paul, initiated on her part by either jealousy or sexual competition, as an attempt to explore his failing marriage and find out where it is heading. From a sexual perspective, the marriage is not inadequate, and it does further allow Paul into the picture from Carole's perspective, even if he were initially purely a vehicle for her ministrations. But psychologically, it is the death knell of their marriage. I would argue this is not because the threesome happened but because it exposed the issues at hand and, in that way, was a catalyst for the ensuing changes.

As a consequence, Graham, previously an exclusively masculine character, is thrust into a quiet and moody disposition. Jung would see these as hallmarks of an "anima" state; when a man's femininity is controlling him. There are sexual features that reinforce this. With Carole and Paul, he responds in a typically masculine way, but with Emily, he is more the recipient as his feminine features come to the fore. From a sexual perspective, it is of interest that in neither case did he receive a blowjob, the seemingly prototypal male prerogative in porn. Carole's attention in this regard was toward Paul, with only a sucking acknowledgement toward Graham at the end. With Emily, there was even less, and his attention to pussy licking is more dominant. These sexual features serve to reinforce the psychological features, or more accurately the psychosexual ones.

Emily's situation reflects Graham's in many ways. The sexual combinations are an exact mirror (with the caveat of no sex between men in mainstream porn) in that the missing 'fourth' of the man: woman, masculine: feminine balance is the missing 'man' in Emily's scene and the 'woman' in Graham's, they being the inner or contra-sexual aspect of each respective porn star. Emily discovers her dominance and power with respect to Helen, possibly deliberately on Helen's part, and takes this into herself with which then to engage Graham.

You may be interested that the issues of Graham's shortage of blowjobs and the 'missing fourth' only came to my attention when I reviewed what I had written in anticipation of what I am discussing now.

The final sexual scene between Emily and Graham represents a resolution of sorts. Each is now exercising their contra-sexual features and establishing a bond. That this may in itself be transitional could be reflected in their premature departure. It is a stage of development that many get to and stop at, so I won't deny them their time together. It is just that if and when each develops their internal balance and the psychological projections are withdrawn, they'll have a new level of challenge. How far they will get with that is anyone's guess, as many people stop at this stage of a relationship because of the fears that facing the contra-sexual might bring to light: ("God, I'm not gay am I?") From the psychosexual perspective, we will be exploring these issues further with Carole and Paul.

Mick is an interesting character, in more ways than one. He seems exclusively masculine without much femininity and indeed, with a couple of exceptions, this is exactly what he is: The archetypal masculine. As such, he is less than personal and more a figure that represents various psychosexual masculine functions that unfold and act as a guide and initiator to others, particularly Paul. He has been well cast here from the description that Brian gave prior to the movie. Yet there are some enigmatic features; his comment when at the door before joining Helen and Emily ("My lady didn't pick this one ... or maybe she did!") implies an understanding of the feminine at the complex level of role reversal that is going on. Also, in the final scene, he remains a silent observer, seemingly just watching over ... his work.

A more exclusively masculine figure may not have been able to resist jumping into the action. In addition, his actions in the complex scenes at the Club indicate a feminine savoir-faire; this might need a little explaining.

It is the difference between male – minus the balancing feminine – and masculinity, as a principle. The former might 'jump in' because of the projections and the desire to 'possess' or 'control' them. The latter would not; being the 'archetypal male', or more appropriately 'archetypal masculine', the actions of the woman do not represent a challenge or threat in the same personal way. As a person acting this role, he would have to be comfortable with the integration of his personal femininity to the point that he can 'act' as the masculine principle. In life, this can only be a role: We are human, not gods, although with sufficient maturity, maybe we can attain such a status.

In this respect, Mick represents an interestingly composed complex figure that has no psychosexual development of his own to undertake, and his presence there could be to help the transitions of others with an initiatory hand (or cock). As with Helen, this is implied in what the setting of the Retreat itself and the Club seem to offer; they are seemingly 'made' for this sort of activity, even to ritualistic proportions. Helen acts as a complement to Mick in all these respects, although she does introduce her lesbian skills both to the movie and the other women. At one level this could be seen to be the simple and potentially sexist porn formula of allowing lesbian contact in mainstream porn, but not gay interactions. This may be so, but might there be more to it than that?

I suspect there is; so, let's tackle a ticklish subject. If it is an acceptable mainstream porn alternative and we exclude the sexist possibilities, might it indicate a fundamental difference between female sexuality by comparison to male? I think it does, and we will explore this when we very shortly move to Teiresias' enigmatic comments about men's and women's respective appreciation of sexuality. If that is the case, Helen is "all woman", or the feminine principle and as a complement to Mick. In other words, she also has integrated her masculine side into her personality and is illustrating that the feminine perspective of sexuality is different to that of the masculine. Not less than or better than, just different, and also maybe more mysterious.

The climax (not another pun?) comes (oh my god!) with Helen's role in the final scene, which cuts quite a poetic and dramatic tableau. Helen's relationship with Carole here reveals an intimacy and complexity beyond the one she had with Emily, and which, although present, is not so readily apparent in the one between Mick and Paul. If what I have discussed here is the case, it puts a different slant on the lesbianism in mainstream porn and also indicates that a deeper function is that it introduces to the viewing men, or women, a feminine aspect – even mystery – that they need to be in contact with. If this is so, then gay sex does not hold the same position or serve such a similar function and maybe why it is not present in the mainstream.

My impression is that such an enquiry would reveal much about homosexual dynamics that is largely excluded in the current predominant Freudian view. I am reminded of Tristan, the female director's comments as described in *The Porn Report*, when she describes her anal penetration by all ten co-stars (both male and female – don't ask, dildos I presume!), in the movie that she also acts in, as the "ultimate feminist gang bang". There may be some deeper mirroring and inversion going on here than initially met the eye.

As an aside, and given my (and psychology's) definition and positioning of terms, I am interested in the terminology of the feminist movement. Feminism, as defined here, is only one pole of a pair or spectrum. In its exclusivity it omits – even negates – the masculine. Because women contain both masculine and feminine aspects, the psychological rule is that such neglect, or repression, sees the omitted opposite return via 'the back door'; that is, with aggression and in an inferior form as compared to the position it is challenging (masculinity as seen in men), even to the point of an unaware identification. It could be argued that many of these features have and continue to exist in the feminist movement.

It may well be that the confusion we are experiencing with man and woman, male and female, and masculine and feminine is not only due to the lack of clarity in defining them and which depth psychology is seeking to rectify, but that we are taking an analytical (masculine) approach in the first place. From this perspective, we use man and male, woman and female synonymously; in other words, man is the male of the human species (with rabbits he is a buck) and vice versa for a woman. By contrast, masculinity represents a principle. Let me repeat that: masculinity represents a principle, like in a lot of nouns in languages such as French, Latin and many others, where we call them "genders".

As a principal, masculinity is not the same as the male of the species, it is pure and uncontaminated by the feminine principle, although paradoxically complemented by it. Obviously vice versa for femininity. So, with the common identity of male with masculine and female with feminine that depth psychology, via Jung, has shown to be erroneous, is there any other way to get beyond this analytically induced confusion?

Now, with all these possibly still somewhat confusing perspectives in mind, let's move on to the deeper dimensions of both male and female sexuality, as evidenced in the Teiresias myth, and possibly a way beyond the confusion.

Teiresias was chosen by Zeus and Hera to decide the question of whether the male or female has the most pleasure in intercourse. And he said:

"Of ten parts a man enjoys one only; but a woman's sense enjoys all ten in full."

Please excuse the repetition:

I have taken the relevant passage from the myth as a platform to the next section and omitted the remainder, which comes up at other varying points on our journey.

Recall in our initial look at sexuality from the depth psychological perspective (Chapter Three), we came on the male: female, masculine: feminine issues and placed them in analogue form, a principle we also expanded on earlier in this chapter. I propose that the analogue method of exploration is more fruitful to this discussion for one simple reason: it gives equivalence to principles such as masculinity and femininity.

Earlier, we discussed the fact that masculinity and femininity were not equal (the same) but equivalent or of equal standing; they are archetypes, after all. Equivalence and equality are not the same thing; they are subtle differences, but they are important to grasp in our ongoing argument.

I may be splitting hairs here, but there are other subtle dimensions in the quote above. The question posed by Zeus and Hera is about male and female enjoyment of sexuality, but Teiresias' reply refers to man and woman. These can be seen as the same thing, but remember: man is male, but not all males are men (decidedly few if you think of rabbits). So, what does that matter, you may ask? Well, Zeus and Hera are gods and not of the human species, to whom Teiresias' reply is directed.

The implications of this: Maybe it is that males that are not human have the same pleasure as females, and this loss is the human condition? Maybe it sheds some light on the Garden of Eden myth? Maybe it reflects the patriarchy and the loss that that achievement brought? Maybe it indicates that the gods truly are equal at a sexual level and that Zeus and Hera are representative of masculinity and femininity – with a little patriarchal sexism thrown in? Or maybe there are other angles, depths and twists to this that have yet to be seen ... There is no direct answer to any of these questions individually, but collectively they may point beyond our rational and analytical perspective to something mysterious within sexuality.

Which is what I think Teiresias' reply does. As I indicated earlier (Chapter Three), it is not that man enjoys one of the ten and woman the remaining nine; it is that she enjoys all ten and he just one; not one of the ten, but maybe one-tenth? There is not a separation here; there is an implied full complement that woman has ready access to and that man has only a fraction. Now, given that both man and woman have a feminine principle, it means man has access to it also, even if somewhat more problematically. I wonder if it is this that makes Hera mad? I further wonder whether this explains the integrated portrayal of lesbianism in porn? I also believe that is something that men of wisdom know to be the truth: that women do enjoy sex more. (I'll duck for cover for a moment here!)

This all starts to get delightfully paradoxical; which, by the way, is characteristic of the feminine principle! It's as if we are halfway between the animal kingdom and the gods, with the male and female of the animal having a balance in their sexuality, because it is undifferentiated. At the other end of the spectrum, the gods, as masculine and feminine principles (or archetypes) do as well, but now differentiated (I briefly reflect on Mick and Helen here). Mankind is kind of in the middle, struggling with the differentiation process, and this is where the gods may help 'inform' him and her. Deal with sexuality and maybe we become as gods ... more of this a little later.

Are you enjoying all these little twists and turns? I know I am having a ball. And isn't this just the nature and a profound feature of sexuality: Play.

Let's take this a little further and back into porn. I am also now going to be looking through a masculine: feminine lens, not a male: female one, so bear this in mind with your reactions to what I might express.

The number ten implies wholeness and the feminine is round (a breast, a womb). Masculinity is straight, a line (a penis) and one. Feminine sexuality is total; the whole body is erogenous, whilst the masculine is focused on the (male) genitals. Although a little Freudian, the masculine principle emerges from the feminine and, at a deep level, desires a return. Is this reflected in the Great Cycle of Existence – birth to death? Note that the Great Cycle has sex in its midst. Does this make masculine sexuality obvious and that of the feminine mysterious? I think it does. If it is from the feminine that the masculine sexuality emerges, is this femininity an image of the soul?

Does porn explore these questions, even if inadvertently? I believe it does. When Emily and Helen were fucking each other without a man involved (and you can fuck without a penis), weren't they exploring the masculine: feminine dynamics? I won't go back through the movie in any detail, but your reflections of it may come to the conclusion that, as a whole, it is exploring these issues. By now, it won't surprise you that it is my conviction that sexuality, and hence pornography, has enormous influence, even a fundamental one, in exploring these questions and the changes in ourselves, our culture and even our species.

You could examine all these questions with a Freudian orientation and come to some more definitive (Freudian and masculine) conclusions. This certainly is valid, but is it only the one of the ten? If we take a Jungian approach, are we then looking more to the ten? When we look at a blowjob, particularly if deep-throated, is it more than issues of the devouring mother and castration anxiety? Why on earth would any healthy man desire it, if that were the case, and I assure you he does. Could it relate to a sacrifice of the masculine perspective in a ritual context to that of the feminine, a re-entry into the divine?

As I close this section you will note that there are an awful lot of questions above. This has been deliberate; it is designed to get you to ask deeper questions about sexuality than maybe you hitherto have and to accept that unanswered questions, anomalies and paradoxes are part of the feminine principle itself and, hence, are the language of the soul. Ultimately, sexuality is mysterious, I would suggest. I am developing a view of sexuality that is psychosexual (sex and soul) and archetypal (spirit), when you may argue that it is simply an instinct. You are right, but it is not all sexuality, is it?. But let's have a look at it from the instinctual perspective to see what surprising rewards that may bring.

Konrad Lorenz, who has defined the field, tells us that there are four instincts. These are commonly described as feeding, reproduction, aggression and flight, and can be amusingly referred to as the four "Fs" of feeding, fucking, fighting and fleeing; a useful mnemonic if nothing else! Lorenz is referring to the animal kingdom and what this perspective achieves is to see these instinctual drives in the same light: animalistic. So, if they are experienced in the human sphere, they are seen in this way and judged as base, inferior and the like. From a typically mechanistic psychological view, they are infantile, primitive or regressive. All in all, not a very encouraging perspective, and sex is there in the midst. Sexuality then gains a perspective that equates it with reproduction, which I will define as "generative". Anything that doesn't meet this requirement is, therefore, "degenerative" at this instinctual level.

Jung describes these instincts somewhat differently (he gets around, doesn't he?). The major instinctual groupings, or drives, are: hunger, sexuality, the drive to activity and reflection. These are comparable to the feeding, reproduction, aggression and flight groupings. There are some subtle differences though, because Jung is referring to the human 'animal' specifically. The drive to activity equates to aggression, for example, but elevates the drive from a base to a more human perspective by the implication of an emotional component. As a consequence, aggression can be seen as more than mere anger, but also to be purposeful and with masculine features. A similar analysis of reflection leads to an association with the feminine. I would argue that hunger (feeding) and sexuality remain gender-neutral.

This is an interesting point in the expansion of the aggression instinct, so what about we do something similar with sexuality and see what we arrive at?

Reproduction I have described as generative and implies a degenerative aspect from the human perspective if not directed toward reproduction (the Catholic Church's position ... strangely Freudian). If we compare this to aggression and anger, then sex is not seen in a very good light. But Jung's description is far more human; he broadens and elevates the scope to sexuality, which includes but is not defined by the equation sex = reproduction and that everything else is simply less than this, or degenerative.

Unfortunately, and reinforced by the continuing dominance of the Freudian equation of sex with pathology (physical or mental illness), we still incline to the Lorenz position, which is a shame. Jung's view is far more expansive. It is reinforced by the fact that he also considered there to be a fifth instinct in the human sphere: Creativity. If we look back at the drive to activity instinct, we may see another feature of instincts: that they overlap each other.

This last fact is an interesting one to examine because a lack of appreciation about how instincts operate at the human level means we can misinterpret and 'animalise' a lot of human behaviour and endeavour. Sexuality can contain elements of all the other instincts; the association of feeding and oral sex is but one obvious example. Take aggression and sexuality, which overlap in some other very obvious ways and which porn takes advantage of, sometimes frequently. Also embedded are the masculine and feminine principles, perspectives on dominance and submission, and even sadomasochism. It's all there; everything you've ever seen is in porn, but were afraid to ask! Maybe this orientation makes much sexual practice less alien, negative, destructive or even perverted.

We could take any or all of these arguments considerably further, both in the field of depth psychology or in the psychosexual examination of issues such as fetishism and perversions. Unfortunately, this would take us too far away from the main thrust of this work and we must leave it there. However, you may care to use it as a basis to explore any interesting line of enquiry that piques your fancy. I am going to suggest that Jung's approach takes us away and upward from the commonly held position on the instincts: It humanises and even begins to spiritualise them and, obviously, I am now going to focus on sexuality to back my argument from here.

If you care to take any of the scenes from "Retreat" and look at them with the above view of instincts, I think you will find it quite revealing. In a brief overview, we can repeat the relationship between oral sex and feeding, although there are times it could be aggressive or receptive (reflective). The gender (masculine: feminine) principle overlaps these two instincts, whether it is a man or woman giving or receiving, which augments the gender arguments above. Spanking takes the aggression theme a bit further toward that instinct, yet in the context of the scene (Emily and Helen) it remains primarily sexual and used to play on the gender theme and the masculine: feminine inversions that occur in both women. Reflectiveness marks the scene between Emily and Graham, but it would be stretching things a bit far – at this stage – to say that love is included.

What? Love is an instinct? You've got to be kidding me! Actually, I'm not saying that it is an instinct, but I am also not kidding you. What I am saying is that the seeds of love are in the instincts themselves. To do this, I will briefly divert into the depth of the psychological notion of archetype, as espoused by Jung.

Archetype is a word derived from the Greek, meaning literally "first modelled, or moulded". Archetype could be considered connate with the more familiar words stereotype and prototype. Jung resurrected the term in the twentieth century and applied it to his psychology, which embraces a "collective" – as opposed to personal – and more spiritual dimension to human existence. The archetypes form the organising foci within the collective background, which become familiar to man as universal themes and principles, such as "mother", "warrior" or even "sexuality".

Archetypes, according to Jung, are innate and universal psychic dispositions that form the background from which the basic themes of human life emerge. Being innate and universal, their influence and action are seen in the form of myths, symbols, rituals and stories of human beings. Like the instincts, archetypes are present beyond our acquired experience of life; although our personal development will further mould and inform the universal pattern to our own experience and so individualise it, much like we described earlier with the analysis of the masculine: feminine gender principles.

Archetypes are the components of this collective dimension and serve to organise, inform and direct human thought, feelings and actions. From an energetic perspective an archetype is eternal and universal, is latently bipolar and has a self-regulatory function. The bipolarity indicates archetypes can be seen as either good or bad, positive or negative, nurturing or depriving depending on our relationship with them, and hence often governed by personal experience.

(As an aside, Jung used the full term as the "collective unconscious" for this collective. I have already voiced my difficulty with the term unconscious and so, in many ways, I prefer his original term of "objective psyche". This latter term is continuous with its complement, "subjective psyche" and illustrates the bridging aspect of psyche, or soul, between personal and spiritual life.)

It might be useful to add yet another perspective to this mix before we look further at how instincts relate to the archetypes. In philosophy and comparative religion, there is the notion of the Perennial Philosophy or the "Great Chain of Being". In simple terms, this sees the physical and the spiritual dimensions to be the two ends of a spectrum, rather than opposing principles or world-views. This spectrum can be expanded and elaborated in varying ways, all of which are similar and commonly reflect the temperament and disposition of the commentator, as well as the time he or she lives in. I am going to give you mine, which obviously matches the arguments of this book.

I will extend the physical – spiritual spectrum to include the emotional and mental realms as: physical–emotional–mental–spiritual. I am also going to stop there in this analysis, the nature of which could fill a book, and ask you to accept it as a sound working model for our purposes. I am further going to elaborate on this model to say that each level up the chain includes the position below and extends beyond, or transcends it. So, the emotional includes and transcends the physical, the mental includes and transcends the emotional and the spiritual includes and transcends all of the levels below. As an aside, I see the somewhat marginalised Western concept of 'soul' to relate to the personal dimensions of the mental, emotional and physical levels and to be the bridge to the spiritual.

Back to the instincts:

If we see the instincts–archetypes in a similar manner, then I think we have a formula that says the archetypes include yet transcend the instincts. We can also see that the depth psychological perspective of instinct–archetype is a direct parallel of the Perennial Philosophy or Great Chain of Being. So, maybe it is not so far-fetched to say that love was in the scene involving Emily and Graham, yet is possibly in an even more evolved form in the last scene with Carole and Paul?

It is a truism to say that porn explores sexuality from the instinctual level but to say that is all it does or can do is a gross mistake. Of course, it can remain entirely instinctual. To achieve this, all it needs to do is exclude an emotional dimension and it will remain cycling in the physical and instinctual levels exclusively. I consider this to be the porn end of the erotography spectrum, according to my earlier definitions (Chapter Two), and on the scale degenerative–generative–regenerative to be distinctly degenerative. Without access to creativity (another instinct) and the emotional level, the movement of sexuality up the physical–spiritual, instinctual–archetypal, degenerative–regenerative spectrums will become frustrated, self-absorbed and in danger of obsession and addiction. Indeed, all sorts of mental disturbances, as well as perversions, can be seen to arise from this dynamic. In this respect, Freud was right; it's just that he didn't and couldn't have seen the whole picture.

If porn is to be more than this it needs to engage other dimensions. Jung, in his definitions of instincts, already implies the connections with the emotions. This is reflected in the connections of these emotional areas in the physical brain as well as in the pattern of the Great Chain of Being. More than this, we know it commonly to be the case with sexuality; that sexual involvement leads to emotional entanglement. This is one dimension that porn takes distinct advantage of and encourages emotionless sexuality if at the degenerative end of the spectrum.

Look at what happened to Brian. He initially had a strong sexual response to the movie, taking his trousers off and masturbating. But as the movie progressed, he became increasingly emotionally engaged, as judged by his responses and reactions. The last scene almost leaves him in an altered – ecstatic – state of consciousness. I would suggest that the movie has taken him a long way up the Great Chain by engaging him not only sexually and physically but also emotionally, as witnessed by the lessening of his sexual response, a common occurrence and hence often why it is avoided in porn.

Incidentally, I feel this dynamic explains a lot of sexual difficulties (erectile dysfunction, premature ejaculation) in men, as they may be becoming better acquainted with their femininity, but unable to handle it. They need rituals of transition if this is the case, not Viagra.

This response also caused him mental reflection, particularly toward Val and his marriage. There is a subtle bridge going up the Great Chain that I would like to highlight here and has a direct bearing on gender issues. Emotional engagement leads to contact with our 'other half', the contra-sexual principle inside us. This definitively cannot be done without an emotional consciousness in its own right, one implied in Jung's view of the instincts but repressed and denied in so many walks of life. My belief is that, if you deny a person contact with their emotions, you deny them access to the soul. I think this is why Jung equated the soul image with the contra-sexual image in men and women.

I further think the soul image is beyond such classification and that once the gender principles of masculinity and femininity are fully engaged the soul image is feminine for both men and women. I believe this is compatible with spiritual experience and is reflected in sexuality, which in and of itself can be a path to the spiritual, as should by now be evident.

We are here in the vexed area of moods, extending to the currently fashionable psychiatric diagnosis of "bipolar disorder". What I am indicating is that this bipolarity and the moods that indicate its engagement are the soul wrestling with the gender issues in an internal way. For example, when a man is moody, even depressed, he often displays feminine characteristics. Indeed, we commonly define femininity by emotional states. A woman may be moody in an opinionated and judgemental way that appears more masculine. Without all these inner connections, our mental states remain detached and isolated from the physical and prey to dualism, as seen in the mind-body conundrum and reflected in medicine as a psychosomatic illness. Obviously, Freud was on the right track seeing instinct and sex as behind such illnesses as hysteria; he simply didn't go far enough.

Without these connections, the mental perspective is prey to dualism, in a subversive way, and takes that as its world-view, backed by judgement and even bigotry. This position is isolated and vulnerable and reflects a patriarchy not connected to its femininity, which it fears and wants to repress and to which it is paradoxically attracted. These features are in the Teiresias myth and are reflected in Zeus and Hera's actions and reactions. Also, remember the anomaly of men with right-wing political views being as attracted to porn as often those of the liberal left? I wouldn't consider them as having an equal attraction and I would further suspect that there might be more of the porn at the aggressive end of the spectrum in the attraction of those from the political right. Just guessing ...

Ultimately what I am ascribing to sexuality is an archetypal dimension. Actually, all instincts do have it, according to the arguments above; it is just in the human species that we begin to appreciate it in a conscious way and one that demands self-responsibility. I have defined archetype above, so let's see how that applies to sexuality.

An archetype is timeless and exists across all cultures. Well, sexuality certainly does that. An archetype is bipolar, and sexuality is certainly and inherently that. An archetype is self-regulatory. Does this apply to sexuality?

If you take the instinctual position, it would seem not. It would seem that we are driven by sex; instincts are called "drives", after all. Yet that is regulatory at one level because it is driving us toward reproducing. The issue is where 'we' fit into the equation. My suggestion is that if you reject sexuality then it remains instinctual and acts according to the highest principle therein: reproduction. Now, it is interesting that this is the position the Catholic Church also promotes, which means that within this Church sexuality remains an instinct and opposite to the religious position. Divide and conquer, so the saying goes; divide sexuality from spirit and you divide the person, then you have a mortgage on the soul. This is the province of the priest, as it is only with his intervention that you can connect with spirit in the Eucharistic mass. This position is further reinforced in a general sense with anything that is inclusive of the sexual, such as the body and its rejection in Western culture and religion.

Science has helped in this division by denying even the existence of a soul, reflecting from a different angle the estrangement of it within Western religion. In this scenario, sex remains an instinct, mechanical and inferior. Science thus forms a strange bedfellow with religion by denying access to spirit with the estrangement or negation of soul and its connection to sexuality.

If I am right and sexuality is archetypal as well as instinctual (as all the instincts are) and it is perforce self-regulatory, how do we see this? The answer: In pornography. Porn is the "return of the repressed": It is sexuality denied demanding its existence and expression in and of its own terms. Porn displays the full repertoire of sexual expression, not only for archetypal completeness but also for us to experience its fullness and determine our own position with respect to it. Of course, most porn is not created for this reason and is not its intention; but as a phenomenon itself, it shows the denied, denigrated and frustrated position of archetypal repression in all its glory.

That porn is confused in intent, as well as in content, is of no surprise. We must get beyond that and see what as a broader principle – an archetype – it is telling us about our attitude and relationship to our sexuality. To do this, we must have the individual courage to reconnect with our sexuality in whatever way it presents itself to us. For me, as with many, it is with the assistance of porn. Yet always remember: Pornography is the vehicle into a full and wholesome connection to sexuality and our individual responsibility is to discover what this sexual potential is for each and every one of us. My belief, experience and knowledge are that such an exploration will significantly assist the reinstatement of the soul in Western culture and, with it, our individual connection to the spiritual world without the need of a priest (who may have an ambiguous and confused relationship to sexuality anyway).

Sex as sacrament?

If what I am saying is the case, what avenues do we have to assist us in this process? We could look to other cultures where sexuality does not have this same problematic position and will do so in a future chapter. Certainly, many have actively taken that route, commonly into Indian spirituality, and Osho Rajneesh, as a modern example, exemplifies this with his emphasis on the fundamental connection between sexuality and spirituality. His movement would bear a more detailed analysis from this perspective. Yet we are not of these cultures, they may serve to instruct and illustrate these issues to us, but – archetypally – they are not of our Western culture and disposition. However, if as I have argued, we have been so effectively severed in this regard in the West, where do we find a path?

What I think porn does is provide us with the raw material for this process. No, I'm not completely right here; it is the raw material itself and also contains something precious if we know how to unearth it. The savvy amongst you will notice that I am lapsing into alchemical metaphors and I am going to use alchemy itself as the principal map. First, a little examination of why that should be appropriate.

According to my comments above we need to find the threads in our own culture and history that indicate pathways in the retrieval process. As sexuality is demanding archetypal reintegration and we have seen that soul has either been made relative or even denied in the West, it is sound, even imperative, to see a connection between the two. This is (partially) reinforced when we look at other cultural traditions and gives us

194

a point of comparison. Doctors of sex and the soul are traditionally the medicine men or shamans if we look at pre-Christianity. Medicine has come a long way since then – not necessarily in terms of progress I might add – but has come to view sex with a scientific and pathological lens, which is not always healthy. (Isn't that a paradox?) Religion has become more concerned with power and delivers this by controlling a person's sexuality; particularly with medicine's rejection of proprietorship (Freud and psychiatry notwithstanding). There is the additional feature, or intent, of denying access to his or her individual soul.

The patriarchy of the last two thousand years, which is reflected in our myths and culture, has had an enormous influence in this regard. My argument is, and by resonance with the astrological Age of Aquarius, that this dominance is coming to a close and that the return of psychosexuality, initially most prominent in the nineteen-sixties, reflects this both literally and symbolically. If we can't get to the figures and traditions of pre-Christianity, because Christianity has all sorts of repressive concerns of its own that might block such an exercise, then where do we find them?

I contend that it is in the religious undercurrents of history, both ancient and modern, and as reflected in particular figures and their paths, that we find clues. Religious undercurrents exist in the mystics, who were versed in other traditions and employed tools such as alchemy and astrology. The witchcraft phenomenon and the Inquisition are most informative in this regard: the former, in particular, illustrates the confluence of the feminine and sexuality. In medicine, there are figures like the medical alchemist and astrologer Paracelsus who do not cease to go away (a modern study of his life and work was published in 2007). The relationship with magic is also significant and although Aleister Crowley may not be the best advertisement in this regard, he bears more detailed examination, in my opinion.

This latter comment (about Crowley) brings up some interesting popular misconceptions. These are that magic is inherently dark and the work of the devil (by association and implication, so is alchemy) and that women are sexual temptresses who lead men to evil. I find this particularly interesting as it imputes a power of matters sexual to women that only a repressive patriarchy, backed by the full force of the Church, is able to deal with. It must have felt threatened and frightened. It is of further interest that, according to recent changes and my analysis of them, it has failed in this regard.

That sexuality is associated with such wide practices and disciplines as alchemy, magic, shamanism, mystical practice, and folk medicine (to name but a few) is highly telling of its primacy, range, power and potential for change and transformation within individuals and beyond. It is no wonder that vested interests have had to exercise immense powers, including psychological techniques (which, ironically, border on the darkly magical, or sorcery) to control sexuality.

Of all these, I will choose alchemy as the main path of enquiry for reasons that will become apparent; so back to the raw material of sexuality. Pornography represents the return of the repressed and its darker features, initially inevitable, make it available to and provide support and justification for all the powers that have hitherto kept it repressed. My thesis is that this is no longer working or possible and is exemplified by factors such as technology and the Internet.

In alchemy, the raw material is contained and kept in a container called an athanor. Here, the alchemist provides various chemical agents, heat and patience, and under astrological direction he or she works toward the transformation of the raw material – commonly lead – into gold. It was Jung (he crops up again!) who reinstated alchemy in the twentieth century as a historical tool that paralleled the work of the depth psychologist. Jung saw that alchemy reflected the images of personality change and growth from an inner or psychological perspective. He even used alchemical patterns in psychotherapy.

Collectively we must contain and 'work' with the raw material of repressed sexuality, because most of it is 'shit'. (Another alchemical term for the raw material, but it might also infer anal sex?) The chemistry we add, and the work we do is our own. This work is looking at the material and experimenting with it in differing ways, reflecting on our involvement and motives, so that we can progressively purify what we are dealing with. It requires our energy (heat), courage and patience. It is also fundamentally mysterious and often under the guidance of a mentor (a psychotherapist in therapy, or me here with your sexuality).

The gold is not literal; it is symbolic. The raw material of pornography is gradually changed into a creative and expressive sexuality that flows through our lives and relationships leading to soul realisation, spiritual maturity and states of grace and love. Do you find all this too much? Are you thinking that the bow I have drawn is long indeed? Maybe it's because I've led you to the outcome without going through all the stages, which, in one way, is impossible in a work such as this. Yet there is something I can do, and that is provide the map: it is just that the map must be applied to the territory for the alchemy to work. You have to walk your talk. Well, let's go back to "Retreat" as a metaphor for the raw material.

The raw material is what each person brings to the weekend for 'change'; sometimes without knowing it. The choice of the term is interesting because a 'retreat' is often associated with a religious institution. In this situation, it acts as the alchemical vessel to contain the raw material so that changes can occur that are creative, purposeful and even spiritual. The director is the alchemist and Mick and Helen are the chemical catalysts he (or she) has 'added' to the mix to assist the changes. There are two patterns that emerge to differing outcomes: Emily and Graham, Carole and Paul. It is these patterns that will reflect the mapping and will be referred to as we proceed, as I take you through the alchemical stages. Before we do this, there are some parting reflections for this chapter in the form of the validity of what I am to undertake, so let's explore these.

You may have accepted my arguments about the whole psychosexual perspective to a greater or lesser extent. There are issues you can reflect on and see how they apply to your own life and how you view the world; also, whether this perspective assists you in your personal development and relationships, both sexual and otherwise. You may have followed me on the various angles I have taken, particularly those of a psychological nature. However, I suspect if you have any difficulty, it is with the use of pornography itself as the subject matter.

Specifically, that I should construct a narrative and try and 'sell' it to you as a vehicle of self-growth and spiritual realisation. One argument could be that I have composed the story to suit my own ends. This argument is valid, though untrue at the obvious level because it was a spontaneous creative act. The next line of argument is that this may be the case, but my background in other fields would incline me that way. Yes, they would, and for this, I make no apology. However, what if I told you that this story arose out of my exploration of sexuality itself and my personal journey through pornography as the core of this development?

In this respect, I am unashamedly presenting "Retreat" as a creative act that incorporates all of the features I am espousing, which will emerge from a faithful exploration of sexuality, even if that is through the route of pornography. If this is the case, isn't it an irony that it is the porn itself that does this?

7

Sex and the Single Soul

We've arrived at a transition point in our enquiry. Following the last chapter, I experienced an emotional pause. I felt I needed to take stock of what had been described and discussed to date and put it into some sort of order as a platform for the second half of the book. I had a sense that the depth psychology perspective, particularly that of Jung, had provided a deeper window into sexuality, but that there was a need to integrate what had been explored before advancing. In some ways, this is difficult, and the pause is relative, as many of the themes we're exploring will continue into the second half of the book.

For example, mythology has informed us to date and will continue to do so the deeper we move into the topic. Why? Because mythology reflects the stories of our lives in a collective and cultural manner, and provides the sort of broad scope that our enquiry demands. The Pandora myth has been left simply explained: An expression of the relationship between the gods (world of spirit) and mankind, as well as having a distinctly sexist twist, to which I have provided a sexual implication. I even propose that Pandora herself could be a metaphor for the pornographic phenomenon. The Teiresias myth further reinforces the sexist issues that have dominated the last two thousand years or so, which we have had cause to question, but beyond that gave us insights of a more eternal nature about the relationship between man and woman, as well as a broader understanding of feminine sexuality. There is also more than a hint that the whole psychosexual domain has a fundamentally feminine flavour.

Depth psychology itself has modernised this mythic and cultural perspective into a language that is more readily understandable to modern man (the term 'man' is inclusive of woman ...) and taken sexuality a fair degree beyond the dualistic and resultant sexist position that has so dominated the recent scientific and rational era. Or at least our application of these insights with respect to sexuality because it was not done in any detail by the pioneers of this dimension themselves. Reich certainly did from the psychoanalytic end of the spectrum, going well beyond Freud's mechanistic position and we will have cause to return to him. Jung did not; nor have his followers to any significant degree. James Hillman, in the wake of Jung, has certainly re-established the position and primacy of the soul in the psychic economy, as well as the "language" of the soul, which he perceives as imaginative, symbolic and – initially at least – having a feminine quality that we have associated with psychosexuality. It is thus also deeply emotional in nature.

Hillman we will also be returning to as he not only placed a central importance to the soul, but also made use of mythology extensively. Although this was primarily Greek, as our enquiry has been to date, there are some limitations in this that we will be exploring as we look at myths from the Teutonic (Germanic, Scandinavian or Northern Traditions) and Celtic cultures. Hillman also makes many references to alchemy, again following in Jung's wake. Why is this?

I suspect it is because there is only so far modern depth psychology can go in isolation. The deeper the enquiry the more other maps are either necessary or facilitate the exploration. Of these I would nominate alchemy and astrology; the former we will be making significant reference to as it has sexuality deeply embedded within it. These are tools that have been made use of throughout mankind's history by those of a mystical and magical disposition; that is, those who incline to an inward (esoteric) path to self-discovery and spiritual realisation. In the recent Piscean aeon, their presence and availability have been couched in secrecy, often for the necessity and even safety of the practitioner. This is mainly because the established religions have had a controlling dominance regarding spiritual pathways and sought to negate their existence, by a variety of sometimes frightening means. In the current era, and aided by people like Jung, these disciplines have re-surfaced, and their importance has been identified.

There will be disciplines from another – Eastern – culture that we will be including in the enquiry, mainly because the negation in our recent eras in the West of these pathways has been so complete. Perspectives from other cultures will be informative because they are inclusive of the psychosexual. However, these must be seen relatively: Eastern culture, in general, is not our own. Yet because it has an unbroken tradition – compared to the West – that goes beyond our own historical disruptions, we can explore its patterns to discover our own sources and re-establish the cultural connections that have been severed, and so move on in our own traditional idiom.

This last point about disruption, although covered earlier, may stand some further clarification, as it is an important perspective to understand in our overall enquiry. The rise of the monotheistic religions (Judaism, Christianity and Islam) developed out of the prior polytheistic and pagan religions. (Pagan indicates heathen and is a Christian term that is somewhat pejorative toward the natural and animistic spiritual traditions it superseded; I will continue to use the term, as it is one we are familiar with.) This period also encompasses the aeon of Pisces, which we are now just leaving and about which I will have more to say. In summary, this period (the last two thousand years) could be considered to have been the domain of the patriarchal perspective.

The patriarchal era can be considered to be masculine-dominated and to permeate both religion and state with power and control. In the earlier part of the era, this brought a new dimension to spirituality but latterly has tended to segregate the population, with a small group connected to the "power and the glory", with its attendant riches and control, and ability to deny the population at large a direct relationship with the divine. This effectively created two tiers in the overall religious system, with those championing the 'inner' perspective – a direct relationship – scattered amongst the mystics, magicians and alchemists, who often remained within the prevailing religious structures. The folk traditions (witches, folk medicine and the like) connected with shamanism ('primitive' healers and magicians) and the religious cultures that preceded Christianity also maintained this connection, although mainly outside of the formal religious systems.

What has all this got to do with sex, you might ask? Well, have a look at where sex is usually distributed in this carve-up. Isn't that a major tool of accusation toward magicians, 'primitives' (pre-Christian cultures) and, most particularly, the witches and the folk traditions? Also, notice how this also refers to the body, as opposed to the 'higher' mind, and also ... the feminine.

My understanding of this outcome is that any notion of soul has been progressively relegated within formal religion for the reasons of power and control, and that many of the features that identify and even define soul – body, sex and the feminine – are similarly relegated. Or, more correctly, if these features are denigrated and despised, then the individual will have only a limited capacity to engage and relate to his or her own soul.

These mechanisms have, of course, been utilised with more than a liberal dose of guilt and shame, should the more obvious power and violent mechanisms fail.

What has not helped this process of soul reconnection is that, as the modern era approached, science made an emergence and came to dominate our worldview in the twentieth century. Art and creativity – often associated with the feminine anyway – took a similar position to soul, as science did not only deny the latter's presence, it negated the very existence of soul by rationalising it away. I suspect this emerging pattern, along with the declining power and control of formal religion, continued the trend previously described; that is, until depth psychology discovered its hovering presence in sex and mental health (Freud), ancient spiritual tradition (Jung), the body (Reich) and the creative imagination (Hillman).

I have further indicated that science and religion have been able to maintain the status quo because the patriarchal perspective has dominated what I have called the Great Cycle of Existence – birth, sex and death. Although overlapping, birth and death have become the province of science and medicine behind the hospital doors, whilst sex has been the major vehicle of religious control. This factor, combined with similar mechanisms to control the feminine, art and creativity, has effectively maintained the status quo to the end of the twentieth century.

Medicine has assisted in this endeavour: how? Well, look at birth; does this or does this not presently disempower women, thanks to the – often misogynist – obstetrician? And what about the psychiatrist with the artist? Or, indeed, with anyone who undertakes an introspective approach to spirituality? I wonder how many a potential mystic languishes in a psychiatric hospital, or is kept disconnected from his or her visions by drugs?

The very fact that the medical and academic professions still remain dominated by the mechanistic and rational approach to sexuality that Freud promoted indicates, to me at least, that depth psychology has possibly not gone as far – yet – as it could do in exploring and reinstating the feminine, creativity and our non-Christian heritage. These have been left to feminism (although now largely historical, I would suggest), the New Age and various atavistic approaches in health, healing and religion: a mixed bag indeed.

What I am proposing here, if only for the convenience of this enquiry, is that we put these various facets together under the title: "Psychosexuality". This provides a continuum with the depth psychology traditions and underpins the ancient concept of soul. However, I am going to leave the details of psychosexuality here, for the time being, as I believe we need to explore the symbolism from "Retreat" a little further to flesh out the argument. I also believe that a wider archetypal perspective of traditions that are inclusive of sexuality and an analysis of the symbolism there lying deep within our own heritage (next chapter) may help support a broader and more complete picture of psychosexuality (Chapter Nine). We are left here with two terms that could stand a little further definition.

Psychosexuality is a term I have employed to define sexuality in its relationship to soul. I have chosen to use the traditional prefix of "psycho" to assist in its rescue from the clutches of academic and rational psychology. (Of tangential interest is that in the modern vernacular a 'psycho' refers to someone who is psychologically dysfunctional, or 'mad'.) The modern scientific definition of psychology can now be seen to reinforce the trends in science and religion that I am at pains to reverse. Although it is somewhat difficult to use the prefix psycho in this regard, I think it must be done and championed. Maybe the fact that it is connected fundamentally with sex in this definition may help the overall restoration process.

Psychosexuality refers to a complexity of factors that include – at least – the body, bodily energetics (animism, life force), the instincts in general, emotion, and to tackle issues such as pleasure and pain, eroticism and aesthetics, and from there to see that they comprise a modern vision of the soul. This vision sees the soul as the microcosm (as in alchemy), or the dimension of the spiritual that is confined to or relates to the individual organism. Further, it is through the soul that the individual connects with the spiritual or divine.

Archetypal sexuality is the view from the collective (Jung), spiritual or macrocosm (alchemy) that is inclusive of the sexuality of the individual, or their psychosexuality. Archetype has been earlier defined (Chapter Six), with the disciplines that illustrate and explore these somewhat mysterious archetypes, such as mythology and symbolism; those that manifest it, such as the shaman and the magician; the tools that express it, such as prayer, contemplation, ritual and ceremony; plus the systems that encompass it, such as alchemy and astrology. With respect to the specific archetype of sexuality, it is the themes of the myths and the symbols that express sex that are of significance, such that these themes are expressed in appropriate systems (inherently, as in alchemy) and maybe more specifically in sexual ritual, initiation and ceremony.

How the individual, through his or her unique psychosexuality, engages with, appreciates and expresses the archetypal dimensions is how the two dimensions of the individual and the collective unite and reflect each other. This tradition, that the microcosm reflects the macrocosm, is at the core of the mystery expressed in alchemy.

From a philosophical perspective, we are moving to the post-modern era. This can be seen as integrative, holistic and a development from the previous position that was characterised as rational, mechanistic and reductionistic. The latter position is what continues to currently permeate disciplines such as medicine and psychology. Philosophy can be seen to "set the agenda" or anticipate the change and development of these and other disciplines in an emerging era, and to be an intellectual and academic reflection of that new era.

Coincidentally (but maybe more than just coincidentally ... as archetypes are also characterised by synchronicity), we are moving from the aeon of Pisces to Aquarius, which traditionally and symbolically contains these features and reflects the changes underway. One feature, holism, could be defined as "The tendency in nature to form wholes that are more than the sum of the parts by creative evolution", as in the Oxford English Dictionary. I like this definition and even enjoy the symbolic inflection as well as the fact that it has sexual connotations; then again, and in the spirit of this enquiry, I am inclined to see sex everywhere! Or maybe it is because sex, in an energetic manner, simply is everywhere and it is just that we need to put that lens on to view the world.

Isn't this the basis of much in our modern culture, from advertising to humour, such that the pornographic undercurrent in our culture is hardly a surprise? Am I implying that the sexual perspective is part of this transition? Well, it has to be, if we consider it in the spirit of integration and holism; in fact, I think its inclusion is fundamental and essential.

Let's sharpen the lens to the depth psychological, which, by definition, would be reflective of these changes and be of a similar tone. My general argument is that we are moving to a post-modern psychological and psychiatric world, it is just that these disciplines at a formal and academic level haven't caught up yet. I have set my position within that of depth psychology, but feel the need to modernise the developments of the twentieth century to be included in the changes, as reflected in philosophy ... and astrology. This holistic philosophy, I would argue, and as contained in the definition, is inclusive of the mysterious and reflected in the reinstatement of the soul, and sexuality in particular.

Is that one reason for writing this book? Well, yes, it is. I am firmly convinced that sexuality needs to reintegrate within the mainstream on its own terms and in a manner that has not yet been achieved. I argue that pornography is reflective of these changes and that a detailed examination of it will be creative and assist in this process. I am further convinced that such a holistic reintegration will change the frameworks of psychology and psychiatry and, from there, inform the paradigm change that medicine itself needs to undertake. These may be bold claims, but I feel works such as this enquiry set such an agenda.

Taking after Jung, we could arrange the male: female, masculine: feminine in a quaternary. To do this, get a pen and paper and put *male* top left and *female* top right. Then bottom left, underneath male put *masculine* and then *feminine* directly underneath *female*. Now connect each word with lines to each other, such that you end up with a square (or rectangle) with a diagonal cross symmetrically inside. Maybe add a wavy line across the middle with the upper half called *outer*, or *world* and below *inner*, or *soul*. This is by way of a diagrammatic image that summarises much of what we've discussed to date and may be useful for your own psychological reflection of both inner and outer relationships. Don't forget the dynamic called projection; that is where we see the inner figure in an outside person. That's usually where the trouble starts!

For example, we could examine this as a progressive process, or in stages. That is, and taking the male's position, the integration of his femininity occurs in stages through differing relationships with women in his life. The dynamics of projection would remain the same, but hopefully, with increasing psychological maturity, any relationships would become less tangled by projection and seen more as they "really are".

In simple terms, this could go something like the following: The initial sexual attraction is of a more instinctual nature ("lust at first sight") and fairly indiscriminate. It would contain projections coloured by personal experiences of women in his upbringing, his mother in particular. With the progression of relationships, and aided by sexual contact, he would gradually divest himself of these personal images and progressively identify with someone who is more like his internal feminine. There is a direct implication here that sexual experience prior to a marital or equivalent commitment is psychologically advantageous.

As we have already discussed, this stage is imbued with all sorts of difficulties of its own. It is more emotionally charged, as the soul image is primarily emotional in nature, and this is how Jung and others perceive the internal contra-sexual principle to be experienced when initially encountered. So, there are connotations of "she's my soul-mate" that characterise such a connection, which is particularly reinforced if the situation is mutual. I call this the stage of Romantic Love. Also, as the soul is the window into the spiritual world, these attributes can be recognised as a "past-life connection", or whatever. Don't laugh; I've seen all of this and more as a justification for a sexual encounter that may be simply lust at first sight or fundamentally instinctual. (However, the issues of soul-mate, past life and even karma are much more significant than such trivialisation and should not be dismissed because of this.)

Obviously, such stances can be taken to avoid facing the full implications of what is going on. It is always easier to have another person carry our projections, however impossible that may be to sustain in the longer term. It can also be recognised that the Great Chain of Being, or the Perennial Philosophy, can be a useful guide to determine the level – physical, emotional, mental, and so on – at which the projection may be operating. What I am indicating here is a progression from the physical to the emotional levels that simultaneously negotiates the personal background elements and arrives at a position where the image (even in projection) is more that of the soul (as defined by Jung), and hence connected with the spiritual or archetypal world and a bridge to it.

This last perspective highlights something important and which many traditions utilise: This dynamic pattern can be exploited to gain access to the spiritual world and use sex as one of the mechanisms in a ritualistic and initiatory way.

Too far-fetched? Not at all. Eastern spiritual tradition has a continuous and uninterrupted system that employs this. In the West, as we have argued, there is an undercurrent of this in the more esoteric (inner) dimensions of conventional religion with the mystics and traditions such as alchemy, as well as systems like magic. In fact, this chapter is but a bridge to all this ... and more.

As an aside, if we reverse the role perspective and take the female's position, an interesting anomaly occurs. According to Jungian theory, the contra-sexual principle is the "soul image". This would render the image of the soul for a woman as masculine. Yet universally and at an archetypal level, the soul image is feminine, and I believe this Jungian theory anomaly may be more than the fact we live in a masculine-dominated culture. Because our psychosexual exploration increasingly supports the position that the soul image is indeed feminine for both men and women, what could be the solution to this?

I suggest that contact with the internal contra-sexual image is the bridge to the collective and spiritual domains, a position traditionally assigned to the soul. So, at this level of development, the soul image of a woman is indeed masculine.

However, as psychological maturity deepens and the personal aspects of the archetype become integrated (that is, withdrawn from projection), the individual personality attains a balance and fulfilment at the individual level and the soul appears more from the spiritual perspective. I would argue that this is inherently feminine and that the myth of Teiresias reinforces this and conflates it with sexuality. My impression further is that this development is achieved by the integration of romantic love. Then the individual is capable of moving in the domain of the soul to explore the spiritual relatively unencumbered by psychological projections.

Let's make use of alchemy from the psychosexual perspective. What we have arrived at could be considered the Lesser Work of alchemy and is the initial union of the masculine and feminine principles, via the male and female, beyond the primal and instinctual sexual. I have termed this Romantic Love because, as a metaphor, I think it encapsulates much of what this stage is about, is one you may have a clear intuitive sense of, and which I am elaborating on.

A brief look back at porn will identify the vast majority of it exists at the instinctual level. This speaks volumes in itself about the lack of integration of sexuality, even at this instinctual level in our culture, that we have such a mass of this material. If nothing else, and with the right guidance, this level of porn can assist the instinctual integration of sexuality; particularly where that is still problematic in society at large. There was a time, anecdotally, when the French father would take his adolescent son to the local bordello (brothel) and leave him there for a day or two. In a somewhat humorous fashion, this symbolises an instinctual initiation of the psychosexual elements in the young man. Maybe to 'get it out of the way' so as not to form an inappropriate and premature union, even marriage, as a result of an unwanted pregnancy.

In traditional pre-Christian society, the Great Cycle of Existence, or birth, sex and death, is expanded to birth, sex, partnership (relationship, union, marriage) and death, and ritualised: How? Such societies celebrated the year with ceremonies for the solstices and equinoxes, which are positions of the sun with respect to the year and loosely equated with the seasons. In between these times were four further points, more related to the moon, and hence feminine in contrast to the sun and the seasons. The Great Cycle is consequently seen to be governed by the feminine principle because these four ceremonial times celebrated the four aspects of the cycle described above. You may recognise here how a spiritual orientation is taken by using an archetypal pattern, reflected in nature and the cosmos, to guide the individual through transitions in a ritual manner. Such is the lost wisdom of the ancients.

You may ask what the importance of this is. From our perspective in this enquiry, it is the differentiation of sex from relationship and marriage. Please note: I did not say separation. This differentiation allows an independent insight into sexuality without it necessarily being considered a preliminary to marriage, a mistake that is all too obvious in our society and condoned by formal religion. There are distant memories of this on May Day in the Northern hemisphere, and in the recent past, several writers with a Celtic bent have indicated that the sort of rituals that marked this ceremonial time were primarily sexual and even orgiastic, recalling Dionysus from Greece.

Back to porn: My concern is that the exclusive focus on the instinctual level of its portrayal, important though I may consider this to be (in the right context), is that if it remains confined to this level so then it cannot progress. This factor is the genesis of obsession and addiction – maybe as a pattern, it is the genesis of all addiction – when the energetic focus cannot escape the instinctual. This would, according to my argument, naturally lead to the view that ritual and ceremony is an essential component in overcoming addictive patterns. There is much food for thought here, as well as more than a little evidence.

The porn industry as a whole may be disinclined to offer any dimension beyond the instinctual and there are obvious motives in its position here. This is not uniformly the case, however. For example, so-called women's novels are often focused on the romantic and the erotic, and the anti-censorship feminists, as well as those who have involved themselves in the industry, have introduced this dimension to porn. This has been supported inadvertently – because I'm sure the producers of the same have not had this in mind – by porn that explores themes such as fetishism, bondage, discipline and sadomasochism within the mainstream industry. Although their motive may be to attract consumers to the more perverted end of the sexual landscape and so create ready-made customers, I argue this may have backfired.

How could this be? Well, the facts and my arguments don't support such a movement across fields of sexual taste, but of a more detailed exploration within the existing range that sometimes incorporates these themes. The industry has recognised this to some extent, and the range of products reflects this now with a more integrated diversity. There is another factor in operation here; the range of products will include other instinctual dimensions of the psyche and this may produce change. How so? Because the consumer then explores his or her instinctuality across a greater range and thus integrates that level more completely. It is then possible for the psychosexual energy to flow onwards, particularly if other rituals of change assist this.

An interesting digression that sheds further light on this issue is the physical age of the female porn star. They are sometimes referred to as "Young Bunnies" (a dig at the magazine "Playboy", maybe?) and, indeed, mostly they are. In fact, there is a play on the "all models are eighteen years of age or older" caveat a little too strongly for my liking, as it almost implies the reverse and vicariously looks back into the paedophilic spectrum. Of course, this is understandable if there are adolescent males scouring the Internet; but I find it excessive. The added factor is that a considerable number of young porn stars would be in the industry for their own sexual exploration and without a vision of relationship, which I think reflects in the way they act and the instinctual level they are portraying.

This is, again, predictable from the psychological orientation of the industry toward consumption; but is unfortunate, as it doesn't readily engage the erotic end of the spectrum, the emotional dimensions or the exploration of sexuality in the context of relationship. You will have noticed in "Retreat" that I have engaged all of these and you might argue that I have taken an idealised and unrealistic position. To some extent, that criticism is valid, although I would argue that in such sub-genres as feminist and couples porn, there is such an attempt and that my personal history (with respect to Private) indicates that it is a consistent theme in the mainstream. I would even argue it was a significant factor in the success of Private.

Ironically, once again, fetishism and the inclusion of other instinctual elements may also help in this direction. Some of this is for similar reasons to the ones already outlined, but it could be that such activity requires a more mature porn star and necessarily makes the sexual activity more complex and drawn into further levels of relationship and depth.

I would also like to offer my own reflection on the age issue. I am more drawn to the more mature porn star and exactly for the above reasons. I would also like to add that you might consider "Retreat" idealises porn, but it is on a continuum with where the industry could head; a more integrated psychosexuality in mainstream art and theatre. Is this too much to ask? If my contribution indicates, at least in principle, that this is possible, then couldn't it be considered an example of what may be to come? Although I must admit with the second half of the movie that I might have extended the reasoning beyond the range of what may be possible presently; then again, I may be a prophet of what is yet to come ...

Emily and Graham come together in some sort of romantic association at the completion of the first half of the movie. Whilst I have indicated, even somewhat cynically, that this might be only a stage and present them with some future problems, let's allow them their day in the sun. I think the reason they had to leave the Retreat was because ongoing exposure to the others may present a problem. There is the recognition that, from Emily's perspective, Helen and Mick could be well beyond her sexual development, and from Graham's, Carole and maybe Paul are ready for further exploration beyond where he wants to go. From the dramatic position, this tidies up the first half with a – relative – state of union and completion, yet leaves the door open for further exploration.

It will be of interest to see how the first two scenes create this impression and the subsequent solution. Let's start with Carole's seduction of Paul and Graham and, further, let's enjoy the dramatic perspective; that is, see the narrative as authentic – as in the mainstream – and not just as a text or excuse to hold the sex scenes together. As we have discussed, this requires an existing maturity and ability on the part of the porn stars, which I have assumed. This may require a small leap of faith on your part, but I argue that it is entirely in the realms of possibility and something I have more than fleetingly observed in my own consumption. It is also, of course, why I have given most of the porn stars an age range at the end of their predicted careers in conventional porn.

In each of the first two scenes, I am going to focus most particularly on Graham and Emily, as it is their union at the completion of the first half that is of current interest. The involvement of the others will be considered but will be more truly explored later in the context of the second half of the movie.

Carole is the initiator of the first scene and this seems a little premeditated, although her motives may not be entirely clear to us; indeed, they may not be to her either. We are given the impression that her marriage is in a questionable state and this is further discussed at the close of the scene. The overall impression is that, as a personality, she is taking the initiative in a way that was intimated earlier and using this to confront her marriage. Although this has already stepped out of the conventional limitations (assuming it was sanctioned in a Church ceremony) with affairs on both sides, this is the first time they have engaged in a more complex act. I would also suggest that part of Carole's frustration is that Graham wants her to be his feminine image and she has a distinct masculinity, which does not accept that role, although she may have in the past.

It is interesting that Paul would assume Carole's advances are born of experience and this may imply that he has more sexual experience than he is either given to show or that is discussed in the movie. Paul remains somewhat enigmatic well into the movie and there is a sense that his background might be more complex, as identified by Brian's reflection of him. He certainly doesn't baulk at Carole's advances, which suggests a confidence in this area in that both he and she must know that Graham will shortly return.

The sex itself is almost a classic porn threesome. Although

Carole is in the hands of two men, she retains a lot of the direction of events by her hand signal to Graham and within the sex itself. For example, she responds to the double penetration by the two men with her own bodily and pelvic movements. In the past of movie-length porn, it would have taken at least a couple of scenes to get to something like double penetration. I always had the impression there was a formula, almost a 'rationing out' with something like two straight man-on-woman scenes, a lesbian scene, a man with two women and then a woman with two men scenes, and finally an orgy involving all participants at the end. The orgy has tended to go out of favour, it is possibly too complex for the genre to date and the focus has gone to more complex single unified scenes such as described in "Retreat".

The overall impression is that the men 'share' Carole and she, relatively, does not seem to favour either of them. This is symbolised in the double penetration, where the men alternate in their penile attention to her pussy and arse. She enthusiastically embraces both men in this, and it provides the culmination of the sexual union, with a lot that preceded it, almost foreplay to this and something that has allowed the erotic excitement levels to rise, such that the physical act itself is easily performed. There is no apparent sadomasochistic dynamic operating here, only Carole's excitement and pleasure. This may add a little to the resulting post-coital confusion and reflect that, at this stage, Paul is not the object of her desire; it is the need to sort out her marriage.

Carole's acceptance of the men's cum on her face and in her mouth is almost a porn 'must have'. She shows no difficulty with this, and her looks support any number of possibilities – such as pride, further seduction, or empowerment – it does not appear to be a demeaning act, and Carole is not coerced; exactly the opposite. And this is my summation of the facial at this stage of the movie: there is more to it than meets the eye (did you like that one?), and we will be exploring this feature in much more depth.

Here I would like to return the focus to Graham, as the consequence of this sexual adventure is that he is left somewhat confused and bemused, and we have indicated this is not the necessarily desired result of Carole's actions. She is left relatively empowered from this threesome, with a widened sexual experience and a sense of freedom. Obviously, she is now prepared to look to a largely unknown future, whereas Graham is still affected by the seeming inevitability of the relationship breakdown. Although Carole had previously, as in the car, displayed some clear masculine tendencies, these did not seem to detract from her femininity.

Graham, by contrast, has displayed a predominantly masculine persona, at the very least, without many overt feminine features. He would appear to be psychologically less mature than Carole and this is borne out by their respective emotional positions following the threesome. In this respect, the threesome catapults Carole into a new dimension of her psychosexuality, and we leave her there with the hindsight knowledge that she will be exploring it further.

How is this symbolised in the threesome? Paul presents a different picture of masculinity to Graham. This is symbolised in their working relationship prior, and in the scene, these features are brought into the same arena but become inverted. (Inversion is almost a psychosexual 'law' and is frequently present in porn.) It is likely that in the workplace the rather patriarchal structure that was evident in the interactions in the car would not have allowed Graham and Paul such emotional proximity or even equality. In this sense, the patriarchal perspective keeps a man not only distant from the woman, or his feminine nature, but also from a man who displays strong feminine features, which it might be argued that Paul does; even to the point that Brian thought he might have been transposed from the gay movie scene, although subsequent scenes will make him revise that possibility.

This puts an additional twist into homosexual dynamics and illustrates how the feminine principle – Carole in this case – may bring these opposites into an even more acute perspective, as it is unlikely Graham would entertain any such intimacy with Paul unless this were the case, as indeed does the porn genre collectively. Maybe this has added to Graham's confusion, as the confrontation with his own femininity seems to be on several fronts and brings up the fear that he may be gay. No wonder he is relieved when Emily seduces him, he is able to context his newly found emotional state into a heterosexual context. This might be a resolution, but it could also help to suppress the fear of being gay. We'll never know.

That's a little walk through the psychosexual possibilities and you might well have seen more, as may Brian. The final point in this scene describes something alluded to earlier in the pattern itself. There are two men and one woman: from a balanced perspective (see your diagram), there is a missing fourth, another female or more appropriately, the feminine. With the above exposition, it would seem that Carole and Paul represent the more integrated female and male aspects, respectively, and this is one reason they move away from the pattern of the first half of the movie to re-emerge in the deeper exploration of the second.

Graham is the masculine principle personified; it would seem. Yet he is a man and contains a feminine aspect that is not initially present but begins to emerge in the scene. In this search for psychosexual wholeness the feminine needs to come in and in a balanced way, that is, as Graham's femininity. Up till this point, maybe Carole has 'carried' this projection for him but has increasingly become frustrated with this and this is possibly why Emily has gained Carole's attention in her attraction to Graham. This being the case, the presentation of his wife as the temptress in this scene would add further to his confusion.

The outcome of these various dynamics is that Graham is confronted with his own femininity, which we have additionally seen in his projections onto Paul. Up until now, you may have appreciated the psychological dynamic of projection, in that it is 'held' or 'carried' by another person. Some may wish to do this in an active way; take the muse or the film star as examples. Others may not, as it may (I stress 'may', as consciousness of what you're doing is a big factor here) limit their own individual development or create a fear that it might. Certainly, that seems to be the position that Carole has adopted toward Graham, for whatever reason.

As a result, Graham is left with nobody carrying his projections. Carole doesn't wish to and Paul is disinclined to do so – I'm being polite. As a result, he is left with them; in the trade, they are involuntarily 'withdrawn'. The consequence of this is that Graham becomes emotionally disturbed: Whilst at the projected level, his sexuality had been instinctual and essentially unemotional, now it has moved away from other people he is left with the emotional turmoil of needing to face this within himself. The degree to which he does this before Emily enters his life is questionable.

In many ways Emily mirrors what has happened to Graham, so they seem a fitting match (I'm not a cynic). Emily's tryst with Helen and Mick contains less in the way of the complexity of the first scene. Why is this? Mainly because Mick's role is largely as a connection point between the two women, as was Carole with the two men. However, there is a fundamental difference here as the two women are able to relate in a sexual way and explore masculine aspects in a manner that is disengaged from Mick, who then seems more of a catalyst than a significant psychosexual 'involvee'.

As we have discussed, this is one of the fundamental differences in porn that sexual activity between women exclusively, or involving men, is acceptable in the mainstream genre, whereas gay male sex is not. As we have further seen, this difference cannot be seen as simply or even fundamentally sexist and may relate to the differences in the mystery and expression of feminine sexuality as compared to the masculine. From an obvious level, you may see that, were Graham and Paul to have engaged sexually, they might have gone through similar and parallel changes that Emily and Helen do. At a deeper level, I believe there is nothing that such a male engagement can inform any entering woman, whereas the entering man becomes witness to something that I believe is more fundamentally inner, mysterious and of a different order. You may beg to disagree ... maybe a controlled experiment might help you?

The contact between Emily and Helen is a classic one. One woman takes the initiating and dominating role, although from a conventional perspective, she is the dispenser of pleasure by performing cunnilingus (pussy sucking and licking) on Emily. Emily achieves an orgasm, relatively easily in Brian's opinion, which makes him wonder about her lesbian proclivities. Whilst Helen seems more distinctly lesbian with her initial overtures and engagement with Emily, the subsequent scenes show her in a more balanced light, such that she takes more of a catalyst role, like her partner Mick.

This is because Helen allows the roles with Emily to reverse, which also says something about the dynamics of feminine sexuality that may also indicate it as being not as obvious or even present in masculine sexuality, and another reason for the difference between the two. Please don't forget that the difference between female and male intimacy isn't confined to porn; it is present in varying degrees and extents in the mainstream and life in general. It can hardly be that life mimics porn in this culture; it is more likely to be the reverse.

Emily's response is also somewhat paradoxical. Although Helen has been dominant and taken the initiative, her attention to Emily is quite gentle and giving. By contrast Emily's newly found dominance is expressed with aggression and power, with smacking and the way she manipulates Helen's genitals. Rather like Graham when his sexuality starts to become emotional as a result of projection withdrawal, Emily discovers an emotionality that she gains from this interaction with Helen. The projection withdrawal here is the masculine elements in Helen that Emily then begins to see in herself. The difference in the emotional response for Emily is that they have masculine characteristics of power and aggression. By contrast Graham's were more feminine with sadness and moods.

Mick's involvement adds a further dimension to the flow between the two women and brings the dynamics back into the heterosexual arena. Emily retains her strength, however, and another sign that Mick has a subtle integrated femininity is that he allows her to direct the sexual play and to unite with his wife. This seems a fitting close and leaves Emily free to move to the next stage of her development, which is to occur shortly. The cumshot on the pussy, whilst an open display of the masculine, is also an honouring of the feminine and it is one that Emily also partakes in. Her licking, eating and sharing Mick's sperm with his wife has symbolic overtones that again bring a sacramental quality to the cumshot and its reception.

Once again, the scene is defined by a 'missing fourth', in this case the masculine. As with the earlier scene this is obviously present in Mick, but subtly and mainly in Helen, which is from where Emily retrieves hers. This provides the balance that reflects and mirrors the first scene. Again, you may see further dynamic interactions in the whole interplay.

What is emerging from all the above are two levels. One level is the balance and reflectiveness of male: female, masculine: feminine. These resonate through the two scenes and are one expression of depth psychology's view of psychosexuality. In this they match Jung, but with some reservation, in my opinion, and a lot of the above may have made your head swim a bit if you were trying to grasp the dualism in an intellectual manner. I think Jung is too inclined to a dualistic position and this may over-ride other possible perspectives. Whilst I think this is an enormous step forward from the mechanistic and mechanical perspective of Freud's psychoanalysis, I think it has its own limitations, though it has allowed us a detailed exploration of the situation to this point.

Why do I think this? Because the equations are almost too balanced and I do have a difficulty with the equation man: feminine: soul and woman: masculine: soul as I have already indicated. This is reflected in my opinions regarding the difference between masculine and feminine psychosexuality and is further reflected in the dynamics and interactions with the two scenes we have discussed to date. This leads us into a second level where such dualistic order that, although 'balanced', still has a masculine ring about it. I believe the second level goes deeper than this and requires a perspective that goes beyond such gender issues and encounters the psychosexual dimensions in a more holistic and genderless way.

However, we are yet to get to all that, so let's return to the last scene in the second half. Well, that's if you don't consider the anal scene with Mick and Helen, which I will look at in due course. I am referring for the present to Emily and Graham's encounter in the woods.

The whole atmosphere is more romantic and this is reinforced by it taking place outside in a natural setting; even the description is softer and more sensual. There seems little detail to explore here from a sexual perspective, as it reflects the psychological states each has found themselves in. The difference is that Emily is employing her masculine discovery to a romantic end, which Carole did not. What's the difference? The difference is that Carole was already aware of this, but was frustrated that Graham didn't tolerate this and wanted her to be just the 'woman' of his life. Carole did not want that, so her masculinity contained anger and power and was, to a larger extent, already integrated with her femininity. She basically wants to go further in her exploration and is already beyond Graham, whereas Emily is at a more equal stage of development. Carole wants to go beyond the romantic stage; Emily is just discovering it.

Graham is in the reverse position and such issues as the lack of cock sucking reinforce the changes. He is happy to follow Emily's lead as, in contrast to Carole, she is employing her newly found masculinity to engage his femininity. The main issue here is that this is predominantly in projection, which is what characterises romantic love. In a classical sense we move from lust, or instinctual love, to "this is my soul-mate", or romantic love. This is implied, but more in the integrated background of the developing relationship between Paul and Carole.

Are Graham and Emily at the stage of romantic love? Not entirely, as they are each displaying contra-sexual tendencies that they have only recently discovered and are employing, mainly in projection. Although there is a sense that this is subliminal, it has provided the mechanism to get them together, and it may be that they will regress to a more conventional role-playing in the future: or it may yet be the seeds for further growth.

It is just that, in this movie, Paul and Carole will explore this further development, as we have seen. Brian has considered whether the Emily and Graham conjunction has anything particular to offer his uncertainty about his relationship with Val, but is also inclined to see that Carole and Paul offer more. Obviously, this is a dramatic and narrative technique to have these stages contained in the same movie, alternatively it would have to employ a long time sequence; otherwise we might have followed Graham and Emily further along this path, rather than seeing it in Carole and Paul.

It is obviously doubly convenient, because this allows for the sort of partnership changes and complex sexual interactions that characterise porn. The alternative of a long time sequence with these developments occurring organically is not quite so attractive to porn, unless it employs other involvees. On the side, Brian wonders whether that has been the unrequited motive that he and Val had in engaging more complex sexual scenarios. Of course, it is not all as clear-cut as that. These figures in the movie are essentially symbols of stages of psychosexual development and are there to reflect back these sorts of issues to the viewer, which they are more than adequately doing with Brian.

Paul is an interesting character, thinks Brian. He further recognises he is identifying with him with respect to his own development and that his attraction to Carole may also parallel what is happening with Val. It is interesting that both have drifted from getting involved in threesomes and foursomes of late, and Brian considers that this may have been due to the lack of emotional maturity on the part of those others involved. He reflects that with a Mick and Helen, maybe things could have taken a different course!

Paul has some similarities of developmental maturity to Carole in that he is aware of his feminine nature and may have been through the romantic stage. Emily obviously has not, and maybe her dissatisfaction was that he didn't see her in that projected feminine way. His masculinity is somewhat soft as Carole's is somewhat hard. In reverse, Carole has a lesser identification with her femininity – possibly in reaction to Graham's need – whilst it is strong in Paul. In a sense they are in a bit of no man's land after shedding their respective partners and wondering where to go next. This is where Mick and Helen step in ...

Talking about Mick and Helen ... what are we to make of the scene involving them? Indeed, what are we to make of all their interactions together and differentiated from the manner in which we have seen them to date; that is, as symbols and catalysts for the other participants? The arse fucking scene goes right back to basics, it is sexually instinctual and confronting as well as providing a contrast to the scene between Emily and Graham. Maybe that is the point, that the instinctual not be lost with the emergence of romantic love. This is a huge problem psychologically in our culture, such that we split the two and when this romantic phase develops, many a marriage falls apart.

This is a further argument for adequate sexual experience and instinctual integration prior to any partnership or marriage, such that a union can be grounded in a more mature perspective that is more likely to be sustained. Ideally, and because of our collective stage of evolution, it is best that a romantic union be appreciated before such a choice. Irrespective, society isn't perfect, although a little sexual ritual and initiation would go a long way.

The fucking of Mick and Helen encompasses and surrounds that of Graham and Emily could be read many ways and is fundamentally symbolic. One interpretation is that such a romantic union rests on the foundation of the sexual. A second is that a couple with an apparent level of higher sexual integration, like Mick and Helen, are able to enter into an instinctual act and not 'romanticise' it. That is, they engage in it for what it is. The outfit seems both a play and a satire. The ejaculation in and around the arse reflects the base instinctual level, and maybe has alchemical overtones.

In the midst of these overlapping themes, I will use some alchemical metaphors to begin a further explanation of them. There are several "conjunctions" in alchemy, when the opposing elements come together in a union. Each conjunction is known as a "complexio oppositorum", or union of opposites. In symbolic terms this is the masculine and feminine principles successively coming together, moving apart and coming together again in a cyclic, ascending and evolving manner. We can picture this like two mirror spirals around a central column and this also looks strangely like the DNA molecule. However, from antiquity we have an even more potent symbol, as seen in the myth of Teiresias: the two entwined snakes.

In these successive changes one important thing to bear in mind is that each stage of development supervenes the one before; that is, it goes beyond it yet includes it. If not included, the potential for regression always exists. This is what Mick and Helen's scene illustrates, that romantic love includes the instinctual sexual on its own terms. You will also notice that this all mirrors what I referred to earlier as the Great Chain of Being, which is the backbone of alchemy. Alchemy is essentially an ascent of the individual up the Great Chain. Whilst traditional alchemy sees these changes in the making of gold from base metals, I am suggesting that another alchemical metaphor can employ sexuality. I would further suggest not only that it can but also that it actively did. What we have here is the resurrection of these motifs in a porn movie. How interesting!

The first union in alchemy is the sexual union of the instinctual. Here is the animal level exclusively, yet it is always wise to remember we are part of that kingdom. So, we can anticipate two sub-levels to this union: the animal (instinctual) and the human (lust). The next stage in alchemy is the romantic union of opposites, which involves the discovery of soul. Together they comprise what alchemy calls the Lesser Work, as described earlier. Whilst the first conjunction – the instinctual sexual – is contained throughout the movie, the second – romantic love – is scattered around and emerging from the instinctual.

The second conjunction is most obviously present with Emily and Graham, with the irony that the contra-sexual elements are what brought them together and may provide the seeds for future confusion or growth, depending on their respective awareness and strengths. If the projections become progressively withdrawn and personal integration occurs in both parties, then the Lesser Work of Romantic Love is complete.

Carole and Paul give the impression that they have integrated and are now moving beyond this stage so maybe the scenes of the second half of the movie will explore what is known in alchemy as the Greater Work.

The Director's Cut

Part 2

Jan cut a fine figure of a man as he returned from the bar, putting his wallet back into the small shoulder bag that seemed to accompany him everywhere. Carole was observing him closely, as the "fine figure of a man" was more literal than symbolic; he was indeed a fine man, almost epicene. He was fine to the point of delicacy and he could be seen equally as a woman dressed as a man, she thought, especially with that light and musical voice. Although, at first glance, he was obviously male, there was a subtle radiance that was distinctly feminine. No wonder he had attracted a little interest with some saying he was a female transvestite. A man of contrasts; Carole decided to hold judgement.

The drinks followed a short time later and it was tacitly understood that the visit to the bar had opened the account for the evening, probably on the expense account, she further surmised. Carole was becoming intrigued by Jan; he aroused a subtle energy in her, only vaguely identifiable as sexual. She reflected that this might just be a result of the upstairs bedroom scene filmed here at the Club, with the surprising arousal of her sexual responses to the two women, which she enjoyed putting into practice in the last scene with Helen and Paul.

She speculated: I've always played the full-on woman role with respect to the studs and in my life away from this business. Of course, I can be ballsy, but I've never seen that in a sexual sense. Yeah, there've been times when a part demanded that I lick out a cunt, or be licked out, and toys are always fun; but it had never been my scene … until those scenes! I feel I'm stepping on something about being a woman that may have eluded me to date and this strange guy has somehow brought it out in me. Funny, though, it hasn't lessened my desire for cocks and I got into Paul's tit-fuck and facial at the end in a really dreamy way. Some food for thought here, gal, and not just from Paul's yummy spunk!

Carole looked up from her drink to see Jan's eyes fixed on her. A small tingle went up her spine and she looked down again.

"You asked about my involvement in mainstream?" Jan eased the tension.

He was looking at her but quickly engaged the whole assembled company, being the four from the Retreat and now joined by Graham and Emily, all seated in one of the quieter wells set below floor level in the large room. In fact, it was difficult to gauge the size and extent of the lounge, because there were various wells, nooks and crannies, with varying degrees of privacy … as Carole recalled! At various times the porn extras could be seen in their alternative functions as waiters, barmen and waitresses. The dual purpose of the Club was well known in the business; it functioned both as a private club and as a venue for porn productions, although it did have a public persona with another bar and common restaurant. By contrast, the Retreat was used exclusively in the business, not only for film production and photographic sets but also for any associated activities such as team bonding!

It was not uncommon to see others from the trade there and, now the filming was over Carole could see Rick Hale, a stud with whom she'd had a two-year relationship at the bar with – possibly – his new lady. Carole didn't recognise her, so she may not be in the trade … but she was a looker and would fit in the business, so it may have been one of Rick's motives in dining here with her, to see if she wanted to "get into acting" following his testing of her sexual attributes, maybe? Carole smiled; he'd done the same thing to her many years back, but not until after he'd turned her on with his cock did she know he was an actor: Well she did, but she thought it had been mainstream, not as a porn stud. She smiled, caught his eye and they acknowledged each other. She briefly thought about going over and giving him a peck on the cheek, but his glance told her that may be indiscreet at this point in time. She was also more interested in hearing about Jan's mainstream experience now anyway.

Jan's story didn't surprise her, although it seemed a little vague and enigmatic. He had also been involved in modern music production and her ears picked up when she heard that the piece that was played in the upstairs bedroom scene was one of his productions. Instead, his revelations were more about his desire to see the creative integration of sexuality into cinematic mainstream. Carole chose not to challenge him at all about this yet; she simply sat back and let the others fire the questions that filled in the immediate gaps. But she did notice that Paul was equally silent.

Then Jan deftly brought the conversation back to "Retreat" and stated his intention; to respond to Carole's query over the champagne, but, more importantly for him and the anticipated Voluptas series, to undertake a de-briefing of their involvement. He delicately asked for their approval of this request and was not in the least surprised that they were in unanimous agreement. The consensus was quite simple: this was a rare event and a possibility for them to explore their experiences, as well as where they were individually and collectively going in the business.

They were commonly left up in the air after shoots, and if challenged sexually in ways that surprised or even shocked them, there was little forum for expression and discussion. Any 'interviews' were confined to the industry and its desire for self-justification and promotion, and not very creative or therapeutic for the porn stars themselves. You could hardly say that you didn't like swallowing cum, could you? Carole had thought to get more politically involved in the industry and had been invited to help direct. However, she felt she still had some acting performances in her to fulfil and she still really got off on the varied sex!

Jan took a sip from his scotch:

"I know Graham has to go early and catch a flight for a shoot in Budapest, so whilst we still have the benefit of his company, I'd like to get some feedback on the scenes up to the Club?"

"Well, my role was fairly uncomplicated, except toward the end." Carole volunteered first, partly to settle her unease. "You told me to identify with my role as Graham's wife, which didn't happen a lot in the study scene, but started to affect me toward his departure. The tears weren't an effort."

Carole sat back and allowed Graham a voice.

"Yeah, it was something similar for me, although it got to me from the word go. When I came back in and you were sucking Paul, my erection faltered a bit and I had to really lick you out to get it full on again. It's funny, I knew that this was part of the scene, but when I imagined myself as your 'real' husband being sort of cheated on, it got me emotional. I know you asked us to try and be in the part," he said, now looking at Jan, "but the emotional and physical responses were a slight surprise."

"But the actual sex wasn't a problem?"

"No, routine stuff, really." Paul spoke for the first time.

"Yes," said Carole, "I'm a sucker for a good DP and these guys really got into the rhythm!" A collective chuckle followed this revelation, which allowed Jan to move into other areas.

Obviously, there was no sense of impropriety in any of the physical and sexual acts to date. Mind you, he was dealing with seasoned performers who had long ago clarified their boundaries in the business and, by their reputations, could afford to keep to parts and roles that didn't compromise these.

"The emotional tone resurfaced in the scene with Emily, too," Graham added, almost as an afterthought.

"Ladies?" asked Jan, looking at Emily and Helen.

"Familiar territory for me and Mick, I presume?" Helen glanced toward him, but the remark was based on prior experience and their sexual liaison that was well known to continue past the set. It was also what made the arse fuck scene in the kitchen so easy to integrate into the movie, thought Jan.

"Touché," added Mick.

"I felt like a bit of a teacher with Em," Helen added. "Even though I know muff-diving is well within her repertoire, she acted so innocently it became fun to watch the changes. What made it more so was that we've never done a scene together before. So, I suppose, I had a slightly different sense of myself as a sexual woman. That is a little odd; as you know, I've come into sexual mainstream from a strong lez background. When I first got into this business, I didn't want an erect cock anywhere near a scene I was acting in!"

"What made you change in the business?" asked Jan.

"Well, like most of us I suppose getting into porn was an escape; a challenge for rigid upbringings, plus an opportunity for paid uncomplicated sexual experimentation," answered Helen, "so, over time, I reckon I got rid of the distortions and traumas of my upbringing and thought I could enjoy what I originally despised. This took a while, though, as in the early days my naiveté got me into situations that directly or indirectly reinforced it."

"Directly?"

"Yeah, sometimes it was more like rape, particularly when I first started with men. It was like they played on my pain and fears, so a gang bang could easily turn into a really painful experience, physically and mentally."

"But you stayed with it?"

"Yeah, but that's my inherent personality. I'm no martyr, and deep down, I knew I'd like men. I also knew I could do this without losing my taste for women!" Helen smiled at her own joke as some of the others laughed.

"OK, I suppose you all have stories like that?" A collective nodding followed. "Do any of you want to volunteer more about this aspect of the industry, or shall I press on?"

"Press on, Jan," Carole said this time, "We've all done our therapy, one way or another."

"OK, thanks." Jan took a further sip and there was a pause of a few seconds. "What about you, Em?"

"Well, I was a bit up in the air at the end really." Her response caused Jan to frown a little and engage the others. "It's not that there was anything physical in the acting that was unusual or any different from what I've done heaps of times, it was more the way it was strung together. Although Mark has asked me to keep to gentle scenes since Joe's birth last year, nothing I did went beyond that physically; it was more my emotional response and somehow having different perspectives about where I am as a woman now."

"Can you explain a bit more?"

"Well, in the past, I may get the straight scenes first, and the lesbo stuff comes as a reaction to tough stuff in the straight scenes, like a justification." She took a mouthful from her white wine; all eyes were on her as she continued. "This was kinda the other way around. It was like I was taken into my femaleness, woman-ness, in a different way and then it made relating to Graham so much more balanced and easier. I don't think I've ever felt quite so empowered on a set, yet it was soft and gentle with no aggression in any form by then, although I felt clear and purposeful. It was like the scene with Helen got it out of me or softened it; I can't be sure which."

"You know I found myself feeling really soft for you at that point," Paul chided in, "and that extended to Graham as well. I know that started a little in the study, but I didn't have any idea of where to take it, so I kept my attention on Carole. Not really a hard thing to do!" Laughter accompanied this whilst Carole looked down at her glass quite demurely. "Seriously though, I started to really feel for Graham in the scene and then Em when she went to the lake. I was almost touched by the outcome, but I had this sense that Jan had more in mind for me, so I kind of kept my feelings in check and refocused."

"I know we've touched on this, but did any of you find the sex itself a challenge?" Jan was moving the subject matter around, seemingly at random.

"Not in this part of the movie," Carole replied.

"No," said Graham, "it was more that the emotional aspects complicated it."

"Yes, I agree," was Paul's support, "that's why I kept my focus. I felt I could have got a bit destabilised, although in the second half of the movie, I get to see there's ways of dealing with this."

"The spanking was interesting," said Emily, "I normally get aggressive, but I didn't find it difficult to maintain the pain and pleasure edge with you, Helen."

"No, it was spot on."

"I might repeat myself and ask this question again when we talk through the Club scenes, but the idea at this stage wasn't to create sexual challenges, more emotional ones."

"Well, you almost succeeded in softening me up!" Mick was being facetious … but with a grain of truth. "Also, because you didn't outline what the scenes in the second half would be like, it maintained an expectation and tension I haven't fully experienced before on a set. It has happened with particular women and encounters, where there's an air of the unknown, even mystery, and you don't know where things are going to go when you get into it. What was also clever was doing the scenes in a sequence that matched the movie."

Jan looked pleased. "Well, before I sort out some food … I presume you'd prefer to stay here to chat, the restaurant could be a bit crowded tonight?"

There were collective nods of agreement.

"How do you think the viewer would respond?"

Paul, every bit the philosopher, stepped up to the question: "Well, that depends on who, how and why. I'm going to assume it's a user-friendly mature male who's looking for a little extra to his porn. If it is, I bet he started off excited and ended up a bit like us guys; somewhat affected and intrigued."

"A good summary, Paul, I'll order some food."

Jan had wondered whether they might explore the second half of "Retreat." However, as things do, by the time the food arrived and Graham said goodbye, they appeared mellower – assisted by the drinks, no doubt! Jan took stock of the situation: nobody volunteered any queries or questions about the subsequent scenes. Instead, and collectively, they talked much more amongst themselves about the issues that had been raised to date.

Jan realised this was like a de facto therapy group; they were exploring their involvement, experiences and reactions in a more wholesome way than would normally be the case after a shoot. He felt directing the conversation further would disrupt this flow, so he concluded that it wasn't the right time. When he came to that conclusion, another idea had fashioned itself, which he put out to the assembled company as the evening drew to a close.

"We still have a lot we could discuss, but now doesn't feel the right time."

"Yeah," responded Carole, now clearly the spokesperson of the group. "I reckon we're still digesting heaps, so what do you suggest?"

"Well, the movie will be in the can soon, and the company will have it on the shelves as soon as … maybe six weeks. What I'd like is a bit of critical feedback and maybe some response from the critics, industry and sections of the public. I don't think this will cut across adjourning at this point, and I'm aware some of you are heavily committed for a few months?"

Collective nods from most assembled, except Emily; noted by Jan.

"What I suggest is that we have a more extensive debrief in several months, it gives time for "Retreat" to get a good audience without premature concern on my part for a follow-up. I'll get my PA to contact you and arrange this? But what I would like to do is get together for a weekend at the Retreat and also run some ideas about Voluptas across you, based on what the debrief brings up and where it takes us."

There was a general affirmative consensus, with a little logistical input from some of the group.

"OK, well, I think I'll leave you children to play," said Jan, "as it's way past my bedtime!"

8

Archetypal Sexuality

You know, I really loved writing the title of this chapter! Why?

Well, I was exposed to the Jungian notion of archetypes as a modern depth psychological compensation to our loss of an accessible spiritual perspective in the West. So far, so good, but then, as a conceptual framework, archetypes in psychology seemed to get as bad as the religious systems they were trying to replace ... superior and arrogant, intellectual and patriarchal. Psychologists of these traditions would deny this, of course. So, as an old-fashioned iconoclast, being able to connect archetypes with sex is quite delightful ... and necessary.

As I have been at pains to discuss earlier, one of the losses of the twentieth century was that sexuality was left to the Freudians in the separation of the giants of Freudian psychoanalysis and the broader depth psychologies. So, here's another attempt to repair the damage, which, of course, is a major theme of the book as a whole.

We're now going to depart from the more analytical perspective that we've taken to date with respect to depth psychology and look at the approach essentially pioneered by James Hillman, who champions the soul's view of both the world and spirit. If we are to look at the spiritual aspects of sexuality, which is what archetypal sexuality propounds and examines, we must initially get the right perspective.

In the wake of the patriarchal era, this perspective has initially and inevitably been rational and intellectual. Not that this is inappropriate, just incomplete. Beyond its domain, such a limited mental approach can lead to progressive confusion. To some extent, this is the orientation that has been adopted in earlier chapters, partly because it is valid, but also because it is an approach we are familiar with and can be a bridge to where we are going. Taken too far, however, it can inflate the mental perspective and allow psychosexuality to adopt a lot of the characteristics that we are trying to get beyond.

In the psychic economy, and as shown in the Great Chain of Being, there are various levels between the body and spirit that could collectively be conceived as comprising the soul, or soul complex. The mind and intellect are components of this, but unless the soul and its activities are seen in their entirety, the rational mind will assume an importance beyond its station, which I indicate it has done in the patriarchal era.

More than this, I would be inclined to see the body within the soul complex, with the world and spirit comprising the two ends of the chain, or spectrum. This then gives an impression of the external world as the manifestation or reflection of the spiritual world and mediated through the soul. As this book is not intended to be a mystical treatise, I'll leave the various arguments for these outlooks on one side at present; it's just that you might find them useful and provide a conceptual framework for what is to follow. Just don't feel disappointed if you can't get your head around them; such issues have sent some great minds mad (Van Gogh: "I put my heart and soul into my work, and have lost my mind in the process.")

Hillman is inclined to see the main activity of the soul as imaginative; that is, reflected in the images that it produces or, more correctly, are produced within it. It took me a while to get beyond my rational outlook to see what he was saying. In later years, I increasingly appreciated and understood him; I think he is a genius yet to be fully appreciated. When I did, I then understood that even thoughts were an expression of imagining. This book is a creative act of primarily imaginative material. We own thoughts and believe them to be things in and of themselves and see them as property, such that we believe we can copyright them and accuse anyone else who may express similar ones as a plagiarist. Thoughts stem from ideas and the imagination. Maybe ideas stem from the world of spirit and filter through our imagination as acts of creativity. To believe we own them is a gross – and spiritual – hubris. Such is the extent and difficulty to which the patriarchy has led us, particularly when the soul is relativised and even excluded from the overall picture.

Ideas and images are to be seen metaphorically, analogously, humorously, imaginatively, symbolically and creatively. They dance on the edge of our vision and in the theatre of our minds to inform and instruct us in our journey through the Great Cycle of Existence, which the soul traverses. I can't explain to you how to adopt these stances to gain a closer appreciation of the activity of your soul; all I can encourage you to do is accept them on their own terms, listen to their language and experience and enjoy them. They may then explain themselves.

The perceptive amongst you may notice something subtle and interesting. We are moving from a masculine to a feminine perspective, which is, coincidentally, the gender image of the soul. Maybe Teiresias was right, and it is with the view that "a woman's sense enjoys all ten in full" that we need to view and experience the soul rather than the restrictive one of "man". If so, maybe that gives us not only a fuller understanding of the soul and its activities, but also one of another order or level of being, which conforms to the supervening principle of the Great Chain of Being; that is, to transcend yet also to include what has been moved beyond.

Ideas come from intellect, which I see as a higher function of mind and which connects with the spiritual. We are unfortunately inclined to conflate thought with intellect, a grave mistake. Basic thought is a rational function of the human condition and requires no appreciation beyond day-to-day existence and its travails. In this respect, thought is mundane and equivalent to our five senses, or so believe the Buddhists. Intellect requires an integrated soul perspective, that is inclusive of body (sensation, feeling and thought) yet also requires the emotional and associated functions. Ideas and the intellect can be seen in this 'higher' state and as a connection of the soul with spirit; yet when devoid of emotion, femininity, the body and sexuality, ideas become mere thoughts and the intellect is not truly alive.

Enough sermonising! Back to sex: Well, not directly, but how sexuality is embedded and encoded in myth, symbol and metaphor, the various languages of the soul. What I am proposing is that if we lack an integrated position with respect to sexuality, then these may be useful tools to further explore the subject and facilitate such integration. We must engage these dimensions directly, such that the images bring us to the ideas and the intellectual perspective that defines the archetypes, and subsequently bring us into the world of spirit.

Snakes are symbolic of ... If we take a Freudian approach, we could say the penis. So far, so good: So, anything long and straight is a cock? I once had a dream that portrayed me holding a broom handle, which I told my analyst:

"What do think that is?" he asked me.

"A penis," I replied.

"Why?"

"Well, long and straight, and I'm holding it, just like an erect penis." Note my careful choice of language for my revered analyst.

"You have sexual dreams, don't you?"

"Yes!"

"So why would your unconscious bother to disguise a cock as a broom handle?"

The old codger had less trouble with the terminology than I did!

I had just received a very rapid education in symbolism, not only about the content of a symbol, but also its function. The Freudian approach is rational and mechanistic; images, particularly dream images, are not. A sign is just that; it points to something known. A symbol is more than that; it points to something mysterious. In analogue terms rational: irrational, masculine: feminine, sign: symbol, literal: symbolic. So important was the message I have quite forgotten what we discovered that the broom handle might have symbolised. In hindsight, I am inclined to imagine that it was the handle of a witch's broom! Or maybe that's just my fantasy because of the current subject matter ... and if it is does that matter? Is that association just the soul being playful?

We came across snakes earlier with Teiresias, and they were mating. So, well, maybe Freud was partially right, let's say one part in ten. Maybe it is as simple as that; the snakes are expressing sexuality. If so, then sexuality embraces the male and female, or masculine and feminine, as we explored earlier. The myth shows that Teiresias had experience with both genders and that this ultimately gave him a position of wisdom, though not without some sacrifice! The association with death is interesting, as by killing the snake he experiences its essential gender nature when he is inducted into the feminine.

Death and sexuality are associated, thus indicating the Great Cycle of Existence. Death is symbolic here as well, indicating sacrifice to achieve wisdom. We will be coming to the great god of the Northern Traditions later, who sacrificed an eye for the attainment of wisdom and seership, and also had the experience of being a snake in a ritual that involves sex and love magic. The symbols move across cultures and are, therefore, archetypal. Do I need to remind you of the French metaphor that sexual orgasm is "la petite mort", or "the little death", and is in the feminine gender in that language?

Back to our own culture: Two entwined snakes; does this remind you of anything? I'll jog your memory: what about DNA? DNA is our life code within the Great Cycle. Yet it also transcends it, because we pass it – interestingly half – into each future offspring ... through sex, of course. We won't be going into any detail here, but if you're interested or already know biochemistry, I would ask you to look up or remind yourself of the other interesting features of DNA. For example, there are four bases that pair off together, but only with a specific partner. This reminds me of the diagram you did in chapter seven at a psychological level and even some of our initial discussion of pornographic imagery.

Our offspring thus contain our DNA and transcend our individual death, so in this symbolic sense, we are immortal. Maybe DNA is a symbol of the soul that connects the physical with the divine, the temporal with the eternal? If this is so, it is more than an irony that the symbol of the medical profession, the caduceus with two snakes twined around a central pole, should then have a feminine quality associated with it.

In Greek mythology, the caduceus was the staff of Asclepius, who was the prototypal doctor, although in a very shamanic and magical guise. It was a simple staff that had only one snake around it and one that alchemy has subsequently elaborated into a mystical Christian motif: the crucified Jesus as a snake? The double snake motif is more associated with Hermes, who was the "trickster god", the divine messenger, the bringer of dreams and the agent of wealth and death, as well as trickery. I find it interesting the medical profession has chosen this version; it is a more elaborated and complex symbol than that of the single snake and, in my mind, takes us away from the association with the archetypal healer, Asclepius.

Myths and symbols are very fluid, as we see if we explore this association in Greek mythology a little further. Asclepius was given a gift from the goddess Athene; this was the blood collected from the spine of the decapitated Medusa. Remember Medusa, the Gorgon? Perseus killed her by looking into a mirror and cutting her head off with a stroke of his sword. Medusa was in the underworld, and Perseus was doing this act as part of another myth, but the blood that was collected contained the power of life and death and was put into Ascelpius' hands: The blood from the right side of the spine, being associated with life, and that of the left with death.

Life and death? A bit like the two snakes fucking that Teiresias treated so inappropriately, or so it would seem at face value unless looked at symbolically. Here Greek meets Eastern myth in a time when the mythic structure transcended cultural divisions. A little later, we will explore these connections and their significance, but in the present context, the life and death metaphors relate to the two sides of the spinal cord, which are envisioned in the East as two entwined snakes. This is further reinforced by Medusa's hair, which was composed of snakes and anyone who looked at her directly was turned to stone, hence Perseus using his shield as a mirror.

The power of the snake ...

You might begin to appreciate that there's more to mythology and its symbolic expression than meets the eye. So, let's close this section with an interesting twist and irony that you may already have detected. The DNA molecule, at a symbolic level, resonates with the symbols of cultures past in a quite direct way. DNA was only discovered scientifically in 1953. Did the myth and symbol inform its discovery? Or, further still, is DNA seen in a literal way and the symbolic depth not appreciated? Or yet more: were the myths an intuition of the structure of DNA? Or, more mystical still, did the myths express the creative process that has resulted in our mechanistic view of DNA and, hence, life ... and death?

I feel it is time to provide a little further explanation of where we are headed by way of a summary and before we head off into another culture. Currently at the core of pornography is a judgement; you either like it or you don't. If you don't you are siding with the prevailing mentality and have social and cultural acceptance, even if it is a diminishing and minority mentality. This prevailing mentality, in my definition, is patriarchal, mechanistic, power-driven and repressive. From the religious perspective, it requires acceptance of authority and its framework of personal and spiritual development: it is exoteric. It inclines to view the instincts and pleasure as inferior, wrong, bad and leading to moral decrepitude and madness: it is the safe path.

If you do like pornography, you have been and maybe still are a relative outsider; though this is rapidly changing. You have had to deal with moral issues and personal conflicts at a core level, maybe incompletely, and suffered them deeply. The resulting illness, even madness, could be considered a result of such indulgence; although by now you may recognise that my position is that the prevailing mentality is more truly the cause of any such madness. Personal and spiritual development is symbolic rather than mechanistic and is driven by inner guidance: it is esoteric. It sees the pleasures and instincts as tools for spiritual realisation. It is the path favoured by the mystic, magician and artist: it is hardly a safe path.

The latter view is not simply the product of Western culture in the last aeon. It has always been present and stems from the shamanic cultures of pre-history. It has usually been sanctioned or at least tolerated. The Western position – now losing its grip – has been further to the right-hand path (and I'm not talking just politically, as you will see), and this 'other' or alternative left-hand path has been despised and rejected. Things are beginning to change: Our initial foray into myth and symbolism, with their expression in alchemy and related traditions, indicates that the view from the left has remained a significant undercurrent and a thorn in the side of the dominant patriarchy. It says something of the strength, even the fundamentality of this undercurrent that it has withstood the torrent of rejection, negation and attempts at extermination that have been thrown at it.

I am not advocating a swing to the left and a rejection of the right. In a spiritual sense, the path of the right to spirituality, which includes asceticism, denial of sexuality and the like, is a valid route in spiritual development. It is just that it is one of basically two paths, and we may be moving to a time of co-existence if the cosmic and astrological changes are anything to go by. I suspect pornography reflects this. We have one-third of the population as active consumers, and maybe, with increasing acceptance, this will grow to one-half. We have three-quarters who see nothing wrong in the consumption of "non-violent erotica". Maybe this is the half who enjoy it and a half of the remainder who don't, but are broadminded enough to recognise its validity or at least to tolerate it. We are left with a quarter that doesn't. That's not the majority.

If we go back beyond the Piscean/Christian aeon, we find references to the position of the left-hand path in myth, archaeology, anthropology, and history and can trace them into the aeon and the present with the traditions (tolerated or despised) that have maintained it. However, I think it will be invaluable to explore one tradition from another culture that stems from the dawn of time and would have been commensurate with the traditions that forces in the present aeon in the West have attempted to extinguish.

Tantra is an Indian cult; it is not a religion. In recent history, it covers the present aeon but extends deep into pre-history well beyond this. This is possibly a further three to four thousand years and by inference, from an archaeological understanding, a further twenty thousand years. It is commensurate with the shamanic traditions of probably all pre- and non-monotheistic cultures, and their rites and practices. Let me set the scene with a – rare – quotation or two. I do not like the ready reliance on quotes to support an argument or position for a multitude of reasons, but in this circumstance, it is to provide an image, or flavour of what Tantra is like.

> *Here is an Indian description of what a Tantrik (sic) saint looks like to an outsider. He is so happy as to seem crazy; his eyes roll, reddened with wine. He sits on silk cushions surrounded by works of art, eating hot pork cooked with chillies. At his left side sits a girl skilled in the arts of love, with whom he drinks and repeatedly has ecstatic sexual intercourse; he continuously makes music with his vina (a stringed instrument), and sings poems; all of which he weaves together into rituals. Everything such a man seems to be and do gives violent offence to the conventionally minded. And that, in fact, is part – but only part – of the point. For he himself has to break any lingering attachment he may have had to even his own conventional attitudes. What he is doing fundamentally is rousing all the energies he can discover in his body, emotions and mind, and combining*

them into a vehicle which will carry him towards enlightenment: enlightenment being that state of knowing the truth about the origin of things and men, and their meaning, as clearly as experiencing the street. He uses every possible means, adapting every conceivable emotional stimulus and act to his purpose, on the assumption that things which you actually do repeatedly, and which have associated with them a powerful sensuous and emotive charge, change you far more effectively than anything else. And only if you combine together many different kinds of doing is the change radical.

(From Philip Rawson: Tantra)

(Enlightenment is) not to be achieved by shunning or avoiding our desires and passions, but only by transforming those very elements which make us fall, as a means of liberation.

(From Ajit Mookerjee: Kundalini)

I don't know about you, but this is not the image of a saint that I was brought up with! If you found yourself reading the first quote and picking up on the 'strangeness' factor, try revisiting it from a couple of angles. The first might be to replace the word 'saint' with 'practitioner' and see how the remainder seems to you. A second would be to notice whether you judged what he was doing and where this judgement comes from. Maybe you are actually attracted? Lastly try reading it as if it were you actually in the saint's role and get a feeling for what is happening.

My own feeling is that there is much in the above description that I find attractive and which at various times I have been made to feel guilty about. Yet at a deeper level there is something about it that feels 'right', or natural. As we move into the Tantric world, I would like you to see if you can suspend any judgement and criticism about what is being portrayed to you, see how much you are attracted to it and whether it also feels right to you, too.

Cult: "System of religious worship; devotion, homage, to person or thing." (OED). I mention the term 'cult' again, not necessarily because of its proximity to 'cunt' (joke), but because it has been usurped by the religious patriarchy and used as a term of denigration toward spiritual practice that does not conform to what is deemed acceptable. I would further point out that, in general, cult refers to spiritual paths that may have individual and autonomous avenues for spiritual attainment thus usurping the 'authority' of the priesthood. I would also add that the word 'cult' is the basis of 'culture'. In all this, the distortion of meaning is similar to that of 'myth', which is considered something untrue in its vernacular usage and is a verbal tool used in a similar psychological manner by the scientific rational community for dismissive purposes. Again, we see this strange alliance between science and religion over the domain of the soul.

So here we go on a whirlwind tour through the Tantric world: See whether you can appreciate the images at a symbolic level while simultaneously absorbing information. I'll try to assist in this process. This will be necessarily a vastly simplified tour, primarily because it is to serve as a comparison to and a vehicle for the unification of such forces within our Western culture.

At the base of the spine lies the coiled and dormant cosmic energy that is the supreme force within the human organism, considered feminine and named Shakti (pronounced and sometimes spelt: Sakti). The ultimate ambition is to awaken her so that she can ascend the spine and join the pure consciousness of Shiva (masculine, also pronounced and sometimes spelt: Siva) that pervades the whole universe and it is to this end that Tantric practice is directed. The actual coiled energy is referred to as Kundalini, which means "coiled up". Symbolically the coiling is of a snake in three and a half circles spiralling around the central axis of the spine and sometimes with her tail in her mouth. As a brief aside, to which we will return, the snake eating its own tail is referred to in the West as the Ouroboros and is a consistent theme in alchemy, where it may also be symbolised as a dragon.

There are many practises that are employed in the awakening process that are collectively referred to as yoga. These include bodily positions, which we most commonly associate with the term Yoga in the West, but also include other meditative and physical practices. The general flavours of these stated practices are ascetic and to the right in the spectrum earlier described. They are also referred to as the "right-hand path" (which I introduced you to earlier), where practice is primarily metaphorical. Common to all yogic practices of both paths is the use of the breath and breathing practices to act as a stimulant to the Serpent Power (another term for Kundalini). Also common is the view that the body is the core psychobiological instrument through which cosmic power reveals itself.

Tantra specifically makes use of sexual practice to awaken the dormant Kundalini energy and allow Shakti to ascend the spine in her journey back to the source and her unification with Shiva. This is the "left-hand path", lunar and magical, and involves a literal practice that evolves from and returns to the symbolic. Why do I say 'journey back' and 'returns to'? Because her presence in the body is a result of a 'fall' from unified consciousness and Tantra represents recognition of this state, an intuition of prior unity, and then practice to awaken the energetic possibility and affect a re-unity. This has interesting resonances in the Western notion of the Fall, as in the Garden of Eden, and even sheds a different light on it. Maybe we have understood it too literally as a myth, and Eve's apple could be the divine nectar? The union of Shakti and Shiva can be considered an inversion of the cosmic process of creation and manifestation. Tantric yoga also specifically associates this whole process with sexual energy and employs sexual acts in practice.

The dormant Kundalini resides in the base chakra, which in the physical organism is in the region of the perineum, just in front of the anus. (This may bring an interesting perspective on anal sexual practice as we move on.) A chakra is considered to be a centre, vortex of energy, or consciousness located in the body. Do you notice how Tantra sees 'energy' and 'consciousness' somewhat synonymously? There are varying views about the numbers of these chakras, but generally, six are seen in the body, with a seventh just above the head.

Each chakra has specific features in terms of a number, colour, sound and associated images. These are too varied and detailed to go into here, and the interested reader is referred elsewhere, but they serve as aids to meditative practice. It is important to remember that the chakras are not literal or primarily physical, although they do have interesting associations in this regard. They are associated with what is considered the 'subtle' body, which is a sheath connected to various and progressively more subtle bodies that you may care to envision as surrounding the physical body, but at an increasing distance and with increasing subtlety.

The chakras themselves also become progressively less physically symbolised as we progress up the spine, thus mapping the increased consciousness that the Kundalini energy sustains as Shakti continues in her journey to unite with Shiva.

Another aside: In this vision, Shakti is the dynamic aspect of the pair, Shiva the passive. I wonder if this sheds a further interesting light on the comments of Teiresias? The dualism and sexual connotations are further reinforced with the consideration that there are two major entwining channels that surround the central channel of the spinal cord. The channel on the left is lunar (moon and female) and white in colour. The right channel is solar (sun and male) and red.

As Kundalini rises through each chakra there is a unique quality that is produced, resulting in the sounds, colours and images that collectively symbolise that chakra. It is important to emphasise that these symbolic features are the result of the experience of the energy itself, which are then documented and used as maps for other potential initiates to guide them more safely in the process. It shows that Tantra is fundamentally a practical and experiential cult that accesses the subtle and symbolic from the literal. The movement of Kundalini through each chakra produces these characteristic physical and psychic signs in its upward ascent. You may also note resonances with what I earlier called the Great Chain of Being.

As an interesting aside, when such energetic movement occurs spontaneously, it can be disturbing to the recipient. If it is as the result of psychological trauma, it may even be shocking. You may intuit all manner of psychosomatic and psychiatric possibilities here and it is of interest that Tantric practice and Kundalini yoga can be most informative, adding a perspective that provides other possibilities to the healing mix and even maps to assist in it. Many Western medical and psychiatric practitioners have been and continue to explore these possibilities and correlations.

Wilhelm Reich's approach to the body was also primarily sexual, you may recall. He reinstated the primacy of the orgasm, which has a literal resonance with the symbolic union of Shakti and Shiva. Because Reich had a negative, even dismissive view of matters spiritual, he wasn't inclined to include such associations in his work. It hasn't stopped others and won't stop us either. In essence, Reich's views on health derived from unlocking the 'blockages' in the body by direct physical and breathing techniques. As he moved into more cosmic interests of his work, it was practitioners such as Alexander Lowen who pursued these ideas in more detail, as he practises and documents in his "Bioenergetics". From a Tantric perspective, we could consider that the 'blockages' are preventing the energy from moving through the relevant chakras. The overlap in perspective is considerable.

As you can see, this Tantric system is packed with complexity and symbolism. No wonder it fills thousands of yogic treatises! From here, we will be selective and pick out the features that pertain to our ongoing argument, but be assured that I will not selectively neglect anything that may negate it. I am confident that, to date, I have found nothing in these disciplines and their symbolic expression that does form a basis of negation.

One of the most important points I would like to stress is the absolute inclusion of the body in the process of spiritual realisation, a significant reversal of the Western negation. Further, this inclusion is also inclusive of the feminine and sexuality. Indeed, this system – which, I remind you, has an uninterrupted history and tradition throughout Eastern civilisations – requires the body, sexuality and the feminine for spiritual realisation. Am I beginning to repeat myself? I hope so, but the repetition is inherent and makes the argument compelling.

What the Tantric system does is see the physical and psychological processes as undivided. The chakras, although subtle, have a physical representation in the body by virtue of their position, as indicated with the base chakra (the home of the dormant Kundalini energy). Many Western commentators have made associations between the chakras and the endocrine (hormone) glands, which give the impression that the hormones may be conveying the chakric 'message' or intention. Also, there are nervous system correlations, such that the encircling channels of the spine could be identified with the sympathetic and parasympathetic systems. Beyond this, you may also see the image as similar to the caduceus and DNA ...

I would suggest that the immune system could be included in this picture, as an extension of the nervous system. All this indicates a complex and energetic interaction at the physical level, which is fundamentally holistic. Western medicine has even identified this unity in the discipline of "psychoneuroimmunology", or the interrelationship of the psyche (psychology), nervous and immune systems, and within which most commentators would include the endocrine or hormone system. In this view, the psyche component can be seen to extend from the physical and form a holistic unity that parallels the Tantric world.

I will briefly pick out one chakra for special reference, as we will be returning to it and have referred to it frequently – although indirectly – already. The sixth, or Ajna chakra, is the so-called "third eye" with a physical location in the central brow slightly above the level of the eyes. The physical location correlates with an endocrine gland, the pituitary, which lies a short distance behind. The pituitary is a kind of master regulator, or conductor of the overall hormone system of the physical body.

The third eye is where the two channels come together, and so represents a state of union of opposites, as in alchemy, but of a high order, as the next stage is the seventh chakra, which is above the head, beyond the body and is beyond all dualism. Symbolically, the third eye is related to 'inner vision' and we might recall that Teiresias was 'blinded' by Hera. As this blinding is, in a symbolic sense, a gift of closing the outer vision to awaken the inner, it puts a new slant on the actions of Hera and Zeus; maybe these two gods are not as oppositional as we have presumed, more complementary? Maybe there is a deeper wisdom implied here, and one that resonates with Indian culture? Odin, also known as Wotan the great god of the Northern Traditions, sacrificed an eye for the purpose of inner vision.

The sixth chakra, therefore, represents a high state of personal evolution. Is this equivalent to the evolved soul, the mature Shakti reconnecting with her lover? I believe the correlation is very strong and compelling, but we can get overly structured in these views. A further interesting feature is that the pineal gland, a little deeper in the brain, is associated with the seventh chakra, which we may see as the pinnacle of spiritual evolution and which Descartes, the philosopher who championed the split between body and mind in the West, saw as the "seat of the soul". Actually, the division that Descartes created was not between body and mind, as commonly understood, but body and soul. The pineal represented, in his view, the point of connection of the body with the soul. Maybe he should have had a detailed look at Eastern mysticism, it might have helped him!

Overall, the chakras provide a symbolic theory of the psyche, or soul, and should be seen in that light. That the pituitary and pineal glands happen to be rich in hormones and maybe agents that help altered states of consciousness is of further interest. For example, growth hormone in the human pituitary has strong features of eternal youth. The pineal contains traces of dimethyl tryptamine, or DMT, which has and is still used in some ancient cultures to induce spiritual states of consciousness. All this is a book in itself, I just thought I'd whet your appetite and pique your interest a little.

Is this the elan vital, the elixir of life, the fountain of youth, the gold of the alchemist, the divine nectar? How does this relate to mead (of the Teutons), wine (of Dionysus) and that alcohol can even be called 'spirit'? We will return to all these questions as we progress. Which brings us back to sex, that, after all, is the core of Tantric practice.

Here's another quote from Rawson (mentioned above), which sets the tone:

> *Raise your enjoyment to its highest power, and then use it as spiritual rocket fuel.*

(From Philip Rawson: Tantra)

Tantric practice is fundamentally sexual. We need to see the man and woman in the forthcoming descriptions as embodiments of the masculine and feminine principles. That is how the practitioners view each other and a sexist undercurrent will limit the extent of what could be appreciated. It is also important to point out that whilst Tantra is initially practical, it matures into the symbolic levels and images, which is not the same thing as fantasy.

Let me clarify, even if these are only my personal and subjective definitions. We confuse fantasy and the imagination. Indeed, imagination is in danger of being debased in a similar manner to the words myth and cult. Fantasy is idle and instinctual; based on memory, personal experience and having features of wish-fulfilment. It is the routine activity of an unreflective consciousness. Imagination is more reflective and creative. There is an emotional engagement of the individual with the imaginative process and its expression in creativity that indicates a relationship and even partnership, such as I envision between my day-to-day self and my soul. Vision is a deeper level of this process, where the I-soul complex is the recipient of ideas, images and experiences that feel fundamentally 'other', or spiritual in origin.

You may detect here an energetic reversal between fantasy and image. Fantasy reflects our common orientation of looking at the world in a linear manner, seeing objects as in the present and radiating to the past, but seeded in wishes for the future. The imagination turns this vector around, and in the continuum, imagination-vision looks into creation and its manifestation. It is fundamentally spiritual and requires the active participation of the soul. Recall that, in the Tantric vision, the feminine principle, Shakti or the soul, is indeed also the active principle.

The chief symbolic system Tantra uses is sex, infused with transcendent love. This is that the two practitioners unite so that their union produces in each the connection with the divine. You may recall an earlier contentious position that I took regarding my own experience of and orientation in pornography: that it was aimed at my own inner realisation and that this realisation was the abundance that would flow out into any relationship? Maybe that is not looking quite so contentious now.

The sex is ritualised. Surrounded by art and music, the ritual makes use of meat, fish, a particular grain, alcohol and sex ... sounds like an evening at the Club! Meaningful jokes on one side, it is the indulgence and fulfilment of the senses that is here symbolised. The main focus is the arousal and controlling of vast – cosmic – energies. The sex is classically between a man, embodying Shiva, and a woman, embodying Shakti. It is important to recognise that rites can also involve several partners in an orgiastic setting, where sexual contact may even be at random. Not only does this recall pornography, but also the pre-Christian rites we alluded to with May Day and the like, as well as Dionysian ritual.

For the purposes of our description, we will keep to the man and woman union in a simple ritual context. Human beings are, in the Tantric view, closest to the female aspect of creation when we reflect on the imagery contained in Kundalini. The woman is the embodiment of the goddess and attracts the main focus. It is further considered that it is only in contact with a woman that the Tantric practitioner can progress. As an aside, I wonder whether this is a further comment on the exclusion of male gay and inclusion of lesbian sex in porn?

The core of the practice is the use of sex to stimulate the awakening of Kundalini at the base of the spine. Sexual practice is associated with the retention of semen by the man to concentrate the power, with the focus on the woman's orgasm as the symbol of Kundalini's arousal and movement up the spine to the ultimate union of Shakti and Shiva, whilst the man's semen is symbolically diverted up his own spinal cord to this union.

My personal opinion is that because retention has this symbolic dimension, it should not be taken literally; that the actual physical retention of semen may not be a necessity and, in some circumstances, even unhealthy. Indeed, some Western practitioners of a depth psychological and magical orientation would see actual release as a desired outcome. Maybe it is a question of both/and again, rather than either/or? A paradoxical viewpoint may also help resolve such logical difficulties.

There's much, much more to this. The texts are full of illustrations of sexual postures that are fundamentally yogic, so maybe the porn stars varying postures could be more than simple dramatic effect? You may also recall my comments about these practices being illustrated on temple walls available to young and old. One final point worth stressing is that the sexual partner in Tantric practice is not usually the life partner, but someone relatively unknown or in a relationship where this is the specified means of contact. In fact, it is considered that someone with whom there is a romantic or personal involvement would not be suitable. In this respect, whilst Romantic Love is a stage in psychic evolution, and as witnessed between Graham and Emily, it can also be an obstruction to further growth. Tantra recognises this and avoids the complication, or so it would seem.

You may find all these comments and positions challenging. I invite you to remain open-minded and consider two things. Firstly, how much, even though at an instinctual level, does pornography reflect a lot of this imagery? Secondly, and as I have cause to do whilst writing this section, how reflection on sexual unions that you may have experienced and could describe as 'cosmic' (please excuse the New Age joke) reflect these patterns? If you don't believe you've had any, then maybe go back to my descriptions in the early chapters. Don't forget though, Kundalini experiences are not confined to sexual practice and you may have experienced something similar spontaneously, as a result of a shock, or even in a dream.

A final quote from a Tantric text:

What need have I of an outer woman?

I have an inner woman within myself.

Whilst this may reflect a 'realised' Tantric practitioner, doesn't it also remind you of our discussions of gender in earlier chapters?

A few final comments before we leave this intriguing world. We have taken a rather pure view of Tantra, the "girl meets boy" angle. This keeps it relatively pure and symbolically accessible. We have alluded to greater sexual complexity with varied and apparently indiscriminate sexuality up to the level of orgy, and as reflected in pornography. If we step outside of the pornographic mainstream, then do they also explore other psychic avenues? Well, yes they do. The more fetish end of the spectrum is often included in the ritual dress, so we can leave that. What about things that we may even consider perverse?

Whilst we have associated the embodiment of the woman with the goddess Shakti, she is, of course, not the only goddess of the Indian pantheon. Most cultures that exhibit a pantheon see the archetypal mother, or feminine, in a threefold aspect as mother, daughter and crone. One is the nurturer and nourisher, the second has orgiastic potential and the third the paradoxical goddess of the underworld and death, whose equivalent in Western culture is the crone or embodied in the witch; magical overtones indeed. Tantra would not be complete without these dimensions and they do exist, as our understanding of the Great Cycle of Existence would predict. It also brings the spectre of Tantra toward the magical traditions of the West, within which the mysteries of sex and love are deeply embedded.

Kali is this equivalent goddess in India. She is the destroyer and devourer as well as life bearer. Her paradoxical nature exemplifies much that is embedded in Tantra, such as the entwined paths up the spinal 'mountain' of life and death. (Incidentally, doesn't the mountain metaphor of the spine recall Teiresias on Mount Cithaeron?) Whilst we may equate Shakti with the daughter and orgiastic potential, Kali represents the deeper more mysterious aspects of the feminine, even death. It is not surprising then that Tantric practice should also include worship of her? Some practices may seem somewhat unusual, such as sexual intercourse in a graveyard, but maybe it puts a lot of the apparently more extreme pornographic practice in perspective.

It may be worth bearing this in mind when we look to the

domains of sadomasochism, bondage and discipline. An interesting point of contemplation might be: which aspect of the goddess are my consumption and I serving?

Now I am going to move into a rather enigmatic area of symbolism that both transcends and unites the differing mythical and cultural outlooks into sexuality. This symbolism is the use of the two colours red and white. In general, our perception of the colour red is that it is associated with the female or feminine principle. Why is this so? At one level, it seems relatively simple: red is the colour of blood and women bleed in a cyclical manner called menstruation. White is the colour of semen and purity, so in a dominant and masculine culture would easily be seen as male. This is reflected in the hexagonal Indian symbol of two interlocking triangles with one, red, pointing down and the other, white, pointing upward. Traditionally, the downward pointing red is seen as the feminine triangle representing the pubic triangle and the associated blood of menstruation.

Yet we have a paradoxical situation on our hands, because the left-hand path of Kundalini's ascent is white and female, further it is connected with the moon, as it is lunar. The left-hand path is the magical one and is even represented as dark and dangerous in our culture; we associate left-handedness with concerning psychological features and the feminine, although this also reflects the patriarchal position with respect to the feminine. The right-hand path is red, masculine and connected with the sun. The male: female and sun: moon analogues are familiar; the colour associations of male: female and red: white are less so, as would be the added static: active.

How do or can we explain this? One way is to see that as we move from the literal to the symbolic then an inversion process occurs, which is subtle and complex. For example, if we take the literal position we have outer: inner, male: female, white: red and active: passive. However, if we invert this and take the inner symbolic position, we then have inner: outer, female: male, white: red and active: passive. The last two pairings remain unchanged with the inversion. I also see these features reflected in the paradoxical issues regarding gender that we explored earlier (Chapters Three and Six).

Is your head in a spin yet? Mine was; I went for a long walk with the dogs! What this analogue approach does for me is give me an insight into paradox that a literal and rational approach cannot, and makes me see that any 'explanation' is a rational fantasy. Analogue thinking seems to work with paradox and symbolism in a way that the rational, linear and mechanistic world of the external masculine does not. We are left with the deeply paradoxical inner, red and male Shiva, with whom Shakti has united ... more to come.

I am also going to attempt to explain these paradoxes by linking them across cultures to see the parallels. In alchemy, the symbolism matches that of Tantra and that fact I find intriguing. I will progressively infer that alchemy preserves the ritual aspects of sexuality in a covert form as one of pathways that can be used for spiritual attainment. As indicated, our common and modern perception is that alchemy is associated with a lone practitioner slaving over a bubbling cauldron in an attempt to make gold from lead or another base metal, but maybe he – or she – has other ways of making gold.

Yet all these alchemical processes have been recognised to be psychological, according to Jung, and therefore symbolic. What do they symbolise? Pathways to spiritual attainment. And, as we have discovered, symbols are multifaceted and inherently contain the sexual as a valid path. So, maybe the secrecy and obfuscation in alchemical treatises and literature was also to obscure and hide this fact. If we see it for what it is, then it matches the holistic understanding of India: that sexuality is a valid, but not the only path to enlightenment. What we need to do in the West is not only to restore the feminine, the body and sexuality, but also the magical and esoteric traditions that employ these forces as an esoteric pathway to spiritual attainment. No wonder the Church felt threatened!

From here on I will be using alchemy in this restricted psychosexual context and as a Western variant of the Tantric tradition.

Is it valid to do this? I think the above argument of itself is strong enough, particularly with the further evidence I will offer as the book progresses. There is one scholarly commentator, Dr Brian Bates, who traces the Tantric tradition back in history to the Bon Po shamanic culture and from there sees a close relationship with the cultures of the Northern Traditions by their common Indo-European and Aryan connections, and who further examines some of the Northern myths from this perspective. We will be following this trend and deepening it a little later, but I would like you to accept that the evidence for these connections, influence and cross fertilisation is not just compelling but inevitable, because of the archetypal and symbolic basis.

At this point I would just like to mention an amusing connection with the Celtic mythic structure of Britain in the dark ages, after the Romans left, but before the Christian Church filled the vacuum.

The unjust British king Vortigern was trying to build an impregnable fortress against the invading Saxons in the wilds of Wales; a situation he had brought upon himself. Each time he built the structure it fell down overnight. His druids advised him that he needed to sacrifice an innocent child, who had no father, and sprinkle his blood on the stones to hold the structure in place. Merlin was found to fit the bill exactly, as his mother was considered to have conceived him following the attention of a demon, although she remained a virgin. Well, it may not have been a demon, as that might have been a Christian hindsight correction, otherwise the parallels with the birth of Jesus are uncomfortably close. Also, a demon could be a "daimon"; the transcendent creative principle of Greek thought.

Anyway, Merlin was certainly an unusual child and he wasn't entirely happy with what Vortigern had planned for him. So, he proposed to Vortigern that he explain why the walls were falling down. He told Vortigern to look beneath the foundations where he would find a pool, which he did. Merlin then asked him to drain the pool and that he would then find two eggs, vases or stones (depending on which version you read). Once opened, inside would be found two dragons, one red and one white. They would ascend, fighting, and initially the white would appear to be dominating but eventually the red won out. Conveniently Merlin explained that the white represented the Saxon invasion, which appeared to be on top, but ultimately the red of the British people would win. That saved Merlin's life, but ultimately not Vortigern's. It was left to Arthur who, with Merlin's assistance, completed the prophesy; even though only temporarily.

Can you see the parallels? They're all there ... The dormant energy in eggs, awoken to reveal two dragons: Dragons are the Western equivalent of the snake or serpent. The eggs could be ovaries or testicles? Vases and stones reflect alchemy. The dragon is a potent image, the fire breathing adding to the impression of the power of breath to ignite the passions and their subsequent intensity; even violence and danger. The two channels are there, the red and white, the fighting as a twisting ascent that might also be seen sexually, of course, and the ultimate success of the red. I would point out that this represents an ultimate union, not a combative dominance; but then again, we have nearly two thousand years of Christian and patriarchal influence to deal with, although the conflation of sex and violence is itself of interest.

Has an alchemically informed myth been distorted? Was the original myth an expression of the symbolic path to spiritual realisation? Did it contain sexual symbolism, more than the present version of it does? After all, Merlin is a magician, and his parentage is dark and mythically sexualised. It also throws a little light on Merlin's enigmatic relationship with his sister, Gwendolyn. Could she have been his soror mystica (spiritual sister), the Western equivalent of a Tantric partner? And what of the complex relationships between Arthur, Gwenivere and Lancelot? Could the Courtly Love of the Middle Ages represent the re-emergence of the sexual in the context of Romantic Love? I find all these intriguing possibilities when these legends are read in such a fashion.

In fact, the legends are replete with goddess images, some of a deeper and sometimes darker persuasion. There is the varying image of the Lady of the Lake, she who has gifts hidden in the depths. Nimuë, or Morgana, is Merlin's 'consort', who learns his art, dupes him and locks him underground. Really? Could this be a Christian reinterpretation? What about her being another – maybe more Kali-like – aspect of the goddess with whom he has a Tantric relationship and explores the underworld? Then there is his sister – again – who builds him an observatory on a hilltop (the mountain of Kundalini?) from whence he could view the future and prophesise.

Although all this is very attractive, we won't entirely depart from Greek myths as we progress – after all, it would not be holistic if we did – but I want to use the myth of the dragons as a lead into the Celtic and Northern cultures and their influence and relevance. I want to do this for two principal reasons. Firstly, the myths of these cultural trends have been less subject to Christian influence and are thus possibly more revealing of the sexual elements we want to explore. It would take very little to extricate the dragon myth from the religious and cultural influences that may have followed and distorted it, restore it to its more original form and reveal its psychosexual features and symbolism, which I have already done to a limited extent. As the Greek myths have been more extant in our culture – even though in a sense they may not be our own – they may have received more editing and censorship, whereas the further North in the Northern hemisphere you travel, the less these religious influences have operated. Secondly, the Northern Traditions contain in their myths and elsewhere a more differentiated concept of soul than is currently found in the Christian West. It is one that overlaps the features we revealed in the Tantric tradition and one that, I believe, offers a much more detailed avenue into our psychosexuality.

9

Psychosexuality Revealed

One dictum of alchemy is: As above, so below. This is further reflected in the essential unity of the concepts of macrocosm and microcosm. In the last chapter, we explored the more macrocosmic, or archetypal, view of sexuality with the examination of Tantra, in particular. We will be establishing this perspective within our own culture in the next chapter by a more detailed examination of relevant myths from the sexual perspective. However, this macrocosmic view would be better appreciated by a more detailed examination of the soul from a Western perspective, with specific reference to the sexual and energetic outlook, which I have termed psychosexuality.

A little clarification: I use the term Northern Traditions (also referred to collectively as Teutonic) to indicate the cultural and spiritual perspectives of the Teutonic races, whom I see as existing north of the Alps in Europe, although more exclusively the Germanic races and Scandinavia. Our Western Tradition is this and more; it is also inclusive of some other cultures around the Mediterranean and reflects the modern cultural trends of the West, now inclusive of North America at least. The Celtic races are a part of this overall Northern Tradition: In their present revival, they have become seen to be the entire corpus of British mythology and spiritual heritage, for example, and linked more with the broader Western Tradition. This is a mistake; perpetuated as a result of the reluctance to accept and integrate much of the Northern Traditions, particularly the magical and nationalistic elements, as a consequence of the circumstances and wars of the twentieth century. I believe we must get beyond these distortions, as these other traditions contain much that is rich and can inform our cultural progress in the West, particularly from the sexual perspective which the current Celtic revival can limit.

I believe that such retrieval will inform us a lot about our traditional background, cultural development and spiritual future. As I have already stated, this is because it is often less contaminated by the Christian and patriarchal repressive influences of the last aeon. You may have already noticed how the Tantric perspective shows that the Northern Traditions are more balanced with respect to the body, the feminine and sexuality. It is worth recalling that it was from Scandinavian countries that pornography broke the political and social constraints and entered the mainstream legally. I think this factor is significant, these countries being less dominated by the above influences, the shackles of which we are still trying to completely break.

Rediscovering what the idea and image of the soul was and is in the Northern psyche is not going to be an easy task, such that the ensuing comments can be seen to represent a work in progress. Even though currently incomplete, I feel they can inform us about our inherent sexuality and its place in the soul complex. To this end, some modern explorers of similar issues have assisted me, although more from the magical and cultural perspectives. One in particular, Edred Thorsson, has attempted varying models of the soul or what he terms the psychophysical complex. Of note is that Thorsson uses Jung as a comparison in the modern era and cross-relates his own ideas with Jungian psychology. This is of interest: it adds a certain traditional validity to Jung's ideas and places him in the Teutonic

(Northern) tradition. Hardly surprising really, Jung was a German-speaking Swiss.

Thorsson seems to have a mission however, being the reinstatement of the Teutonic or more strictly Germanic psyche in its mythic and cultural totality. To this end, to my mind, he tends to over-react and could be accused of a nationalism that is easily associated with the darker side of the Germanic psyche in the twentieth century. I will try and be more perspicacious and use only those elements that I sense need reintegrating from a holistic perspective and which inform the major aim of this book; being the full, honoured and patent integration of sexuality within Western culture.

I believe that the notion of soul occupies the middle ground in the Great Chain of Being and is inclusive of the body, emotions and lower mental functions, such as cognition. This picture is drawn not from the Northern Traditions, although present in them, but from therapeutic experience; although somewhat informed by Jung. Whilst I have come to this from a medical and healing perspective, I believe it is archetypal and deserves wider inclusion, and it is this that I am currently working on in a more theological sense. So, I was intrigued when I came across Thorsson's explorations in this area, as most of them resonated with what I was actively working with.

From my professional experience, I have come to the conclusion that we must view the body in a broader conceptual light. It is simply not sufficient to perpetuate Descartes' apparent error of separation of body and mind. If we do, we retain a primarily mechanistic and reductive view of the body and lack its integration with the mind. This causes all sorts of negative and regressive ramifications in medicine, psychology and spirituality; too long – and sometimes too tedious – to go into here. If we sort of 'unpack' the body we find progressive levels of complexity that can be explored from various angles.

Let's begin with Western medicine: The physical body can be extended to the psychoneuroimmunological view, such that mind, nervous system, immune and hormonal systems are seen to act in concert as a unified whole – note the inclusion of mind. If we unravel the nervous system within this perspective, we find the instincts, emotions and moods that rest – seemingly – below the mind and intellect. Remember the two sub-systems within the autonomic nervous system, the parasympathetic and sympathetic? Are the moods that dominate both us and our creativity an extension of these systems with their opposing tendencies? Do they represent the features that culminate in the sixth chakra and its unified dualism?

This 'loosening up' process reveals an energetic background to the body that was explored by pioneers like Reich, who traced this to a view of sexuality that did not confine and restrict it to a mere instinct. It also indicates increasingly subtle dimensions to the body, like the sheaths or aptly named subtle bodies of the Eastern view. It further indicates the primacy of sexuality as the energetic framework within which the body exists. Is this tantamount to saying that this energy is life, and without it, the body is dead? Food for contemplation, at least it allies with the intuition that the life force is somewhat synonymous with sexual energy and this was certainly Reich's view.

Although American, Thorsson explores the complexity and subtlety of the body from the Northern viewpoint. However, he obfuscates any detailed understanding by using Germanic terms in a difficult manner for any outsider to that culture. However, it does give the flavour of concepts like 'appearance', 'shape', and 'persona' integrated within an underlying soul complex (his term). In this view, the soul can indeed be seen to be a complex that contains and unifies all these subtleties.

What about sexuality; is that integrated into the model? Not really, but it is inferred, and in some works, there is an indication of the use of postures, like yoga, that extends to sexual postures, like Tantra. Here, we get into awkward territory because the spectre of magic is raised, and images of people like Aleister Crowley (a.k.a. the Great Beast) come to mind. I'm going to make no apology for this, as you can't separate sexuality from the magical realms. If sexuality is a pathway to the spiritual, as Tantra espouses, then the means are essentially and axiomatically magical. Sex magic? Yes indeed, or maybe evolving to love magic. In simplistic terms, isn't it a magical act to create a child from sexual intercourse?

From this Northern perspective, the body can be viewed as a complex of components that are energetically unified and contained within a soul complex. These components are progressively subtler and operate under different principles to the mechanistic view we have of the body itself in modern times. The only difference I am proposing here to a model that resonates with that of Tantra is that the notion of the soul is given prominence. As the concept of individuality is less pronounced in the spiritual traditions of the East, it is not so emphasised in the treatises and rituals where the individual is seen more as a vehicle of the spiritual.

In Western culture, we have attained an enigmatic view of individuality. In my opinion, it is, as yet, only partially developed, but we cannot deal with this conundrum by regression and a return to a time before it became problematic. For many from the West, I believe that this is both the attraction and the problem of Eastern spirituality. As with our earlier discussion of Tantra, contact with the East can assist the reconnection process with what has been 'lost' but, once established, this reconnection should be used to inform our own culture and its development beyond the problematic stage we currently find ourselves in with regard to individuality.

My belief is that a re-examination of the concept of soul is not just a religious exercise, but that it can help us to the next stage of our individual development beyond the isolated, worried, death-fearing species we currently are. To date, this broader and more soulful view connects us with our contra-sexuality and, hence, more deeply with other people. It can provide us with a broader and healthier view of ourselves and hence be inclusive of others. It gives us a sense of "beyond death", or at least a way beyond the fear of it. Sexuality is the foundation of all this, and more.

In Northern myth Odin has two great ravens that sit on his shoulders. These are interpreted as "mind" and "memory". They sit as balanced opposites, maybe reflective at a bodily level of the left and right brain hemispheres. Or, at a subtler level, the contrasting moods that affect us more deeply than we care to admit. Mind does not consist simply of cognition, perception and will, important though these are. It extends to the realm of ideas that we think we may own, but may also be 'given' to us. Memory is not simply the storehouse of personal experiences, but reaches deep within our imaginations and even to memories that are racial or collective, often misinterpreted as "past lives". These views take us beyond our restricted views of mind and memory, yet overlap two other features recognised in Eastern culture, though somewhat ignored and negated in the West.

The ravens straddle Odin from opposing yet balanced shoulders, reflecting the inner connection of the left and right, female and male. The next two functions to consider are more centrally placed and energetic in nature. The first we are familiar with from Tantra; the breath. The breath is considered to link these differing aspects of soul together and with spirit as a whole. So, here in our own traditional background is the Tantric equivalent, so maybe Bates and others are right in their views of the cultural connections that preceded Christianity.

The second is ecstasy that, like the breath, we can consider to be centrally placed in the body. The term ecstasy literally means "beyond oneself", in an exalted state or one of rapture. Ecstasy is a term that in modern academia has become associated with the shaman as the "ecstatic healer" and so is a feature of shamanic culture. It is also apparent in the rituals of Tantra and will be seen to be present in other Northern and Western myths we will be exploring. This all provides a strong argument for seeing shamanic culture to be the prototype for all the cultural traditions we are exploring; this is certainly my conviction.

We could dip into modern culture a little and explore the term ecstasy further. As terms such as myth and cult have become debased in contemporary culture, I find it interesting that ecstasy has suffered denigration by associating the name with a drug of – supposed – addiction. Traditional shamanic culture makes use of drugs in the enlightenment process but, like sexuality, it is not necessarily routinely so. Of course, ecstasy has effects on the nervous system, but it inclines more to the hallucinogenic and mystic end of the spectrum rather than the conventional image of so-called hard drugs. I think the differentiation of the effects of these differing drugs is long overdue. We may again be throwing the baby out with the bath water, as some may have therapeutic applications in areas like death and dying, but maybe their association with sex blocks this appreciation. Maybe also, drugs like ecstasy indicate that the connection with the personal control of spiritual evolution is beyond the patriarchy's capacity to sustain.

We may yet find a brain chemical that is equivalent to ecstasy. I suspect we will, as we have already found cannabis receptors in the brain as well as some intriguing evidence about dimethyl tryptamine, or DMT. DMT is an essential ingredient of South American shamanic cultures and is contained in a drink called Ayahuasca, but it is probably in other cultural preparations used for the same or similar purposes. The reason I am focussing on DMT is that it has been detected in minuscule proportions in the pineal gland and has been used under experimental conditions to induce visionary experiences. It has not been found to be addictive yet, like other similar preparations, it remains under the "hard drug" classification or list of "prohibited substances".

It is feasible that the use of an external agent like DMT can augment the arousal of Kundalini, if we use Eastern symbolism as a reference. Indeed, this would be the generic intention with the use of all hallucinogenic chemicals, which are also usually plant-derived. However, it is also feasible that Tantric-style practices can be used to stimulate the internal production and release of these chemicals (or, more technically, hormones?) within the brain. This could be the final pathway of sexual practice as well, either under ritual guidance or spontaneous acts. Again, we are confronted with the question about how much this relates to concepts of the elixir of life or elan vital and the related symbols of mead, nectar, honey and wine.

Maybe it is no surprise that the modern drug ecstasy is associated with regular and prolonged musical rhythms, as sustained drumming is a regular accompaniment of shamanic ritual and practice. It may then also be of no surprise that ecstasy is also used for sexual stimulation, which it usually sustains and prolongs; also a feature of Tantra.

Finally, we have the work of some nervous system investigators, such as Roland Fischer. In summary, this takes the autonomic nervous system well into the brain by seeing that the parasympathetic branch is related to meditation, contemplation and peace. The sympathetic nervous system, by contrast, is associated with a strong arousal state, including heightened sexuality. The interesting thing is that when the sympathetic arousal, called ergotropic, is heightened further and further, then the energy naturally moves into the opposite parasympathetic, or trophotropic state, in a balanced and integrated manner. High arousal leading to enlightenment; now doesn't this sound like Tantra!

Whilst we commonly associate the sympathetic to the masculine (high arousal, activity) and the parasympathetic with the feminine (tranquillity, passivity) at the exoteric or mundane levels, there can be an interesting inversion that matches our exploration at the end of the last chapter. Looked at from the Tantric perspective, the sympathetic nervous system would be the feminine and the parasympathetic the masculine, and is more compatible with the Eastern symbolism. Interestingly, it is also compatible with the actual structure of the autonomic nervous system: the sympathetic nerves emerge mainly from the middle sections of the spinal cord, whereas the parasympathetic is from the extremes and also involved in the cranial nerves of the brain, which the sympathetic is not. Both systems are involved with normal sexual functioning. These associations I find intriguing and worthy of further study.

Having taken this tour into the more traditional view of the soul from a non-Christian perspective, even though necessarily incomplete, I would now like to use it in a preliminary manner to define psychosexuality. I would further like to use it to explore the territory in more detail, partly as a summary of what we have covered to date, but also to unify it and differentiate psychosexuality from the various other disciplines and traditions that we have explored, to isolate the relevant features.

All perspectives of psychosexuality must be fundamentally inclusive of the body. It is also imperative that we move away from the mechanistic manner in which we look at the body, which essentially alienates us from it. How frequently do we describe our bodies in objective terms? Of course, the medical profession further enhances this perspective. Tantra does much to honour the body as, interestingly, does pornography and therefore assists the process.

Pornography achieves this in a multitude of direct and indirect ways; I will mention some. The first is one of perspective, not confined to pornography alone, and is the progressive dis-adornment of clothing that occurs so that the fundamentals of sexuality may be engaged in. There is a heightened physical focus that honours the bodily form in many ways, beauty being the most obvious. Although it may be argued that such portrayal makes the consumer feel inadequate, I would add that the obvious beauty that the physical form can present, both male and female, counters this.

I know that a lot of what can be seen in porn you wouldn't describe in terms such as "beauty" and I may be stretching the terminology here. However, I am confining myself to the erotic end of the pornographic spectrum, which honours and even exalts (a shamanic term for ecstasy, remember?) the female form. And not just the female, the man is included in this appreciation: We are a long way from the stag movies with the faceless men still wearing socks and shoes!

In a symbolic sense, the female form is portrayed as the goddess, and I would remark there are many features in pornography, certainly in erotic art, that take this approach. In Tantra, this is further exemplified by engaging the senses with food, wine and perfumes. A lot of this is implied in good porn, and it may be that the consumer might reflect this attitude; take Brian's wine accompaniment as an example, maybe?

The one feature that appeals across the screen is clothing and adornment. These are used in porn to heighten the body, not to conceal it (obviously), and with sex as the object, there is great attention to lingerie, underwear and jewellery. Not only does this heighten consumption, but it also helps the porn consumer in their own dress involving sex, bringing it out of the confines of the bedroom. Clothing of a more fetish nature may serve differing functions; such as different aspects of the goddess complex as well as entertaining other sexually related motifs and instincts.

The body also portrays the energetic perspective so beloved of Tantra within porn. We see sex in the bedroom, outside, employing different settings, varying items of furniture and into nature. At the edge of the spectrum, as indicated above regarding "other sexually related motifs and instincts" we have the dungeon at the Club as a good metaphor. Maybe inadvertently the various positions and acts of coupling engage the postures of yoga generally and Tantra specifically. As with clothing, this can provide an educational or even an instructive element to the portrayal.

Narrative is usually a little light and disconnected, but this does, at least, allow the bodies further expression, as they are the main vehicles of whatever narrative may be employed. This is maybe a long way from the ritual and poetry of Tantra but, I would argue, it is there in embryonic form. This is interesting in and of itself, as sexuality, if openly and honestly portrayed, may automatically engage in a lot of sexual rituals because the energetic forces within sexuality will demand it, sometimes in a quite possessive manner. Care must be taken here, and this is why Tantra is so laden with ritual, instruction and guidance, as the forces engaged are great indeed. In the wrong hands, particularly with those naive or having unresolved agendas, this could easily spill over and lead to damage and crime.

We have already discussed the health issues to an extent with an appraisal of occupational issues in the porn workplace and sexually transmitted diseases in particular. I won't be covering old ground here, but move onto the broader issue of health and illness with respect to psychosexuality. I think this position is inclusive of sexually transmitted diseases (STDs) and, beyond a certain point; it is for other reasons that STDs are focussed on at the public level.

Let's encapsulate what we have discussed above with respect to the body and its energetic correlate, which links to the life force and is symbolised as Kundalini. We will then move up the body and use the Kundalini model to help inform us. I will place a special emphasis on the health and well-being perspective to include what is healthy and unhealthy in psychosexuality as we make the ascent, even to highlighting particular physical and mental diseases.

From a healthy psychosexuality, the body is to be honoured and adorned, such that the stimulation of the inherent energetic component by sexual means can begin its initial development in an open and accepting manner. Should sexuality be engaged in with guilt and anxiety, then the act may be doomed to relative or absolute failure. Eastern influence enhances this honouring and acceptance with appeal to the supportive senses and a ritual containment of the act itself.

Poor health can result here exactly because of the anxiety and guilt. The anxiety may relate to poor gender initiation to this point, which we discussed in some detail in my own case in the earlier chapters. It can be reinforced by bad information and ignorance; increasingly, the former and something that the degenerative end of the porn spectrum serves to support. What might not help a virginal adolescent male is a surf of the Internet revealing sites that tell him that unless he has at least an eight-inch dick then women won't want him (supported by female testimony to the fact, of course), aided by images of male dominance, roughness and violence; verbal and sometimes physical. Hardly a good initiation, is it?

It behoves the males in the young man's life to step forward and help in his grounding, beginning with his father. For the base (first) chakra symbolises this grounding and not the sexual forces. This implies that the sexual forces are to be engaged only when the adolescent (male or female) has a firm grip on reality and has a stable disposition. To arrive at this point demands psychological as well as physical maturity, which is achieved with accurate information and initiations within the demands of life.

It is at the base chakra that Kundalini is considered to reside, so if ungrounded the forces may move to the sexual sphere and produce problems like anxiety. Guilt occurs if we take an isolated perspective to the 'right' of our spectrum and is unfortunately reinforced by the dominant and prevailing attitudes within our Western society, although their grip is lessening. I am certainly no friend of the Catholic Church in this regard.

Grounding also implies nurturing and the feminine influence, in boys as well as girls. The base chakra is thus profoundly related to the instinct of feeding. An extension of this is what we eat and the subsequent well-being of the body at the gross physical level. Dimensions of this include not only the necessary diet and nurturing as we develop to support the physical changes that occur up to adolescence but also the daily intake from there that helps our ongoing physical and mental stability.

Environmental and dietary factors have a big impact not only on our direct physical development but also on the hormonal, nervous and immune systems, all of which are necessary for adequate genital functioning. The genitals are hormonal glands par excellence, even to the point that the individual can be defined by them (he's 'cunt struck', a 'dickhead', or 'led by his balls'). The health of the immune system is, in my opinion, the most important factor in the prevention of STDs. In fact, general psychosexual health, rather than vaccination, condoms and antibiotics, should be the first line in protecting our kids – and ourselves – from STDs; as we are unlikely to engage with the sort of people and practices that harbour them if we have a healthy sexuality. Not an absolute guarantee, but a bloody good start.

Chakric symbolism has a lot to inform us here. For example, repeated STDs or unwanted pregnancies relate to a lack of integration at the sexual (second) chakra level. It is as if the energy is stuck there and the repeated problems a call to address the issues and move on. If the first chakra isn't integrated and there is a sudden awakening of Kundalini without initiation and ritual protection, then the effects can be severe enough to produce a psychosis and even schizophrenia, if so predisposed. Use of illicit drugs in an unritualised manner can produce a similar result and is probably why severe mental disturbance and illicit drug usage are given a sibling-like attention, rather than a causal relationship.

As the first chakra is related to grounding and nurturing the second is to sexuality, and now we have two of the instincts awoken. With the awakening of sexuality, there is the emergence of the emotional dimension. It is of interest to me that in psychotic states the emotional dimension is either lacking (schizophrenia) or disordered (bipolar disorder). It is of further interest to me that in schizophrenia sexuality is not a significant feature, whereas in bipolar disorder it is prominent and sometimes indiscriminately rampant – a further factor in STDs.

What this does is posit an important nexus between emotion and sexuality, such that sexual development and maturity goes hand in glove with emotional development. Don't get me wrong; I don't see emotion residing solely at the second chakra; I see it maybe beginning there, but it is more a feature of the third chakra. Like Kundalini, emotion will ascend with increasing differentiation and maturity. This is a major factor in Western society, that the patriarchal emphasis has been on the repression of emotion and hence the lack of development of a mature sexuality. It is almost a truism that those of the 'right' end of the spectrum, particularly politicians, are prey to all sorts of psychosexual distortions. We even identified it earlier in The Porn Report ... anecdotal, funny, but also sad.

At this level, we also have to deal with the vexed issue of excitement, which demands that the third chakra be balanced. The third chakra is also strongly associated with emotion, more so than the second. It is also the fight or flight instinctual level, where we see the clear emergence of gender difference (the genders are only latently present up to this point), with flight being related to "reflection" at the human level (in Jung's view) and fight to aggression and the "drive to activity", which can be seen as feminine and masculine, respectively.

The first three chakras, situated near the anus, above the pubes and below the chest – all in the midline – complete the tour through the instincts at the animal level and as identified and defined by Lorenz. The first two can be considered neutral from the gender perspective, whereas the third has a more distinct masculine-feminine duality inherent in it. I would consider that these elements and genders are becoming separated and differentiated as the focus moves up the spinal cord. We are still below the chest, so in the realm of that which we have in common with the animal kingdom at large.

There are some interesting physiological features that reflect the symbolism. The hormones that are produced in the genitals and associated with sexuality – take the much-maligned testosterone as a symbol here – are known as steroid hormones and fall into a related class with the stress hormones of the adrenal glands. Hormones and immune functioning are, therefore, very closely related, and aren't we aware of this with respect to sexual functioning? The consequence of this is that stress-related disorders have a significant effect on sexual functioning and relate to a plethora of disorders.

The third chakra introduces some problematic elements from the sexual perspective as it indicates that aggression – or lack of it – is immediately above and intimately connected to the sexual chakra. We have discovered how greatly connected sexuality and aggression are. Here is evidence of it from both a symbolic and physiological perspective.

Lack of integration at the level of the third chakra can lead to digestive disturbances. The 'lack of power' of the submissive employee characterises the person who gets a stomach ulcer. The flow on to the next – heart – chakra may account for the relationship between aggressive disorders and heart attacks. We can even take a symbolic approach to the illnesses themselves, such that an ulcer is the downtrodden employee 'offering up' a piece of his stomach to his demanding employer, or the heart attack is the release of pent-up expression of disordered anger.

I won't go further down this path: too many have, such that symbols become reduced to signs, in the "you have back pain because you don't have enough support in your life" variety. However, it is interesting and instructive to explore disease and dysfunction from this symbolic perspective and use established and ancient models, like that of the chakra system, to further explore this. Although our examination is for the purpose of exploration of psychosexuality, the overlap with health issues is considerable. It is a small wonder that many, Freud included, recognised and explored this connection. My impression is there is much further work to be done in this area.

Sexuality, once Kundalini has passed through the second chakra, remains relatively undifferentiated until the goddess moves onward and upward. In a sense, whilst there may be dysfunction at this level, it is more of the guilt and anxiety type, or more severe mental disturbance there if the energy flow regresses to the first chakra. It is primarily instinctual and with an emergent emotionality, which manifests as excitement. This level of sexuality can be considered polymorphous; it can flow wherever, once stimulated, male or female. Such sexual contact at this level with the same sex is not truly homosexual; it is undifferentiated and may explain some animal behaviour. Indeed, ritual may demand that some forms of homoeroticism be explored at this level and is why it is a feature of adolescence. It is as if the adolescent is trying to discover where his or her sexuality is to flow and exploration of it with someone of the same sex may help decide this. Of course, and somewhat simplistically, if obstructed in this exploration homosexual preference may be accidental rather than a true consequence.

Excitement is the energy flow between the second and third chakras or, alternatively, the sexual and power instincts. Initially, undifferentiated excitement can become fear-ridden if the power aspect (third chakra) is not adequately integrated. There is a spectrum here because, without some contact at the far end, the excitement will become over-confidence and may lead to boredom. Fear adds that paradoxical cutting edge to excitement, as long as it isn't overwhelming. A paradox that explains a lot about the attraction to fearful situations, particularly if this involves sexuality. (You could take sex in public places as an example here?)

Obviously, excitement is a big component of the Kundalini experience. The whole ritual structure is designed to have the excitement engaged and channelled upward, and to engage the various chakras in the process. If there are difficulties with the power and aggression instinct at the third chakra then this can become instinctually repetitive, even addictive. Can you see the beginnings of an exploration into dominance, submission and sadomasochism here?

A brief interlude about chakras: Whilst I am using Eastern terms, I want to stress that, at the present time, this is the most convenient way of describing the psychosexual process. Because of the neglected and repressed Western position, we have progressively, over the modern era, sought counsel from the East in matters of the body and sexuality. Many have imported these ideas and they have flourished in Western magical systems, most notably that of Aleister Crowley and others, which hasn't exactly helped the reintegration process. Crowley helped sexual integration in the West in an equivalent fashion to the Nazis and Germanic tradition, I would suggest.

We are now somewhat familiar with terms like chakra and Kundalini, and even some of the Indian pantheon, as they have been extensively used in the New Age, although maybe this is not always the best advertisement. Others have attempted Western models of the psychosexual energetic structure. For example, I know Thorsson has for the Northern Traditions and Dr Christopher Hyatt in a Western idiom and also a more integrated manner, whilst remaining an extension of the magical tradition. I could be tempted to do so from a more depth psychological, or soul perspective, and I have done this to some extent with the discussion earlier in this chapter and with what follows.

Because of this familiarity, I felt at this point it would be wise to continue with the Indian terminology, as maybe this is part of a larger integration process that includes East and West, but also because it is one that you are likely already familiar with. However, I have not entered into any depth into the Indian symbolic appreciation of Kundalini and the chakras, in particular. I have been inclined to assign them a Western perspective and one that is accented toward psychosexuality and on to the body and health in general. Whilst the purists amongst you may well criticise this, in the larger scheme of things I think it is both valid and a contribution to the overall integration process.

One feature of the chakras is that they can be viewed similarly to the steps in the Great Chain of Being. In fact, there is a place for their ultimate assimilation, as when combined they do comprise complementary views of the Perennial Philosophy. One principle we outlined in the Great Chain was that each level supervened the one below; that is, it included yet transcended it. The chakras can be seen in the same light, such that failure of integration of the first leads to instability of grounding if the second is awakened (schizophrenia classically starts in late adolescence), and sexual dysfunction can occur if the third is awakened without integration of the second chakra. In the West, this is an unfortunately common pattern.

There are all sorts of possibilities and combinations that can occur here. I will pick out a few patterns and structures for illustration, but as the topic itself could fill a book it will be necessarily incomplete. What I hope it will demonstrate to you, however, is that the psychosexual pattern as represented in the Eastern Kundalini system is a valid way of looking at these phenomena: I would add that it is a more creative and less pathologised way, as well.

Sadomasochism is a vast subject in and of itself. I have pointed out earlier the various ways that it impacts on pornography and that whilst it holds a position that can be regarded as a perversion, it has a significant presence in mainstream pornography. I would like to give you my take on perversion, which I have commented on earlier. Perversion I consider to have occurred when the content contains sexuality, but this serves another purpose, such as domination or control. It is thus part of a spectrum, where some of the content of the perversion can be seen contained within a primarily sexual context, through to the reverse, where the sexual content is subordinate to another pattern or dynamic.

In this context, we can see that perversion can include sexuality but need not necessarily stem from or be caused by it, a frequently made assumption and error. If we consider issues such as rape, paedophilia, incest and bestiality in this context, we may get a broader view of them as phenomena not so clouded by our own sexual inhibitions and distortions. The clue to this is that these phenomena serve other gods than the one of sexual satisfaction. In dynamic terms, the energy has separated from any creative ascent and is following its own – pathological – course of action. As it cannot move on, it will regress, recycle and repeat.

Sadomasochism is a perversion when it includes such factors as coercion and being against the will of the recipient, but maybe not if these factors (and as identified in "The Porn Report") are excluded. Slightly murky ground, but I would argue that rape, incest and the like do not have a functional connection with mainstream sexuality in the way sadomasochism can, so represent a different class of perversion altogether: In other words, they are fundamentally not perversions, they are crimes. As, of course, is sadomasochism, if it is against the will or desire of the recipient.

In the language of Kundalini, the energy has separated from its healthy ascent and is spiralling away from its creative focus and flowing into a cul de sac. Yet this does form a continuum or spectrum with the mainstream, so it will be educative to see how this can be, as these features are increasingly involved in mainstream porn and even in what I would consider conservative porn movies.

Let us take just one example from "Retreat", that is Emily's spanking of Helen. Firstly, we need to distinguish it from the perversion end of the spectrum, which we can by the fact that the scene flows from and into further sexuality to a completion and mutual satisfaction. There is additionally no criminality, as

Helen can – but does not – disengage, a factor in its own right. There is no coercion, nothing seems to be done against anyone's will and the scene results in mutual sexual satisfaction.

Is this sadomasochistic? Well, yes, of course it is, but at the lighter end of the spectrum. In Tantric terms, it remains within the pattern of ascent of Kundalini, so how do we explain this? The third chakra is involved with Helen first being the aggressor and then the passive recipient, with the roles being reversed in Emily. There are features of initiation here as Helen gives the impression of being versed in both poles of this instinct, whereas Emily, prior to this, seems more the quiet receptive type, and therefore somewhat disempowered. Helen is taking the role of an initiator and this is a ritual or rite of passage. Emily is able to take the role of aggressor, which is subtly relinquished by Helen, and then to learn how to use it.

The outcome is the balance of the aggressive and receptive features of the chakra, which contain the excited sexual energy. When Mick enters, Emily is able to turn her newly found ability toward him and thus move it into the heterosexual end of the sexual spectrum. The energy is free to move on, which it does with further mutual play and a resulting orgasm, which, as an aside, contains some element of the first – nurturing – chakra, although also has some celebratory features between the two women. I would point out that this balance leads Emily to a position where she can move to the romantic level, symbolised by the fourth chakra, and her interaction with Graham.

Were Emily to have withdrawn from this encounter, then her fear would have got the better of the excitement and the aggression-receptivity dynamic of the chakra would not have been engaged. The fear could have been the lesbian connotation, which puts an interesting perspective on homosexuality that it need not be an end or outcome in and of itself, but can serve higher functions. Male homosexuality can also serve this function and has been employed in magical tradition to suit this purpose.

The issues surrounding excitement are great, as they approach yet overcome fear. This is exactly what Tantra proposes because to face the challenge of each chakra can be daunting, even frightening. Although without some level of fear, the emotion and excitement are not engaged, which is essential to any initiatory process, sexual or otherwise. Once activated, the challenges of the chakra are faced and Tantra proposes this be done in a ritual and symbolic manner, often with the assistance of one who has already achieved that integration. It can be seen that both Helen and Mick show features of such integration and attendant wisdom throughout the "Retreat".

This sheds light on the issue of pleasure and pain and indicates that, in many circumstances, they are the ends of a spectrum and profoundly related. In many ways, the pleasure-pain dynamic can be seen to resonate with excitement-fear or fear: excitement is equivalent to pain: pleasure, and they are just of a different conceptual order, with the former having a quality of emotional anticipation and the latter the outcome. A few metaphors may help a further contemplation of these dynamics. The first is the frequent ejaculation of the executed man with hanging. A second is the ecstatic rapture of the witch – or nun – burnt at the stake. What about the use of flagellation in religious practice?

This completes the tour of the instinctual and emotional levels as we move to the fourth chakra: the heart. The heart chakra reflects the level of Romantic Love in the West, or the second union or conjunction of opposites in alchemy. The heart itself has four chambers, in two pairs (doesn't that pattern just keep cropping up!) and represents a level of personal integration marked by balance, integrated emotion, compassion and a stage of love; though maybe only the first. The Kundalini energy has risen above the animalistic instinct and reached a distinctly human level, although many would argue that some animal species – particularly domestic ones – can also reach this level.

Is this the level of the integrated soul? I think not, there is more work to do, alas! Although it does augur well for relationships, family and the like, and offers a level of sexual development that I believe many of the human race would still aspire to if the amount of romantic rubbish on the stands is anything to go by. Maybe those who consume this material need to get down and dirty, deal with the three prior chakras and get them integrated so that they can meet the fourth in their real lives and not simply in (screen) projection.

The fifth chakra is located at the throat and may be associated with both the thyroid and thymus glands in the body. The thyroid is a hormonal gland and the thymus somewhat mysteriously involved in the immune system. Again, we see these connections between the hormone and immune systems, somewhat more directly at this level, which may have symbolic relevance.

The throat chakra is – obviously – about expression. I would suggest that it is also the centre of creativity and the "creative instinct" of Jung that marks us as human. If this is the case it indicates a level of soul development beyond the heart, which I consider significant. The expression is not just verbal, although it adds an interesting dimension to the acts of sex and love, either directly in the act itself or surrounding it with creative acts such as poetry. My personal impression is that creative acts like poetry are often engaged with the achievement of heart integration and romantic love. This can be seen to support romanticism, but I would suggest it also represents a creative desire for the psychosexual energy to move on even further in its development. It is common to see such an enigmatic and problematic relationship between the demands of creativity and romantic ideals in the artist.

We have already explored the sixth chakra in some detail (chapter eight) and it may be of interest to recall this as we now see it in the context of the culmination of the five that preceded it. The third eye, when 'opened' – that is, when pierced by the psychosexual arrow of Kundalini – is related to psychic abilities. This can also be an accidental opening and thus disordered. One example is the poltergeist phenomenon, known to be strongly associated with adolescent girls prior to the onset of sexual activity.

It is also the domain of the witch and the magician and gives us an appreciation of their use of sexual activities. In many ways, these groups are the Western equivalent of the Tantric practitioner. The demand for the magical practitioner is that he, or she, has integrated the levels below such that the energetic manipulation they partake in will be creative and purposeful rather than dark and destructive. Maybe this is why, in the East, these practices are seen to open psychic abilities, but the practitioner is implored to move beyond (to the seventh chakra), as they can be subtle and seductive. Maybe this is the seat of the imagery and ideas that inform the artist and which erotic art can excite and open. Maybe that is the highest function or aesthetic of porn?

At the physical level the sixth chakra is quintessentially associated with the nervous system, although one imbued with psychic potential and thus subtle levels to the nervous system that transcend the physical brain. Let me add a little speculation in this regard, extending from known facts. The sixth chakra, although located within the brain, is the summit of the hormonal control of the body, such that from here it is difficult to distinguish and differentiate hormone, immune and nervous system function. I would further add that the electrical activity within the brain and beyond remains a relative mystery in the Western world, yet might be the energetic perspective that unites these differing aspects, so as to move on.

Here also the two poles of the autonomic nervous system, the sympathetic and parasympathetic, the active and passive, come together. Does the subtlety of mood reflect this higher integration? Is this the final resting place of emotion? How are all these interconnected? The view from the West is limited in this respect, maybe it would be wise and prescient to explore the wisdom of the East and appreciate the symbolic expression and how it informs us ...

The expression of the sixth chakra is considered nectar, the elixir of life, and the fountain of youth or elan vital. The image may be wine, honey or mead, depending on the culture, yet with obvious overlap and similarity. These images are reflected in the Eucharist of the Church, but are not confined there. They are also present in erotic sexuality and more deeply so in pornography. It is our challenge to dig into the mire of the prima materia (alchemy) to discover and rescue the divine. To these images and symbols, we will return.

As this is the "seat of the soul" and the final chakra within the body, the sixth chakra contains the opposites of male and female in a more subtle form than the lower chakras: In fact, there is a progressive development in this subtlety matching that of the "subtle bodies" of the East. In the West, I would cite this as the place of the third conjunction or union of alchemy, which is nominated as differentiated mature or adult love. Of interest is the difference of this perspective from Romantic Love. This is a love of the adult that I would term Erotic Love in its true and mature form, unsullied by lesser consideration. It is awkward to use this term when it has suffered such debasement, reflecting comments earlier about myth, cult and ecstasy, and their usage, but I feel it must be done.

This erotic perspective engages the aesthetic, and is reflected in an unconditioned morality. It is the extreme yet attainable end of where the pornographic phenomenon can take us, when invited, informed and guided by the goddess of love on her journey to her union with the god.

This, of course, opens up the second half of the "Retreat" movie. Does it explore these issues at any depth? I suspect it does and it would be tempting to begin an exploration of the remaining scenes to tease out the issues we have discussed to date. Talking of teasing, I am going to do that to you, but I am not going to do that – just yet. Such an approach would be linear and serve to unite the imagery and symbols in the scenes with the model we have been discussing to date. This would be useful but would subtly defeat one of the purposes of this work: to fully restore psychosexuality to the West.

I have given an indication of how we are going to do this; it is embedded in the unions and conjunctions of alchemy referred to in the above chapter. We are going to explore these energetic features of the East more deeply within our own Western and Northern mythology, within the sexuality of the Western world itself and as exemplified in porn. It is from this expanded and more culturally appropriate perspective that we will be looking further at the "Retreat".

The sixth chakra marks the end of the journey of the soul as the spiritual aspect – or spark – within the individual. Spark is an interesting term, it is energetic and bright, and this is what the dormant Kundalini is in potential. The soul at this level still retains the sense of dualism, male and female, as indicated by the symbols although in a very unified form. This creates the paradoxical views of the gender of the soul that we explored earlier, yet the paradox remains. It depends on how and at which level it is viewed, and from which position (or discipline). In a sense, we are now moving beyond a gender perspective, as the soul moves on.

The seventh chakra is above the head and is referred to as the crown. Here the energy transcends the personal and individual, and connects with the transpersonal, collective or spiritual. Here Shakti unites with Shiva and dissolves in the world of spirit. In Christian terms, this is the love of agape as opposed to eros. In my terms, it is the undifferentiated love that matures from eros and is fundamentally a unity beyond dualism. In alchemy, this is the fourth and final conjunction and is represented symbolically as the mysterious androgyne.

From these exalted heights, let me complete this chapter by being both a little irreverent, but also by anticipating what is to come. The Christian perspective of agape (pronounced 'agga-pay', from the Greek) is the love-feast symbolised by the final supper; hence the Eucharist. The Eucharist is characterised by the bread and wine: note the white and red symbolism, with the white as the nurturing and feminine bread of the first chakra and the red wine the nectar of the sixth, maybe more masculine and generally reflective of the inner, esoteric symbolism of white and red we earlier discussed.

Yet there is more. (Isn't there always?) The wine is contained in the – feminine – chalice and drunk through the mouth, of course. Agape in the English is spelled the same and means "open mouthed in wonder or expectation" (Oxford English Dictionary). Does this put a different slant on the porn climax of ejaculation into the mouth? We will return. I promise.

When I turned to the dictionary for the definition of agape (the English "open mouthed") the first page I opened had 'bisexual' at the top: An intuition of the androgyne as a more appropriate symbol? After all, there is no Greek god of agape, but there is one for eros, the god Eros himself to whom we shall now turn.

Off Cut

Jan's personal assistant, Mel, had just left his office and it was the end of an administrative day, so Jan went to the seating well near the window, put on some light jazz to match the mood, and poured himself a reasonable malt before settling into the folds of the Chesterfield. He looked at the memo: the weekend at the Retreat had finally been booked some three weeks hence. There were two absentees, neither of which surprised him.

Jan had noticed Emily's reticence at the Club and it was known in the trade that Mark, her partner, wanted her to do lesbian roles exclusively if she were to stay in the business. Mark had been an actor for a while, but had worked in the business for only a short time when his mainstream acting career started to wane. He had not been particularly successful there either, although that is where he met Em on a set. Now in the Real Estate business, and with Joe's arrival, Jan felt this was part of an unacknowledged exit strategy. Jan knew that Emily's involvement in the overall project might be short-lived because Mark's insecurities were palpable during filming, but she both fitted the part and her not altogether unexpected withdrawal did fit his wider dramatic intention with the whole project.

Similarly, Jan knew that Graham was going to Budapest for more than a shoot. Even during filming of "Retreat" Graham had brought the interactions with Jan around to directorship issues whenever they were alone. Jan did have some concern about his involvement with the particular group he was being courted by, as they had a reputation for procuring unknowns and sometimes the normal industry boundaries were stretched a little. He was a little uneasy with this and its impact on the industry as a whole, so had expressed his feelings to Graham, but to little avail; maybe his views might help Graham sanitise that segment of the industry though.

Unlike Emily's position, Graham's interests were not something Jan was aware of at casting. The fact that he was now withdrawing did add to the symbolism of the first half of "Retreat" and fitted where the wider project was to go. It saved Jan having to actively exclude him should he have warmed further to the project. However, and because of his background, Jan had a reasonable appreciation of their relative states of psychological maturity – which was one reason they were selected for their respective parts – so the outcome was both not a surprise and fitted well onto the broader canvas he was painting. Yet what exactly was this canvas? Did Jan actually know, or was he just following his creative instinct? He was on a little unsettled ground, as the malt warmed his stomach and gave him some temporary relief. It was time to take stock and do a little more reflection. He had no evening commitment so would probably just go to the corner Bistro, then have a light meal and early night after his musing.

The unsettled ground stemmed from the last meeting with the group. Jan had decided to end the evening when it became apparent that their involvement in the second half of the film was still barely integrated, if at all. There was always Graham's departure as a ready excuse and he decided to employ it when this lack of integration became apparent. He hoped that the intervening time would help this, but he was a little nervous that it might not. So, when Mel gave him the final memo it did settle his nerves a little to see that all the principal porn stars of that section had agreed to attend and the extras were on Club duty, if needed. Of course, their positive response may have been because of the anticipated Voluptas project, but this simply endorsed his increasing comfort; they would hardly want to step into Voluptas if they hadn't come to terms with "Retreat" or even become a little excited about it!

Jan's thoughts went to Voluptas for a period. As a project, it depended in a fundamental manner on the right participants, and this is why he had been so careful in his casting. Mick and Helen had been relatively easy and were signed up fairly early on. Carole didn't take much persuasion either, as Jan was aware that she was looking for further professional – and probably personal development – that made her ideal, because he knew that she did not want to forego her sexual expression; one reason she had declined some mainstream advances. Paul, he had known in the mainstream. Because of his sexual prowess, he had moved into porn on occasion, which ultimately had lessened his mainstream opportunities. He was thus a little disillusioned, but Jan was watching his development closely, as their relationship was quite close – it could be described as intimate – and when he offered Paul the part, he knew that at an obvious level, this would give him an opportunity to say goodbye to a mainstream that was still too conventional.

Voluptas had been sketched out into some models from Jan's creative mind, with which he now felt comfortable. The next stage would be to run some of the ideas and a couple of preliminary scenes across the group at the forthcoming weekend. He could explore his ideas a little further in the intervening period, now that he knew he had a group he could work with. If that had not been the case, maybe his own professional development would have taken a different turn. He could always continue with the style of "Retreat", as the initial response from the industry was very good – he may even pick up an award or two – and sales were steadily increasing. He knew if he were to do this, he might be relatively successful, but he would also become bored and then knew he would want to find fresh pastures.

Another sip: there was a deeper level of unease in his body that was apparent now that all the other issues had settled comfortably into place. Because he did now feel settled about the first three scenes; well, four, if he considered the kitchen scene and it amused him that he actually saw it as part of scene three. He smiled at himself over this. They had gone well and achieved several things. They had conformed to the relative standards of porn, so would be familiar to the viewer. They had defined the dramatic and narrative aspects he had introduced. Most importantly, they had provided a vehicle of development of the more emotional aspects of sexuality, and the stars had embraced this, even down to the departure of Emily and Graham being now both literal and symbolic.

Also, the first scenes necessitated the use of a creative medium to amplify the emotional content and convey this to the viewer. He had spent a lot of time wrestling with voice-overs as a method. It had worked; because there was a balance of this with the actual bridging dialogue, which obviously was well utilised in narrative porn, and he had used the actual stars' voices. It had thus provided access to the more feeling and sensual areas of their responses to the sex scenes. Even though this was scripted, he trusted he had the sexuality portrayed in such a way that it matched the acting and verbal expression. It was a technique he could now employ more and he felt his approach, and maybe the industry itself, demanded this sort of insight into areas of sensuality and emotion that simple sexual portrayal found difficult and was therefore incomplete. At this level he was settled, so what was the deep unease?

Jan scanned a little of his background and his profound association with and interest in his own sexual development. Over a generation, this extended into various connected fields, such as spiritual approaches that employed sexuality and Western magical traditions. As his own professional development had allowed this movement from more mainstream film production – even though he always explored the edges of human behaviour – it was not without risk. His professional status would come under question, even assault, as he now positioned himself firmly within the pornographic genre.

Jan was actually surprised about the lack of challenge, but it pleased him. Maybe he had enough experience and respect to have gone beyond the criticism and even condemnation he thought he might attract. Of course, there was some, but this was from sections of his profession and media that may inadvertently endorse his transition; indeed, most of his more esteemed colleagues who had counselled him against were now watching his career with interest. Some remained as friends and others in active association; he was proving something of a trailblazer.

Now this is where the unease surfaces: Maybe he has taken it too far, too quickly? Whilst the porn stars were coming to the weekend, it may be for other diverse reasons and he was yet to assess how much they 'got' what he was trying to achieve, which would be critical to and inform the future project. More than he had hitherto wanted or expected, he now realised he had a team approach to maintain and deal with. This he had not initially expected, but he realised that may be a fortuitous consequence of the project and inherent process; it would give him some active and vital ingredients to work with.

Which was what? The first few scenes were relatively straightforward; they had simply taken the routines of porn to explore the theme of romantic love and its development from the instinctual and base emotional levels of sexuality. Although incomplete at this point, because maybe it actually required the later scenes to assist any such 'completion', it was not too hard to follow. Even if Emily and Graham were anticipated 'causalities' at this point and as reflected in the movie, did that mean that the second half was too ambitious? Or, more concerning, was his grasp of what the second half was hoping to achieve itself too ambitious? To consider these questions he felt he needed to re-examine exactly what he was intending to achieve, so that his retrospective analysis of "Retreat" may be more complete, but also in anticipation of the forthcoming weekend.

One of the criticisms of "Retreat", voiced by several in the media, was that the latter scenes had been constructed to fit a theory of sexuality of Jan's making. At one level, this seemed a valid criticism and to be the case, but Jan knew it not to be true, although his protestations of this fact fell on deaf ears so he simply became silent on this point. What he had understood was that the romantic stage of the development of love from sexuality needed understanding in a more differentiated light than was customary in the modern culture, but that was presently quite limited. This limitation did not just extend to the various fields, professions and disciplines that had some input into sexuality, or even dictated it; but it also extended to its limitation to the individual and personal position. From a cross-cultural and spiritual perspective, he found this regrettable.

Jan had undertaken a counselling relationship with a retired priest when he came to this point in his own sexual development and understanding of it. This had helped him make the move into an exploration of symbolism, ritual and magical practice, both personally and intellectually. It had been a very rewarding move, but for many years he had kept it separate from his professional activities, as he felt it was incommensurate with it. Then, as the pendulum in many societal and cultural areas seemed to swing again, he felt it was not only time to bridge this separation, but that he may have a vocational place in a broader reconciliation, which he felt he had achieved personally.

In essence, this marked the content of the second half of "Retreat", which represented his initial foray into this more collective reconciliation. As such, and as dictated by these deeper movements into his own psyche, he had determined not to pre-plan the last three scenes beyond their initial outline. Unknown to the stars, he actually did not have a clear idea about how the scenes would unravel or the sexual detail, but followed his feelings and deeper intuition as each scene unfolded. He also followed the sequence he asked his actors to take; that is, to undertake each scene in the chronological order they appeared in the movie. In this way, he could also enter into the process with them and work with what emerged. This approach was, of course, unknown to the stars, although he knew Paul might have some idea.

By a judicious use of setting – for which the Club was initially ideal – and the employment of ritual he knew he could allow this process with more spontaneity than he would otherwise have considered. This then allowed him to enter into the creative process at a level that was beyond the personal and which the stars could more easily identify with, as they were accustomed to leaving such personal and emotional issues in the change room of a porn set. Jan appreciated that such a break was more problematic within the public mainstream – he had to keep the viewer in mind in this respect – but it was equally important that these transpersonal dimensions could be approached on their own terms. He had paid great attention to detail in the two connected Club scenes, by using props that were familiar to both stars and the genre, but which could also provide that ritualistic edge that the scenes demanded. The inclusion of that musical piece he had recently produced added a nice touch, he thought!

Once within the scenes, it had become a little like a dream. He felt he was directing in response to forces that were flowing beyond him, sometimes through and including him, other times manifesting in the play of the actors and the scenes themselves. This allowed him to be like an artist and to introduce his ideas into the play as it unfolded, to mould them into the unravelling scenes and give a shape and definition in response to the overall pattern in which he felt they were all enveloped. This is what made the last scene so pleasing to him; although it followed and was built on what had preceded it, there was a sense that the personal was both included yet also transcended. A tear came to his eye as he reflected on this, calmed by a sip from the malt.

Now he felt settled. No, it had not been too ambitious to have made this step. If his charges had made similar steps with their integration then the review of the movie coming up in three weeks would be an ideal platform to Voluptas. He could let the matter rest now he felt, with one minor yet important exception: the viewer.

This was the unknown that Jan knew he would have to live with for a while longer yet. The initial reviews had been a bit more critical than the response that was coming from the market. Sales were good and the various blogs that Mel had explored indicated there were a sizable percentage of those who had viewed "Retreat" who were on a similar wavelength to him and what he was trying to achieve. This warmed him; it made him settled for the next stage. Yet this made him furrow his brow for a moment. Because, how oh how, was he going to bring the viewer into the picture, maybe not just symbolically, but also literally? Was the literal that it may just encourage the viewer to undertake steps in his and her literal sexual exploration to engage the deeper transpersonal dimensions in their own lives? Or did it demand some more detailed connection with the viewer?

As yet Jan did not know. He determined to create some possibilities in this regard and then leave it up to spirit to determine; such was his role as the magus.

10

Sexy Myths

There is one Greek myth, with a Roman equivalent, that contains a lot of the features we explored in the previous chapter and reinforces the profound and deep connection of mythic structure beyond cultural and national boundaries. That the myths of the East are the basis of ritual and initiatory sexual practice, aimed at personal and spiritual evolution, is an indication that we have a lost tradition of such sexual wisdom in the West. Further, this wisdom is hidden within the esoteric undercurrents of Christianity and the aeon, and because of its psychic nature, such wisdom is also present in the magical traditions. As the Greek myths precede Christianity there may be much hidden sexuality present in symbolic form.

It is of interest that I had to resort to an old work for the bridging myth of Psyche and Eros that I wanted to use to position sexuality within the Western Tradition. The modern works in my library did not lay it out in its complete form, so I resorted to Thomas Bullfinch (1796 – 1867) and the edition of his mythology, called Bullfinch's Mythology, published in 1978. I am going to greatly abridge and précis the myth by removing a lot of detail, such as the various tasks Aphrodite imposes on Psyche, to keep to the main thrust of the tale relevant to the discussion to hand; although there will not be exclusion of anything that might negate the subsequent discussion. I am also going to use the Greek names in the myth, not the Roman ones, which, quite appropriately, Bullfinch treats synonymously.

A certain king and queen had three daughters, the third of whom was very beautiful, in contrast to those of her sisters. She was given the sort of homage due to the goddess of beauty herself, Aphrodite, who was not pleased that a mortal was receiving such attention that should be due to the immortal goddess herself. Aphrodite enlisted the help of her son, Eros, instructing him to instil in the virgin a lowly passion to negate the present exultation.

Eros took the water from two fountains, one sweet and the other bitter, on his task. A mischievous fellow, with his winged form, bow and arrow, he found Psyche asleep and shed a few drops of bitter water on her lips and touched her side with an arrow. Psyche awoke and looked to Eros who, being invisible, was somewhat confused and wounded himself with his own arrow. As amends, he poured some of the sweet balmy water on Psyche's hair before leaving.

Now it seemed that Psyche was cursed because, although she retained her beauty, she was shunned by Aphrodite and attracted no suitor. Her family consulted the god Apollo in his function as an oracle, and were told: "The virgin is destined for the bride of no mortal lover. Her future husband awaits her on top of a mountain. He is a monster whom neither gods nor men can resist."

Psyche demanded she be taken to the mountain, yet the procession was more like a funeral than a bridal one. There she ascended and we move into an 'altered state of consciousness' with fountains, a palace and the like. This is obviously the domain of the gods.

Her husband came to her at night in darkness and, after preliminaries of bathing, foods, perfumes and music; he then embraced her in love, which inspired a passion in Psyche. He commanded she make no attempt to see him, declaring the risk it incurred to his love for and of her. This quietened Psyche ... for a time.

Her sisters were to place mischief by reminding Psyche of the oracle and the monster description. Whilst she resisted this, it played on her mind and one night she took a lamp and gazed on his beauty. A drop of oil fell from the lamp and awakened him:

"O foolish Psyche, is it thus you repay my love? I inflict no other punishment on you than to leave you forever. Love cannot dwell with suspicion."

As in all the best fairy tales the magnificent surroundings dissolved and Psyche is back in her family's company.

There follows scenes of Psyche trying to make peace with Aphrodite, who sets her seemingly impossible tasks that are achieved with the assistance of the gods, as her son lies in a wounded condition following the accident with the lamp. The last task is dire, as Aphrodite gives her a box with the instruction to engage the goddess Persephone, who was in the underworld, with the words:

"My mistress Aphrodite desires you send her a little of your beauty, for in tending her sick son she has lost some of her own."

Psyche achieves the impossible task yet, contrary to instruction, she looks in the box, keen to gain some of *the contents to attract her husband back. The consequence was she fell into a profound sleep or stupor. But Eros, now recovering and missing his beloved Psyche, finds her and returns the sleep from her body to the box, touches her with his arrow and instructs her to complete his mother's task.*

In the meantime, Eros appeals to Zeus with a supplication, who then won the consent of Aphrodite in the matter. Hermes was instructed to bring Psyche to Olympus, where Zeus gave her ambrosia to drink. She thus became immortal and was united with Eros in eternity.

(After Bullfinch's Mythology: Cupid [Eros] and Psyche)

Boy, is this a loaded myth or what! Notwithstanding the similarity to other myths and fairy tales, such as Snow White and Cinderella, let us look at some of the salient features; although there is much we must necessarily omit. As a porn-inspired aside: I wonder what Snow White was up to in the forest with seven dwarfs?

There are considerable degrees of overlap regarding beauty, both here and beyond. I am reminded of Pandora and the further association with the vase, with it being either opened or looked into: a basis of and in alchemy, perhaps? Related to this myth is the goddess Persephone, daughter of Demeter, who has to spend a period of the year in the company of Hades in the underworld. This is a reflection of the seasonal and agricultural cycle, and is the source of a major mystery tradition in Greece. Persephone resonates with the goddess Shakti, as indeed does Psyche herself. Added to this is the name itself: Psyche is synonymous with Soul.

The mountain reminds us of Mount Cithaeron where Teiresias encountered Zeus and Hera in conflict, or even Mount Olympus, the home of the gods. It is also a significant metaphor of the spinal column up which Shakti ascends and is not unlike Psyche's journey, reinforced as it is by the transcendent and altered state quality of the atmosphere at the top, where she unites with her divine lover. The "husband" aspect may be a Christian interpolation, I would suggest, to sanitise the sexuality. This is all quite closely connected, isn't it? An additional twist is the funeral atmosphere at the beginning, which may indicate that Psyche is symbolically dying to her old way of life, or resonate with the more complex image of the goddess that is inclusive of Kali in the Indian version.

The description of Psyche's pre-nuptials suggests a Tantric ritual, doesn't it? All the necessary elements are there. Of all the fluids present, I would like to focus on the vases from the two fountains and the ambrosia at the end of the myth. At the beginning, the water from the two fountains recalls the two channels of the spinal cord in Tantra and even the blood from the two sides of the severed spine of Medusa. Eros drops some (the bitter) on her lips and pours some (the sweet) into her hair at the end of her 'awakening'. Does this remind you of the arousal of Kundalini? Is the second draught a 'healing' balance to the effects of the first? However, it is to the pornography perspective that I wish to draw your attention; how much can this be represented by ejaculation into the mouth and onto the face and hair?

The ambrosia at the end of the myth is also symbolically significant. Ambrosia: "Food of the gods; anything delightful to taste or smell; bee-bread." (Oxford English Dictionary.) The ambrosia provides Psyche with immortality and one of the terms for the substance released at the completion of Kundalini's ascent is the "elixir of life". The bee-bread recalls another association of this elixir, that is, with nectar, honey or mead. The porn twist ... do I need to say it? Ambrosia is white after all.

Finally, let's return to Eros himself. Eros is a god; he is immortal and invisible, as indeed the gods are – I, for one, don't see them too often! Psyche seems to go through a ritual of awakening symbolised as a marriage and being of two stages. I would suggest the first is almost mundane and possibly representing the Lesser Work of alchemy, as it remains conditional and torn asunder by suspicion. Although a little tangential, how often is romantic love destroyed – or awakened from its illusion – by doubt and jealousy as the projections flounder? This seems to awaken Psyche further, such that her tasks take her into the underworld and a higher order of union with Eros.

Psyche is mortal and becomes immortal. Eros is always immortal. It becomes a union eternal, an inner union of male and female, god and human, and the human raised to the divine. Shakti is the woman fallen into creation who ascends to divine consciousness. Maybe that is Eve's function too, but the patriarchal Church got hold of the myth, truncated and distorted it. How different is that outcome from the one we have and are exploring? The cross-relationships are impressive indeed and help to liberate us from the repressive grip of the patriarchy.

As is the magical thinking: You might have got a bit pissed off with me in earlier chapters with the focus on analogue thinking, which seemed to lead to confusion or, more correctly, into an appreciation of paradox. But maybe now you can see that the world is paradoxical, if we take a symbolic perspective that is cyclical and deeper than the linear and rational one. Analogue thinking is what I have employed in a more creative way here than with the simple gender associations I have given to date. It is flexible and reveals the paradox and mystery of some of their secrets, at least those the gods allow!

There's more ... but I want to dip into Dionysus before we move culture. Alain Danielou is one scholar who has extensively explored the relationship between Shiva and Dionysus. This raises an interesting question: Does the union of Eros and Psyche take us to the sixth chakra only? Does the union of Dionysus with all aspects of the goddess take us into the transcendent 'beyond' of the seventh chakra?

Here are some of the features of Dionysus that Danielou outlines. Dionysus is of mixed birth – Zeus and the mortal Semele – and is the god of ecstasy who was translated into the devil by Christianity. His perspective is of excess in the light of health, such as eating after fasting. Like Eros, he has a night mode, but one of balance as his humour precludes a depressive attitude and marks the deep emotionality of his view of life, as well as maybe making a few statements about how to treat depression! He passed through a mad phase in adolescence and was cured by Cybele, the mother of vegetation, and subsequently becomes a god. This associates him with the mysterious Eleusinian mysteries of Greece, which was a Demeter cult and overlaps one of Psyche's tasks, as indicated above.

This role of madness in transformation relates back to our comments on the first and second chakras in the previous chapter, but also indicates its role in such transformation and is fundamentally shamanic in orientation. Dionysus is a liberator of souls by revolution. This pagan view doesn't react to differences, as we do with monotheism and the rational patriarchy, because it is based on plurality and can deal with paradoxes and opposites. It can be seen why Dionysus is favoured amongst women, particularly when they are inclined to pull down the repressive king, the voyeur in the tree, and tear him limb from limb!

Danielou identifies Dionysus strongly with Shiva and with the soul complex, inclusive of the body. Shiva is profoundly connected with nature and may even be a pre-agricultural figure, which shamanism would also point toward. Shiva can be seen as a forest spirit, lustful and naked. His symbol is the lingum, or phallus. He is the principle of life.

This move to exploring Dionysus is to show the deep connection he has with Tantra and the figure of Shiva. In this respect, and as I have indicated, he provides a deeper or more transcendent view of the divine principle that defines the soul in terms of the erotic, personal and psychosexuality. I would suggest that Dionysus provides a more collective and spiritual perspective that unites with all of the feminine principle, as exemplified in his mysteries. It is possible that at this level the orgies and complex sexual situations portrayed in porn are more Dionysian than Erotic and take us beyond individual eroticism.

Whilst orgiastic activities may appear to lack the emotional dimension that defines the erotic, I would argue that the emotional is taken to a fuller ecstatic level by the engagement of the Dionysian and finally liberates psychosexuality from the confines of the personal. In a profound manner, the divine madness of the seventh chakra is connected to the insanity that can occur at the first. Here the snake swallows its own tail. It is the fundamental energetic perspective of the cosmos that is embraced here. Enough, otherwise I'll be accused of mysticism!

I have made a little allusion to the Christian undercurrents above, mainly from a deprecatory point of view; that is, where I think they may be distortions in the presentation of the Jesus and creation myths as presented to us. I do think that the story of Jesus is essentially mythic, irrespective of any historical considerations. Why? Because it has many of the mythic themes we have explored and overlaps some, his semi-divine birth being but one example.

Maybe I'm overstepping the mark, but it would not be too difficult to reconstruct a sexual theme in the myth. We already have stories of healing, madness and altered states, plus the enigmatic various "Marys". I would suggest that Mary Magdalene may have had a Tantric relationship with Jesus and that the washing of his feet with precious perfumed oil is deeply symbolic. In some views, the feet are considered to symbolise the first chakra and, in others, be connected to the second; these are thus related themes. There is also a direct Tantric undercurrent that passes through the Christian tradition in the form of the Grail legends.

With that brief but loaded interlude, let's move to the Northern Traditions. In pre-Christian Europe, the essential division was between the peoples North of the Alps and those South of them. Collectively we might term these Northern peoples Teutonic, which, in the widest sense, includes the Scandinavian, Germanic and Anglo-Saxon races. The Celtic race began in Northern Europe, migrated to Britain and became contracted to the West of England, Wales and Ireland with the arrival of the Anglo-Saxons, after the Romans vacated in the fifth century. In many ways, in Britain, the Anglo-Saxons subsumed the Celtic culture. With the Viking age (eighth to eleventh centuries) there was a significant occupancy of Scotland, such that the Scottish people (originally an Irish tribe, the Picts being more indigenous to Scotland) could be considered predominantly Scandinavian. The Vikings extended their activity to the West of Britain and Ireland, so have infused and diluted the Celtic Tradition there too. The Vikings were supposedly noted for their "rape and pillage" style of invasion, although the evidence is that this was far more harmonious and integrated than we have been given to believe; a question of the rewriting of history to suit the victor, perhaps?

Around the time of Jesus, the Romans had a huge empire that extended from Palestine and to Britain, but not to Scandinavia and significant areas of Germany. Palestine and Britain were thus trouble spots, being at the edge of that civilisation. What isn't clearly known in our history is that the conflict between the Teutons and Romans was extensive in time and place, such that it seems almost an accident of history that Rome came out on top. The Teutons even reached as far as Greece on at least one occasion.

The cult (word chosen carefully) of Christianity was established in Rome progressively, and, by the time of the departure from Britain, was the adopted state religion. Thus, it was to some degree established in Britain at that time; certainly, the earlier myths surrounding Merlin and Arthur hint at the transition from the "Old Ways" (paganism) to Christianity. In Scandinavia, it was a different matter; the change only really occurred at an overt level after the Viking era, and it can be argued that the ruling classes remained duplicitous in their religious beliefs, as well as the general population retained the old traditions with less conflict of interest. Iceland, from where a significant corpus of tradition comes, was 'converted' even later. The Poetic Edda is a manuscript written in 1270, and many stories pre-date Christianity, allowing a window into the pagan beliefs of the North. Snorri Sturluson, who had a profound interest in the Viking age, although he was Christian, wrote the Prose Edda slightly earlier.

We are left with a body of tradition comprising myth, poetry and history that is less influenced by Roman Christianity the further north we get. This tradition is also retained in the esoteric traditions that may have been overtly Christian, but covertly eclectic, as well as being present in the uneducated and folk classes. I would argue that Roman Christianity is a long way from the mythic and historical patterns lain down at the time of Jesus and retained in the Gnostic Traditions of the Middle East, where there are significant erotic treatises. These works were systematically obliterated in the early centuries of Christianity and have only significantly come to light from 1945 with the finding of the Nag Hammadi Gnostic corpus.

Western culture is an amalgam of all this, but does not significantly acknowledge the Northern influence. There has been an attempt over recent centuries, aided by German scholars, artists and philosophers, to restore the balance. This received a major setback with the events of the twentieth century, particularly the Second World War, when use was made of myth and legend with the support of magical tradition and the runes. This was in an inverted and distorted way and, at a collective level, a chakric interpretation of events might be of interest. We won't go down that road, but I will simply state that the examination and integration of Northern Tradition in Western culture is long overdue.

This is all by way of an integration of earlier comments and a major introduction to the traditions of the North. The dominant figure in myth is Odin, alternatively called Wotan in Germany, or Woden in Britain. He cuts an imposing figure, not unlike Zeus, but with distinctly more direct contact with the human realm. (Zeus' contact with humankind was more indirect, mainly via the genitals of mortal women!) He actually presents more as a composite shamanic figure and this is portrayed clearly in his myth of initiation where he spent nine days hanging from an ash tree to there discover the runes and the wisdom of the underworld, for which he sacrificed an eye. This myth is worth reading, not only because of the parallels with Jesus and the crucifixion, but because it is a window into a pagan culture with a profound tradition that is distinctly shamanic.

Odin is a semi-invisible figure with his one eye partially hidden by a large hat and his body in a greatcoat or cape. The term "din" could refer to a "god-man", or the sort of product we are becoming used to: someone born of the union of a god and a human. Odin was the product of a proto-god and a giantess in a magical union. (Incidentally, the original name of Merlin was Myrddin.) Odin resided or resides in Asgard, the equivalent of Mount Olympus of the Greek gods, and rules the Aesir, or gods. These are the gods of kings, judges and magicians.

The Aesir are seemingly constantly in conflict with the Vanir, with uneasy truces, although this doesn't seem to stop interchange, particularly if sexual! The Vanir are the gods of craftsman and farmers, the warrior class being somewhere between the two but more inclined with the Aesir, with the hall of Valhalla reserved for those who die in a distinguished and heroic manner. The Vanir have their own magic, which is distinctly more sexual and feminine, and centred on the goddess Freya and her twin brother Frey, which may say something about Merlin's relationship with his sister! Freya is the goddess of physical health, eroticism, fertility and magic. This magic is also associated with trance and altered states of consciousness, so is distinctly shamanic as well. Odin was 'taught' – an interesting euphemism – this magic by Freya, which indicates a complexity in her sexual proclivities and her role as Shakti maybe. This magic can be traced through witchcraft into the modern variant of Wicca.

What is already emerging are levels of balance that pre-date Christianity and the patriarchy, and can further inform us in the next stage of our cultural development, the Age of Aquarius, into which we are now progressing. There is a balance of magic, masculine and feminine and the need for interchange. These represent the "right hand" and "left hand paths", respectively. There is a balance of male and female amongst the gods and goddesses, which is reflected in Northern society even to this day. My first visit to Sweden was quite an insight in this regard.

This equality also extends to the sexual: Within the Northern

Traditions sexuality is ruled by a goddess and not a god. There is a frequent interchange between the gods and goddesses, and the gods (and goddesses) with the human world. It doesn't stop there; the elves and dwarfs also get into the act. Freya even sleeps with four dwarfs to obtain a precious necklace. This may provide an interesting turn to the gang bang, as well as the term "pearl necklace", when the man ejaculates on the woman's exposed neck. Thus, sexuality literally saturates the myths, legends and sagas, or heroic narratives. It is unfortunate that the modern reintroduction of Northern myths, "Lord of the Rings", is notably devoid of sexuality. Maybe that is because the author was a devout Catholic? If so, Tolkien has done much to further the Roman cause in the reintegration of the Northern Traditions. In such an otherwise magnificent work, which may yet achieve the status of national myth, I find the exclusion of sexuality a great shame. Maybe the pornographic movie saga, "Lady of the Rings", balances this omission a little; although you may realise by now the ring is not referring to an item of jewellery!

Edred Thorsson is one commentator who considers that the relationship between Odin and Freya is magical and not simply romantic. He emphasises that Freya is not the feminine aspect of Odin and vice versa, pointing to the complexity of the figures themselves and facets that indicate this contra-sexuality to have been already integrated. This puts the relationship into a higher dimension and in the upper chakras. As the goddess of wealth, she is also associated with gold, the ultimate achievement of alchemy. Because of the multiplicity and diversity of their respective sexualities, they are even above the union symbolised by Eros and Psyche. This Dionysian flavour provides a magical reinforcement of the complexities so often portrayed in porn that extends beyond the flagrant and degenerative sexual manner in which threesomes, gang bangs and orgies are often viewed.

Let's have a further look at the literal nature of some sexual and porn terms, starting with Frigg, or Frigga, a goddess of the Aesir who was also the wife of Odin and a prophetess into the bargain. Reminds you a bit of Zeus and he gets around a little, does Odin! Mind you, both are pre-Christian gods, ones who rule their respective pantheons and have a distinctly overt and polymorphous sexuality. Although these guys of the North are by no means sexist, have a look as to what their various partners get up to; highly democratic and distinctly erotic in the magical sense, if not pornographic!

When I was growing up in England, we had a term for fucking called "frigging"; I note it is still in use.

Let's return to the word cunt, which we had some fun with in chapter five, so here's a little more. (Swear words are a bit like porn, they identify the underbelly of society.) How is the shape of the Kenaz rune similar to that of the female genitals, as described by Freya Aswynn? (You might find this lady's name interesting now.) Well, take the letter "K" and look at various permutations. In the older version of the runes, it is minus the vertical stave. In later versions, it is minus the lower right stroke of the letter. Does this remind you of the female genitals? Well, at a stretch, but I would suggest that the rune for "man" in a later version does so even more, as it has the letter "K" minus the lower right stroke, which is placed in the upper left as a mirror of the one on the upper right; something like "Y" with the central stave passing up to the full height of that letter. (Yes, I know I'm making you get out a pen and paper, but indulge me.)

Here you have it: The central stave is moving up between the legs into the genitals, and the side-strokes are the creases where the thighs meet the lower abdomen. And this means "man"? How un-sexist were those old Vikings! Puts a different light on all that "rape and pillage"; maybe that's just the Christian priests

315

unhappy that some of their altar ware was stolen. So maybe the women weren't raped, but said something like: "Yes, you gorgeous hunk of a Norseman, fuck me!"

I'm getting carried away and back in porn land ... so back to the cunt – although it does make you wonder why so many Scotsmen look like Vikings.

Hidden in this rune is the wisdom of Teiresias that the core of the feminine mystery lays within "man". (I'm going to presume "man" is generic and is inclusive of both man and woman, as would be the case in the Northern Traditions.) "Freya teaches Odin seidr, which is a form of witchcraft and includes 'sex magic.' ... The Middle English word 'cunt' relates to cunning ... Cen is described as having a shape similar to that of the female genitals." (From chapter five.) The "seidr" mentioned by Aswynn is the magic of the Vanir that contains the erotic, or "sex magic", which Odin learnt from Freya. (And don't you now wonder how?) Of further interest is the relationship to the word "cunning", as reflected in the slightly older word "ken" or "kenning", indicative of a wisdom that comes from below and the realm of the feminine mysteries. This rune is also associated with "wounding", which may relate to menstruation, but also to the wounding that is a central motif in shamanism as the agent of initiation. Maybe there's more to the cunt than meets the eye?

"Where does the accomplishment known as poetry come from?" asks one god, as recorded by Sturluson. It is a world in which poetry, as here indicated, is considered a high art form; rivalling myth and of magical import. There is a subtle connection here as poetry is considered as 'inspiration' and can be compared to the breath of Tantra, as well as our view of the soul from the Northern outlook. It is a "gift of the gods" and is associated in the runes with sex, wisdom and magic; these are odd bedfellows from our modern perspective, although not from a traditional one.

There is a strange tale told by Sturluson about Odin's journey in search of the poetic mead. The story begins with one of the truces between the more warlike Aesir and peaceful Vanir. (In passing, I am reminded of the phrase "in love and war".) The pact was made by using the spittle from both camps to fashion a human named Kvasir who had "original knowledge" and who is pulled in opposing directions by these inherent polarities from his makers. Kvasir is subsequently killed by two dwarfs, who pour his blood into two crocks and a kettle (three 'vases'), and then mix it with honey to make mead. This mead eventually ends up in the possession of a giant, Suttung, as a result of a trade when the dwarfs kill his parents; dwarfs not being renowned for their intelligence! Suttung places the mead in his daughter's care and installs her, Gunnloth, within a mountain for security; for her, the mead or both, I might ask?

Odin then comes into the picture in search of the mead and his journey can variously be seen as a pilgrimage or a vision quest of the shamanic tradition. To edit the story considerably and as a result of various trials Odin ends up in Suttung's presence with Suttung's brother, who has somewhat reluctantly agreed to help as a result of a trick Odin played on him. Suttung, of course, does not agree to give up any of the mead, so Odin keeps Suttung's brother to his bargain by producing a drill and asking him to use his strength to bore into the mountain. This is done, after one false start, and Odin changes into a snake to pass through the hole, whilst Suttung's brother now tries to stab him, but fails.

> *(Odin, now in his original form) came to where Gunnloth was, and slept with her for three nights, and then she promised him three drinks of the mead. At his first drink he drank up all that was in Odrorir, at his*

second, Bothn, and at his third, Son (these are names of the three vases) – and then he had finished all the mead. Then he changed himself into an eagle and flew away at top speed.

When Suttung saw the eagle in flight, however, he also took on an eagle shape and flew after him. Now when the Aesir saw where Odin was flying, they put their crocks out in the court-yard, and when Odin came inside Asgard he spat the mead into the crocks. It was such a close shave that Suttung did not catch him, however, that he let some fall, but no one bothered about that. Anyone who wants could have it: we call it poetasters share. Odin gave Suttung's mead to the Aesir and those men who can compose poetry. So, we call poetry Odin's catch, Odin's discovery, his drink and his gift, and the drink of the Aesir.

(Snorri Sturluson: The Prose Edda)

Brian Bates recognised the connection this myth has with Tantra and explored this somewhat, with reference to Philip Rawson's work on Tantra. The outstanding issue, corroborated by other texts, is that the three days in the mountain amounted to a love ritual, or sex magic. The woman, as in Tantra, is seen as the holder of power and this is all related to the "mead of knowledge".

Without going into it, there are also Tantric parallels in the myth of Odin being hung on the giant ash tree Yggdrasil for nine days where he obtained the runes. It is interesting that the tree is described as "dripping dew so sweet that bees use it for making honey." Recall the association of bees with ambrosia earlier, and the sweet water of Eros? The three containers are of interest as they relate to a container, atonement and enlightenment (the last is a kettle) respectively. These may have symbolic associations with the second, fourth and sixth chakras, and also to the first three conjunctions in alchemy. The mountain we have already discussed in some detail.

Most significantly we have the initial entry into the mountain, which could even delight a Freudian eye. The drill, strength and subsequent 'entry' seem obviously to represent the penis and vaginal penetration. Maybe even the actual two attempts are significant and indicate that Gunnloth is a virgin? On the first attempt to enter Odin blows into the hole and when some dust comes back, he knows the entry is not complete; I don't think I need amplify this for you by now! Certainly, Gunnloth is more than willing to accommodate her guest. Odin changes to a snake, shape-shifting itself being a common ability of the shaman and magician. Yet the snake also recalls Kundalini. Then there is the three days of prolonged – ecstatic – lovemaking, to which we will return.

Odin affects his escape by turning into an eagle. So, his shape-shifting takes him from a snake to a bird and it may not be a surprise that this is a symbol that Kundalini adopts having emerged from the top of the aspirant's head. Birds such as eagles usually symbolise the world of spirit with their vast souring abilities. Finally, Odin brings the mead to the Aesir in Asgard. Now doesn't all this seem a little round about, as it was from the pact between the Aesir and Vanir that the mead originated? I suspect it in and of itself represents a cycle of ascent and one that resonates with Odin's three days with Gunnloth.

What are we to make of the three days? Bates goes to some lengths to explore it from the sex ritual perspective by referring to other texts that overcome what he perceives to be the censorship that Sturluson has applied. Let's follow his lead, but also see what we can infer directly from the above. Gunnloth is a giantess, so reinforcing the power symbolism. She is at the centre of a mountain and could quite easily be seen as Kundalini. At the very least she is someone who symbolises a sex goddess in her relationship to Odin. The three nights, beyond the magical associations regarding the number three itself, indicate a prolonged sexual ritual and one commensurate with Tantra.

What I find of interest is that Gunnloth, as Suttung's daughter, would, at a personal level, be disinclined to undertake a love ritual with Odin given her father's attitude toward him. This seems quite paradoxical and may indicate her role as goddess free from the personal influences. This is reinforced by her apparent lack of personal concern regarding what happens subsequently; that is, she gives Odin the mead only after the ritual and doesn't promise it to him before. She also cries no tears, neither does she fly into a rage regarding her equally apparent abandonment, nor does she obstruct Odin. It seems she is fulfilling a transpersonal or spiritual function.

Although Sturluson avoids any pornographic accusation by not going into undue detail regarding the sex, beyond the inferences to its intensity and duration, we can surmise that it was Tantric because the outcome is that Odin gains the mead, which we have equated with the summit or outcome of the whole ritual process. All in all, this myth, supported as it is by what we know of the culture, beliefs and customs of the people of the North, indicates a sex or love ritual firmly embedded in the magical tradition. I could go on and support this with much more from the Northern and Celtic mythological storehouse, but I think I have made my point.

Here's a summary of my position to this point: Over the last two thousand years, the Piscean aeon or the period of the Christian Patriarchy – take your pick – there has been a general trend of exclusion of the avenues to individual realisation, even enlightenment, that may threaten the increasing power, control and domination of the vested interests, both Church and State. Essentially this is to sever the connection with the raw materials – sex, the feminine, nature and the body – that might achieve this. The manner in which this is done, beyond some obvious and sometimes cruel methods, is to create an atmosphere of fear, governed by guilt and shame.

Ways of doing this include taking over existing locations, such as pagan sites of worship, where it may be argued that the energies of the planet are conducive to and support such an exploration. In addition, make the 'conditioned' priest the go-between for the masses and the divine. Also, edit the traditions that embody these potential individual accesses to such power. This process was assisted by writing becoming for many centuries – over a millennium – the province of the Church, the State, and their scribes, with all the distortions this may introduce, as well as the editing of the mythic storehouse of the preceding oral traditions, so distorting the ritual structures. Finally label these peoples and their traditions primitive and inferior, and then the dye is cast.

There are traditions that have maintained some sort of contact with these underlying forces. Some have been separate from the Church and maintained contact with the "Old Ways". Even some within the priesthood itself continued such contact. Others have come to this contact from inner revelation (the mystics), either within or without the establishment. Yet others have maintained contact with cultures that have not undergone such changes and misuse of power. More deeply than this I would argue that ultimately such human control of the spiritual is impossible.

The Jungian archetypal view is that there would be a fuller re-emergence of these repressed, despised and neglected elements from this 'shadow', as this is what the quest for 'wholeness' demands. Initially, this is with a force that could be reactionary, even revolutionary and potentially destructive or even self-destructive, depending on the maturity of the advocates themselves. I would argue this stands behind the events surrounding Germany in the twentieth century, but more benignly in the events of the nineteen-sixties, the New Age and reconnection with Eastern culture. I would also argue, supported by an astrological view, that the end of the age of Pisces and the advent of the age of Aquarius symbolises and expresses such a change that is now becoming more mature, creative and integrated.

I have further argued in some detail, sometimes a little tongue-in-cheek, that the pornographic phenomenon expresses many of these changes. It should be seen and embraced in that light, as it contains most – if not all – of the repressed elements that necessitate re-inclusion for the transformation of the individual and society, and hence the future of Western and maybe the global culture.

When we examined the definition of an archetype per se, we found an instinct-archetype spectrum, and I have further argued that the archetypal perspective is fundamentally inclusive of its instinctual origins, yet also transcends them. In archetypal sexuality this spectrum is sex to spirit. If we then look at other traditions, we find that sex can be broadened to include the body, nature and the feminine principle. The Perennial Philosophy and my interpretation of it – along with many other commentators – in the Great Chain of Being, support this perspective.

This position is further supported by the depth psychologists of the twentieth century, with the discovery of the mechanisms that operate at the archetypal level and an understanding of their present distortions. I claim this is a work in progress and that archetypal sexuality is yet to be fully reinstated. I am currently arguing that the pornographic phenomenon is involved in this reinstatement, as it contains many of the depth issues that need examining and should be seen in this light. But I significantly point out that this position requires a full examination and inclusion of all the other elements in such an archetypal view – be they the body, nature and the feminine – in the context of the soul, which is the fulcrum of the sex-spirit continuum.

Yet more than this, it cannot simply be an intellectual exercise, which I think a lot of this psychological thrust has degenerated into and which then is in danger of becoming a tool of the establishment, if that has not occurred already. I believe that of the depth psychologists Freud discovered (more correctly rediscovered) the problem of sex and its relationship to health, Jung charted the deeper territory for further exploration, Reich explored the practical and therapeutic implications and Hillman has – and is still – mapping the soul. It requires us to put this all together and integrate them, yet never forgetting that this territory requires a mapping that is based on the actual ground exploration; it requires – demands – practical appreciation and application. This is where I have chosen to take the least acceptable reflection of these issues (pornography) and explore the territory from that perspective, as all – I repeat all – the elements in this creative revolution must be included for a wholesome outcome.

Now to one of the major themes in psychosexuality itself: The various nectars. Of course, and at one obvious level, they represent the fluids associated with sex. At this level the male semen is seen as a potent and powerful force, such that cumshots are often interpreted as being aggressive and directed toward (pun intended) the domination of woman; that is, they reinforce the feminist and sexist position. Of course, by now you may see they are more than that and hopefully we will continue to unravel this complexity.

If the male ejaculation, or external cumshot, was simply a tool of domination, I believe other facets of porn may have also become more popular. Although urination or pissing has been on the periphery of porn, it has never made the mainstream, when it could be seen to be more demonstratively dominating. I find it interesting that the mainstream has indulged and experimented with this medium. There was a time when legally available porn accepted pissing and the "golden showers" (that is, one or more people pissing on one or more others). What is of interest is that censorship (internal or external, I don't know) gradually eliminated a man or men pissing on a woman's face and into her mouth, whilst accepting it elsewhere on her body. This seems obvious at one level; golden showers are not directly associated with semen and are less sexual for that reason. Maybe that is so, but I would argue if the prime intent of the facial cumshot is sexist and demeaning, then this would have been more popular and attracted those who did enjoy facials to explore this avenue more. I don't think that has been the case and, for this reason, I think the argument about the facial is more complex. By contrast golden showers have now been confined to the sub-genre, even a perversion, because of their relative creative redundancy in psychosexuality.

Female fluids, from the sexual perspective, are less emphasised. There is a stream of porn that does try to focus on the female equivalent of the male ejaculation and whilst some female porn stars seem physiologically well equipped to produce significant – and sometimes projectile – amounts of genital fluids, this also hasn't become an enduring feature. Maybe this is because of the inherent inwardness of the feminine sexuality, or maybe for other reasons?

What about blood? Isn't this representative of the feminine mystery par excellence? That a woman bleeds and then if she stops can produce a child? This is the basis of much in the mystery traditions, particularly those that relate to the agricultural cycle where life, death and fertility are integrally associated with the moon and the feminine cycle. The spiritual component of this we have had cause to examine when we explored the word cunt then referred it back to the feminine mysteries and the shamanic tradition in which it is based, where the issues of wounding and suffering are placed in the context of growth and transformation. Indeed, they have been retained in Christianity, although with the absence of the feminine association suffering has become more of a perversion.

Although blood and semen also represent the symbolic red and white, as well as being the foundation of the Eucharistic feast from the pagan and psychosexual perspective, I am intrigued by the other fluids associated with the culmination of psychosexual development and which, maybe, these base fluids are seen to mature into. There is the wine of Dionysus, presumably red and present in the Christian Eucharist, reflective of feminine mystery and the madness of the irrational with its expression in orgiastic sexuality. Alcohol has been used at all times and in all cultures to a psychosexual effect and may be referred to as spirit, an earlier observation that may now take on a deeper significance. Wine is from the grape and reflects, from another perspective, the mystery of the agricultural cycle and its reflection of the Great Cycle of Existence – birth, sex and death.

The opposites of bitter and sweet with reference to fountain water arise in the Eros myth. The bitter is shed on Psyche's lips and the sweet, as a sort of apology or attempt at restoration, on her hair. Is the second the transformation of the first, or simply the complement? Why the lips and hair? Is it that the ingestion of the bitter (lead, prima materia of alchemy) leads to a transformation with the hair representing that which comes out of the top of the head, the seventh chakra? Actually, Bullfinch says the sweet water is poured on her "silken ringlets", an interesting and enigmatic image. If that is the case, doesn't it put another interesting slant on the mouth and facial cumshot?

I am drawn to two further features of the nectar. The first is the association with honey, sometimes in alcoholic combination as with mead, sometimes alone or with the bee, its maker. Honey is a rich food and has associations with healing and well-being beyond its value as a simple sweetener. Some consider it a natural antibiotic; it can be used for skin wounds and it has other immune system attributes. As does the bee, its maker, such that bee stings are considered to stimulate and strengthen the immune system. Interestingly, this is also an attribute of snake-bites, as snake venom has similar qualities and even magical associations. It seems what doesn't kill you may well cure you.

In these respects, honey has qualities not unlike the elixir of life, or elan vital. The image of the associated fountain is interesting as it is also present in the Eros and Psyche myth and, Brian now remembers, in his dream too. What exactly was it? Whilst he tries to remember, I will reinforce that these are all qualities that we may associate with the pituitary and pineal glands in the brain as well as the sixth and seventh chakras. The ramifications of all this is fascinating and make for a profound mystery.

Brian now recalls that there was an earlier section to his dream:

> *He is looking at an island emerging from the Pacific Ocean and it is initially volcanic. He is then in the city square on the island surrounded by old buildings and with a fountain at the centre. The fountain looks initially pipe-like and symbolic, in the modern sense, but as he watches and almost 'looks through' it, it softens and at the top he sees an octagonal jewel.*
>
> *Then he is in the country of the island where he*

engages the second half of the dream (recounted in chapter five):

> *He is watching a man emerge from a misty background. Although he hasn't met the man, he knows his wife and son, they are the 'original man and woman'. The man is dressed in a dark suit of indeterminable period over a white polo neck sweater that makes him look a little like a priest. He appears tired and worn out. Brian goes to a fridge, which is opened by one of his secretaries and inside is a jar with an unknown content. He knows that he must give the contents to the man to revive and rejuvenate him, but the top is tight and he can't open it. He realises, as he wakes, that he will need something strong like a vice to achieve this.*

The first half is quite symbolic. Without going into too much unnecessary detail, this could be called a "big dream" by the North American Indian, which may have significance well beyond the personal and be relevant to the tribe. In Jungian terms, the initial island emergence and the city would point to what Jung calls the "self" or, in simple terms, the consolidated personality. That may be the case, but Brian recalls that the city reminds him of the old city of Stockholm, which is on an island in the river that flows through that city. This was at a time of excitement and reconnection with cultural roots and he was also impressed in his visit there about the sexual equality and openness of that society, similar to my own experiences.

This gives the image a much more psychosexual tone, and I would think the volcanic eruption could represent the awakening of Kundalini from the "pacific" background. Maybe the fountain reinforces this, as the initial impression to Brian is that it is quite phallic, although the "looks through" has qualities of an altered state of consciousness, not unlike the ascent of Kundalini and as reinforced on Psyche's mountain ascent. This reveals a deeply enigmatic symbol: the octagonal jewel. Eight is significant to Brian at many levels; not least that it had magical associations in his childhood that protected him from anxiety and fear. The eight is also the symbol of eternity and could be the "jewel in the crown" of spiritual development. All in all, the first half seems to set the tone for the second, which is more personal and may represent Brian's role in the whole process outlined in the first half, as a response to watching "Retreat", you may recall.

The misty background indicates something emerging from the unknown; in Celtic symbology this could be the "Otherworld", or the realm of the ancestors, which gives the dream a shamanic association. Although the imagery of the parents and son could be seen in a Freudian and Oedipal light, this would be reductive and uncreative. Brian is more inclined to see the Christian trinity of father, son and Holy Ghost, with the mother reinstated. Brian sees this man as himself, maybe in terms of his own present state of spiritual questioning, or that the religious context in which he exists is "worn out and tired"; needing rejuvenation.

So maybe it is his own religious or spiritual perspective that needs rejuvenating? Stephanie, his secretary, is there. There is an erotic element to Brian's relationship with her, but it has not – to date – been sexualised. In Jung's terms, she may be an anima figure but Brian, now with the psychosexual tone firmly in mind, wonders whether she is, as well as this, a Shakti-like figure assisting him to find something of importance, being the jar in the fridge.

What is in the jar? It is for Brian himself, in the symbolic guise of the "worn out priest". He knows he will have to contemplate these symbols and these issues deeply. Stephanie leads him to the fridge: Is this because the jar needs 'preserving' or is in 'cold storage', or because he has rejected it from the light and warmth? Maybe all of them. He is amused by the need of a vice, at one time indicating the need for power and strength, and at another a humorous play on the sexual flavour and content of the overall dream. He was later to find out that one interpretation of Merlin's traditional name of Myrddin is of a 'vice'… maybe the Old Ways are returning?

The dream is left unresolved; that is how dreams are – they give information, but it is our responsibility as to what we will do with it. Brian realises this. At the core he knows it is about sex or, more appropriately, love-magic.

11

Back to Basics, Forward to Enlightenment

Let me take you a little further and deeper into the mystery of alchemy, which we have made frequent reference to, but which will now become the major background theme to psychosexuality. Although you may associate alchemy with chemistry and see it as its primitive precursor, they have, in fact, very little in common.

Chiefly responsible for the apparent connection was the mediaeval doctor and alchemist Paracelsus, perceived by many as the father of modern chemistry in pharmaceutical medicine. He may well have turned in his grave at this honorary title, but because he made extensive use of his metallurgic background in his clinical practice, as well as within the alchemy he performed, the association has stuck. Added to this is the fact that the major metaphorical theme which alchemy is associated with is the use of metals and chemicals in the transformation of base materials into gold. So, the transformation of alchemy into chemistry becomes complete, aided and abetted by its connection with medicine via the healing arts.

I am going to leave the association there and refer no more to chemistry, only those chemical terms we might be familiar with and because of their metaphorical use in alchemy. An additional reason to do this is because I will argue for the strong inclusion of psychosexuality within alchemy, to the point that I believe that the alchemical metaphors are more a code regarding their connection with sexuality rather than with chemistry. The former makes entire sense to me, the latter little at all.

Alchemy deals with an occult or hidden reality in our daily existence, which is the underlying essence of all religions. This is a far cry from chemistry, I might add, unless you take the materialist position of our everyday existence to its rational extreme and logical conclusion. Alchemy deals with truth, beauty, love and the absolute. The association with beauty is interesting as it is replete in the myths we have explored (in the figures of Pandora, Psyche and Aphrodite) and is also a notable feature of the triad of the East – the good, the true and the beautiful – that parallels what alchemy is working with. Alchemy is about the realisation of our true nature through redemption.

From these metaphysical heights let's flesh these features out a little. The production of gold could be considered almost a by-product of the process, a little like the psychic powers of the Yogi being seen as a by-product of his or her spiritual realisation. The gold is a metaphor for the sun, which is itself a metaphor for God or the divine principle. Gold can also be equated with the fountain of youth, the elixir of life and the key to immortality; overlapping concepts that we have already come across.

The Elixir would not only cure all ills by uprooting the cause of disease, but it would also rejuvenate and finally transmute the human into an incorruptible 'body of light' (or enlightenment).

(Stanislas Klossowski de Rola: Alchemy)

The alchemical adept realized "Omniscience, Omnipotence, and the joy of Divine Eternal Love": challenging stuff and equivalent to the divine principle itself. Hence, the association of the microcosm with the macrocosm, a metaphor so favoured in alchemy.

Secrecy is a big concern in alchemy. It can be argued that this is with good reason when the likes of the Inquisition might be looking at what you're doing. This makes sense at one level, for all the reasons we've already discussed and explored. Yet it is more than this, particularly when we compare alchemy with Tantra, which didn't have the same 'policing' problem.

Like Tantra, alchemy is a mysterious art and is automatically guarded by the natural boundaries of ritual and symbolism. By this I mean that alchemy is 'taught' in a practical and ritualised manner, like Tantra, and that the symbolism doesn't incline to easy interpretation. (As you may have found out by trying to follow me with symbolic 'interpretation' in general throughout this book.) In summary, symbolism may be 'seen' – imaged – as circular or cyclic, whereas reasoning is linear. In passing, note the feminine and masculine symbols inherent in the words? The labyrinth is a metaphor of symbolism, or even symbolic of it: "Complicated irregular structure with many passages hard to find a way through or about without guidance." (Oxford English Dictionary.) In Greek mythology, the labyrinth contains the Minotaur, which is yet another myth, so we'll leave it there, apart from the interesting feature of Ariadne's thread being the guidance in negotiating the labyrinth. I'm only bringing that fact in because of an interesting association: Ariadne is the wife of Dionysus.

I think there is another reason for the secrecy, and that is whether it is secret at all or simply confused by definition. In other words, there is a major argument that the secrecy is only apparent and a consequence of the alchemical process itself. *How can that be?* you might retort; it isn't that confusing in Tantra. Well, even though I have removed an immense amount of material from the description of Tantra, such as additional features, sounds, colours, symbolic associations from the chakras and the intermingling of astrology and the elements (earth, water, air and fire, plus ether in the East), it does seem simpler. Or maybe it is oversimplified?

I sense that, in many ways, the Tantric practitioner did not immerse him or herself in the mystery as much as the alchemical practitioner; partly because there is a tradition in the East that is more easily accepting of the Master or Guru, whereas in the West individual realisation is given a higher emphasis. This individualisation means that what each practitioner discovers of his own process is valid, yet would also make for many differing explanations. Add to this the fact that such discovery is of its very nature symbolic, and then the material would have the quality of a dream and be necessarily confusing to the methodical and rational perspective.

Let's skate through a very condensed and rough outline of the alchemical process. I am necessarily leaving aside much important detail, as I did with Tantra, but once again with the caveat that I will not be excluding anything that negates my overall thesis. Also, I will not be including a lot of the associated astrology, the elements, or the metallurgic and chemical metaphors beyond a point, except where they support the condensed outline. (Please note: this is my personal impression of the field and will necessarily differ from other practitioners according to the reasoning immediately above.)

Alchemy begins with the Prima Materia, or the Stone of the Philosopher. (As opposed to the Philosopher's Stone, which is the completion of the process, an interesting inversion.) This "base material", commonly the metal lead, is seen to have an imperfect body, a penetrating tincture and a clear transparent mercury, as well as to be volatile and mobile. Confused already? Didn't I warn you ... but maybe if you see these features as simply describing what must be purified, it might help. We are raising them to a higher order, which is the transformation process: This is not a literal change and is why there was so much disbelief about gold arising from lead, as it simply can't be done in the literal world without enormous equipment not available to the alchemist of the past. The practitioner goes into a mine to obtain this raw material, under the right astrological horoscope for the enterprise, and then cleans the material with a "dew" collected by ingenious and poetical means, which is then distilled. On the lighter aside, this reminds me of the making of Scotch whiskey, which is often given the name dew! We also came across the significance of poetry with Odin.

This material is then placed in a flask called an "athanor" and the process proper begins with gentle heat, various catalysts and astrological guidance, as well as that of personal experience and maybe the instruction of a mentor. The "philosophical egg" – the raw material – contains the hot, male, red and solar principle with the cold, female, white and lunar principle, which all then interact in the first stage. This can be called the "nigredo" (black) and involves separation and decay culminating in a stage of the union of opposites called the "mercury of the wise". This stage can be seen to be governed by the processes of purification, distillation and solidification and is related to mercury.

The second stage has processes of cooking, digesting and fixation, resulting in the appearance of whiteness. This stage culminates in a second union called "albedo", or white. The third stage has fermentation, multiplication and perfection, resulting in the final union of male and female and called "rubedo", or red. This is the Philosopher's Stone. Confused enough? And apart from all the associated details I have left out, I have avoided – beyond a limited extent – using the complicated Latin terminology so often employed. This all makes it very attractive to get the 'packaged' version – the bread and wine of the

Eucharist – from the priest who has supposedly undertaken all this behind closed doors in a prior and secret ritual in his vestry.

My personal orientation to alchemy was essentially to strip it of all the accretions, such as terminology that may be out of date and disciplines with which I am not greatly familiar, and then to see whether it stood the inspection of depth psychology. This is in a manner somewhat similar to Jung, although with less academic erudition, and then to see how this referred to personal development as outlined in depth psychotherapy. I have found it to be quite valid to the process and see a wide application. With that reinforcement my next attempt was to how it might apply to psychosexuality, as I was proposing that a more appropriate detailed examination and understanding of sexuality in the West may add a dimension to where psychology and medicine are headed, and even assist these changes significantly. At the core of this, then, was the question: Does alchemy relate in a significant and detailed way to psychosexuality, as elaborated within this book?

The first step in this is to ask about the relationship of alchemy to Tantra. The significant missing dimension in alchemy is the practical aspect of sexuality included in the art itself, whilst it is patently present in the East. However, the symbolism of sexual union is there, so does this imply that it is also practically and literally present and has been excluded because of the fear of the Church, or is it simply not there?

There are many ways of looking at this, and the initial one is whether Tantra and alchemy have an inter-relationship beyond Western culture. They certainly do if we take a historical perspective beyond the present aeon into shamanism. They also do if we look to China and Taoism, as well as to the Islamic world. So, this leaves us with the sexual enigma. If we examine the symbolism of alchemy there is no doubt it parallels that of Kundalini's ascent, as defined by Tantra. This is something I have already made reference to, but let me take it a little further.

If we were to examine in more detail and explore other treatises, yet retain our attention around the central thesis of sexuality in alchemy, a more complex picture emerges. The above limited view of the alchemical process provides three stages or unions, to which I would add an initial fourth – in the prior preparation. This provides us with an initial conjunction, or union, implied in the latent gender associations in the raw material. If we do this, we get four conjunctions, which I may briefly elucidate:

> *The first conjunction, or union, is the instinctual union of male and female. This is a fate we share with the animal kingdom, raised to the human sphere, and is symbolically seen as retrieving the stone from the mine, or underworld. It is the 'raw material' of sexual energy with which the alchemical process is undertaken. The equivalent in Tantra is the awakening of Kundalini and the energetic movement from the first to the second chakra.*

> *The second union, described as the Lesser Work, culminates in what I have called Romantic Love and integrates the emotional element. It is what makes us distinctly human. The sexual energy has now been matured to a more emotional state by the fire of the third chakra, which is similar to the heat applied to the athanor, and resting in the fourth chakra. It is characterised by study and practice.*

> *The third union is within the scope of the Greater Work and demands a more integrated perspective of the male and female than the previous stage. Prior to this,*

the archetypal principles of masculinity and femininity exist in projection; by the third stage, these projections have been withdrawn, and there is a greater differentiation between an adult and mature love. This creative act has moved Kundalini from the fifth chakra to the sixth and this could be seen as the integration of the soul. Mythically, it is reflected in the Eros and Psyche myth. Discipline and love are the features here.

The fourth union has some deep ramifications. Also, within the Greater Work the masculine and feminine principles, now truly combined within the soul, move across a great divide and dissolve into a unity that is variously symbolised as the sun, the union of king and queen or, in a more potent image, the divine androgyne. This union is more of a transition and is seen as the movement from the sixth chakra in the microcosm to the seventh, in the macrocosm and the domain of Shiva or divine consciousness. The myths surrounding Dionysus, the relationship with chaos, existential fear and death are shadows that are to be overcome at this stage. The attendant principles are understanding and wisdom. This transition is deeply and symbolically contained in the crucifixion and resurrection symbolism and reflected in the ritual of the Eucharist.

As indicated, I have excluded other elements and disciplines from this view, but I assure you they reinforce the above associations. For those acquainted with the Kabbalah of Jewish mysticism, the resonances and correspondences are similarly outstanding. I mention this because the Kabbalah has been extensively employed in the Western magical tradition over the last century or so, as well as in practical ways such as using the Tarot and sex or love magic.

I have no doubt that alchemy has made use of practical sex magic, or love magic, as part of its expression. This is supported by academic research from several modern scholars. As with the left and right paths, plus the alternative positioning of Tantra with the more ascetic and yogic disciplines, this is not obligatory. We are talking here of the left hand path of magic, sexuality, the body and the feminine; it simply would have to have been present. If not, I, for one, am championing its statement. How do you do this? Well, maybe the simplest way is to map Tantra onto alchemy beyond what I have already done to date and then look to the evidence about the sexual rituals and arts employed.

However, maybe a simpler way is to look to porn for information, so let's do that!

Anal sex, or arse fucking, has increased in extent and intensity in all aspects of porn. If we look at the mainstream, the trend has been interesting. I have made mention of some of this with respect to Private. You may recall that Magazine Fifteen contained a woman with three men in a gang bang that involved dildos and various double and triple penetrations (a cock in the woman's mouth in addition to a double penetration), this was around 1970. There is then an interesting hiatus of several years, with the next anal penetration not until Number Twenty-seven, after which it becomes a more regular feature.

What could be the reason for this? I don't know, absolutely, but here's a guess: Issue Fifteen was quite a rapid change from what had proceeded it, and Milton seemed to have a desire or habit to stretch the boundaries. He may have gone too far with that issue and had to wait another twelve issues to reintroduce it, possibly because of changing cultural and societal attitudes, after which it became more of a staple. I suspect this was some sort of regulation, both external and internal. Yet it remains to be asked why it attracted more apparent censorship than, say, facial cumshots.

Of course, it is not so censored now; in fact, quite the opposite. I won't go as far as *The Porn Report* authors with their "deeply offensive and abhorrent" position, but it is excessive and touches on some concerning aspects of the attitudes of some men in the industry. A comment in a recent Penthouse Magazine from an interview with a notable porn director illustrates this: He claims to have had sex with three thousand women, and when asked how many he had had anal sex with he replied: "All of them".

Within the obvious excess of this are some concerning features, which is beyond our need to explore. There are some things about anal sex that do tweak my interest. Of course, it may relate to issues about gay homosexuality and that might also be interesting to explore, but I hope that I have already argued substantially against that rather prevalent and obvious opinion. I would suggest that it has more to do with the sort of issues that are so loved by the pro-censorship and anti-pornography lobbies of feminism regarding men's attitudes toward women, and which this sort of openly admitted excessive activity serves to reinforce.

Yet we must not throw the baby out with the bath water, as I suspect there is more to this than meets the eye. It is something substantially portrayed in what I would call erotic and aesthetic porn and is significantly present in the "Retreat". My own experience, personally and in discussion with others, is that, when engaged in successfully, it provides a level of mutual satisfaction that cannot be simply or trivially explained, or easily compared to vaginal or even oral sex. By successful, I mean that the obvious potential pain factor is mutually negotiated and a stage beyond reach. I have yet to meet someone, male or female, who, having engaged in anal sex in a mutually satisfying manner, has not continued to have as part of his or her sexual repertoire. If that is the case, what are we missing?

There may be several facets to this, so here is my take on some of them. The first is that anal sex engages the first chakra in a more direct way than vaginal sex, which is more about the second chakra. So, the nature and quality of the response is likely to be different, making a direct comparison at least difficult and at most inappropriate. The first chakra is more about power and the balance of pain and pleasure that can be induced and can lift the level of excitement considerably. I am also reliably informed that the nature of any orgasm produced by anal sex — which it can — is of a different quality. Of interest to me is that this generally remains in the dynamic between a man and woman with the man penetrating her anally, but it is rare in porn to see him being penetrated. Of course, this would require a cock, which is relatively taboo, or at least a dildo. The latter is sometimes seen in scenes that have a fetish and sadomasochistic edge, which reinforces the pain and pleasure dynamic, but it is not common.

I suspect we are back to the feminine mystery element here, in that the Kundalini — which resides in the base chakra after all — is feminine, and that the role of the man is to stimulate its awakening within the women in a ritual context, which is symbolically the feminine principle for both of them. This may be the issue; it forms the basis of ritual, and so its engagement in mundane sexuality may stimulate the ritual capacity of the psyche in a way vaginal sex does not. I'm not implying that vaginal sex can't do this, as, of course, it can; it is just that it may serve other ritual functions. In this ritual capacity, it is undertaken in some magical cults with men being anally penetrated by other men. This forms a ritual of induction and also establishes a power gradient within any magical order.

I suspect the power gradient is the predominant one that is exercised when anal sex is routinely and excessively engaged with in porn. If not routine and excessive, then I think there may be some more subtle dynamics involved, such as the interplay of all three lower chakras, as the first and third seem to have a relationship that may be directly engaged in this way; as illustrated by it being more prevalent, sometimes mutual and supported by other props in the sadomasochistic and fetish end of the porn spectrum. I also suspect that this engagement of all the lower chakras can be an intense challenge, which can either unite and transform them, or spiral out of control in a way vaginal sex does not. I think this – fear – may stand behind many of the critics, rather than the simplistic reasons often given about anal sex.

In the movie, Emily is the only principal woman who doesn't engage in anal sex. Maybe at this stage of her sexual development it is too early, which is a statement in itself. Also, it might present the relationship with Graham with challenges that it is not ready to face and which are reflected and inverted in the contrasting arse fucking scene involving Helen and Mick. Of interest is that Emily has started to gain some power and confidence following her interactions with Helen, so maybe these need more consolidation first, as Graham has engaged in anal sex and this could be on a future agenda.

This engagement was with Carole, Graham's wife at the time, who seemed both comfortable and experienced in anal activity. Not only is there arse fucking, but also, in the first scene, it is with a double penetration. Double penetration would seem to engage both the first and second chakras simultaneously and is certainly a porn favourite in this regard; it is uncommon for even a relatively mainstream porn movie to not have at least one. The logistics for this in routine relationships are obviously problematical, as are some or all of the combinations that occur in the second half of the movie. So maybe the double penetration serves a symbolic function in porn that could generally only be entertained in a ritual context in daily life: something seen in a Dionysian orgy, maybe, and which the second half of the movie exploits.

Carole takes the double penetration beyond the routine of the first scene, when it is part of an extended relationship "play". In the scene upstairs at the Club, she engages in it in a complex round with Mick and the two other men that becomes progressively more ritualised and symbolic and extends to cyclical triple penetration. This is certainly more Dionysian and culminates with the interesting tableau involving Mick and the four other participants. These participants can be seen in both the Club scenes as support actors, or extras, who sub-serve the ritual functions. This is illustrated by the simultaneous attention of the two women toward Paul and then Helen in the dungeon, followed by their more intense involvement with Carole upstairs. This is further enhanced by the two women's involvement with Carole; then the two men's attention to her with Mick, culminating in the final scene where all four are directly and indirectly involved with her.

Of interest is, that at this point in the scene, the actual sex between Mick and Carole has reverted to the – relatively – simple anal. It has a highly magical and initiatory quality, as it pushes Carole into an altered state of consciousness. This is reinforced by the fact that she is not facing him, so she doesn't have any symbolically personal contact. Instead, she is involved in a complex tableau with the other four in front of her.

Following the mirroring of the dildo activity of Helen and Carole, Mick and Paul seem to form a bonding that allows Paul to perform the anal role in the ensuing double penetration in the dungeon. There is a similar ritual pattern with the men serving Helen in the way they do and the involvement of the two women at the end of the dungeon scene, with many similarities to the end of the upstairs scene. The ritual aspect is reinforced by the dungeon itself, with the various outfits, props and masks that 'play' on the anonymity of the sex. There is also the contrast between the downstairs dungeon and the upstairs bedroom and a transition between the two, which Mick unites in the hidden company of his four attendees.

Helen and Carole are the respective centres of attention in the two scenes, with Paul forming more of a 'partnership' with Mick in the first. Whilst Mick also traverses both scenes and seems to move beyond Paul in this regard, this is more than adequately compensated for in the last scene, a fact that is significant in itself.

In summary: What I am pointing out here is that we are in ritual and symbolic territory. I have chosen to use the rather controversial topic of anal sex and some personal conclusions about it to move into the two complex scenes at the Club. In this way the discussion of anal sex was a kind of ritual of initiation into this more complex territory, reinforcing what I feel is its prime function in general sexual activity by heightening the energetic intensity and excitement. I realise some of my comments may be tentative and speculative, but I trust they open up a level of creative enquiry into a topic that, for too long, has been inappropriately taboo and misinformed.

Whilst anal sex can be seen in the bounds of a regular one-to-one relationship, there is no difficulty with literal enactment, although the symbolic aspects may not be fully realised. Anal sex in porn can then be seen as literal and educative, but also to illustrate symbolic dimensions for the consumer. The plethora of it in the porn mainstream, irrespective of my comments above and possibly your response to them, would indicate either the extent of it or the attraction of it in mainstream life. I would further add that this is not entirely a male-viewing phenomenon from my reasonable experience and understanding and that at least bears some further thought. What I have tried to do is introduce the symbolic dimension.

This use of symbolism is enhanced in the Club scenes in many ways, which we have tentatively sketched out above in a general manner. This, at the mundane level, would seem to take the sex into fantasy and so beyond the reach of the average consumer. Yet is that the case? Earlier, we discussed the difference between fantasy and the broader imagination, and I would suggest that it is worth seeing not only the porn described here but also your own consumption in that light. I am suggesting that porn can stimulate your imagination and lead you into the world of symbolism, ritual and the mystery of sex and the feminine, in the manner outlined in Tantra and implicated in alchemy.

From this Tantric perspective, it might also be useful to ask which chakras are engaged in these scenes. I would suggest that after the early but incomplete awakening of the fourth in the scene involving Emily and Graham, there appears to be a regression. Such a regression serves a purpose, as, in the general sense, regression is a necessary flow backward of energy to fulfil functions that may not have been adequately completed before. Maybe Emily and Graham would require such regression in their relationship – or beyond – to consolidate it in the fourth chakra of romantic love.

Energetic flow is thus cyclic and such apparently regressive movement is not necessarily due to a failure of progression: a linear and masculine fantasy. We have all had an experience of 'touching' something higher, losing sight of it and then regaining it with a firmer footing; this is quite natural.

This can be illustrated in the apparent regression in the Club scenes. Here all the lower chakras are engaged, sometimes simultaneously. This might be to complete the energetic tour through them, so that the Kundalini energy can progress upwards. This may well be the case because I would suggest that these scenes contain features of all the upper chakras. The perceptive amongst you may have recognised that the first three chakras seem to resonate with the next three. This is what the Club scenes explore, I would suggest. Routine porn, of course, does not commonly or intentionally do this, as it prefers to retain the energy at the instinctual lower chakric levels to be recycled in a circular fashion; a good marketing ploy.

The fourth chakra appears with the general softness of the various porn stars in their relationships with each other, their sometimes-emotional disposition and in Brian's response with his ensuing reflection of his own marriage. The creativity of the fifth chakra is evident throughout, and the sixth by the various subtle and complex pairings that occur. But is the seventh present? I would suggest that it is in embryonic or preliminary form, but more fully in the last scene back at the Retreat the next day.

What does this all mean for the literal aspect of sex in our daily lives? Does it mean 'acting out' what is seen, or is what is portrayed in porn compensation for not being able to and thus confine it to the symbolic level only? This is a paradox, which you may be able to answer in personal terms, but at a cultural and societal level, I think it raises some big questions. So, let's return to our four principal remaining porn stars and track them through the second half of the movie to see what they might illustrate about this question and more.

I have pointed out earlier that Mick and Helen appear to be fulfilling roles as catalysts in the whole process, and I am reminded of the significant role of the catalyst in alchemy, which is a chemical addition to the mix that helps the changes that are desired, without a change in the catalyst itself. This certainly appears the case with Mick and Helen, as we get the impression at the end that they've "been through it all before". Being a catalyst, however, does not necessarily equate with a more highly evolved state; in this case, Mick and Helen need not necessarily be enlightened themselves – that is, having reached and become consolidated in the seventh chakra or the fourth alchemical conjunction – but have the capacity to help others on this path. In this respect, a catalyst differs and should be distinguished from a mentor, guide, guru or master. The master has achieved this status, or at least can only take the pupil or initiate as far as his, or her, own evolution. If Mick and Helen have not achieved this status, I wonder who has. Maybe our director?

Behind their appearances, there are some subtle signs of a fair degree of psychosexual evolution in them, however. Mick starts from a routine male perspective in Brian's summary of him, although his acting in this movie portrays someone with a subtle balance of masculine and feminine features, some of which we have alluded to already. His role in the early scene with his wife and Emily indicates an ease with such scenarios and a compliance in Emily's direction, as she moves through the changes the scene brings out in her. His involvement with his wife has no personal edge beyond the demand of the scene, as he seems to respond to both women in an uncomplicated manner. Helen takes a more active role in the same scene and brings out the aggressor in Emily. As with Mick, she feels generally compliant to the changes that emerge in the scene, and within Emily in particular, it is as if she almost knows what is happening or is going to happen.

This extends to the anal scene that offsets the tryst in the forest between Emily and Graham. This seems very much a theatrical ritual with the outfit and lack of emotional expression. In Tantric terms, the first and fourth chakras are contrasted, possibly indicating what has not been integrated in the portrayal of the fourth. In alchemical terms, it is a parallel contrast of the first and second conjunctions, or the instinctual and the romantic.

In the dungeon scene, Helen takes centre stage – literally – and is again quite comfortable in that position. She starts the proceedings with a more complex masturbation than Carole, possibly reinforcing her maturity, and then responds to the men's attention as Mick leads Paul into the action, indirectly helped by the two women assistants, with the double penetration of his wife allowing Paul her arse. Then she is left to comfort Paul through the emotional changes the scene has raised beyond what is already occurring within him regarding Carole. In this respect, the image of them together back at the Retreat is quite a contrast to Mick's arse fuck of her in the kitchen earlier.

Mick, having guided Paul to a particular point, which Helen will pick up on in the last scene, becomes the central agent upstairs with Carole and thus mirrors his wife's role downstairs. A further contrast between them is that Helen is the centre downstairs in a more masculine setting, with the reverse upstairs. Yet, whilst Helen was deeply receptive in the dungeon, Mick remained quite active and this continues upstairs. When Carole appears to be taking the initiative on occasion, it is almost as if he has set the scene for this.

Perhaps it is the final scene that illustrates Mick and Helen in their full capacity and the scenes at the Club are almost a precursor to this. There would certainly be more that could be teased out of their roles in the scenes to date, but it is probably best not to overcomplicate and analyse the symbols to death, yet to go far enough to point out their catalytic roles.

In the mythology of most cultures, there is a figure that acts as a catalyst of sorts. In Greece, it is Hermes; Rome has Mercury, and the Scandinavians Loki. I'll pick Mercury to illustrate catalysis, as he is also the name given to one important agent used in alchemy, which has a paired gender identity and is known to us as "quicksilver", as well as being the only metal liquid at room temperature. All these figures have an element of the trickster in them; that is, a person who acts contrarily and paradoxically. As paradox is a fundamental characteristic of the symbolic world, Mercury is able to move in it with ease and is why he is seen as the "messenger of the gods" to man. Mercury, although masculine, is quite sexually ambivalent, and I would suggest that Mick and Helen together reflect the differing gender aspects of the trickster as characterised by Mercury.

Let's now turn our attention to Carole and Paul, whom I see as the major figures in this sexual drama. I say this because they represent the full development of psychosexuality beyond the achievement of Emily and Graham, aided and abetted by Helen and Mick, whose ultimate position in the movie, as with all the best tricksters, remains seemingly unchanged yet enigmatic.

We have already looked at Carole's involvement in the first half of the movie. By reference to Graham, we can predict that she is beyond the romantic stage, as she is prepared to entertain more complex scenarios of a sexual nature that would threaten someone seeking a romantic position. Maybe that is why Graham is so disturbed, as this is what he wants and recognises that Carole does not ... yet is what Emily is emerging into. Carole's emotionality as a result of a scenario in which she shows sexual expertise and confidence is, at first, a little surprising. Whilst at the personal level, we have appreciated this may be in response to the loss of her marriage, I would suggest it is because she has moved into more subtle energetic territory.

The masturbation scene at the Club follows in the wake of this emotionality and acts as a time of integration. Her lack of a desire for a romantic resolution to her emotional state is reflected in the fact she does not choose to pursue Paul, a position he replicates and reflects. The masturbation itself does sexually mirror Helen, though in a slightly lesser light, and possibly indicate something that she aspires to and to which Mick assists her in the ensuing upstairs scene at the Club.

Upstairs, Carole refreshes and dresses up for the occasion, in response to Mick's savoir-faire. There is a sense of a more complex femininity emerging here with her crawling on the floor and taking on the three men; being an extension of what she achieved in the first scene, but more ritualised. The interlude on the bed with the two women reinforces this and serves to illustrate a deepening feminine confidence in her responses, as recognised by Brian. This then moves to the very ritualised and symbolic final part of the scene where the arse fuck propels her into an altered state. In one sense, Carole has reached a pinnacle of achievement. She is previously orgasmic and now with women as well, but this represents something more and is reflected further in the final scene.

Paul is undergoing some similar changes. As already pointed out, his involvement with Carole earlier indicates a level of development that reflects hers, though in a different way. Although he seems past romantic involvement, he has chosen someone like Emily, which seems a little anomalous. This could be because of previous personal disappointment at the romantic level, but it may also be that Emily appears as the image of something he is looking for. This could be a more psychologically mature woman, who seems less concerned about romantic involvement because she has gone beyond it. He is disappointed, though, possibly because he recognises he has fallen for a subtle projection: Emily hasn't got as far as romantic love, and he has confused her not having gotten there with having gone beyond. This is something he now recognises with his own feminine nature and which Carole mirrors for him throughout the movie.

In this way, the first scene sorts these issues out for Paul in a similar manner that it does for Carole. He is also left a little shaken by all this, though not as overtly emotional. He is ready for the scene with Helen and Mick that takes him into a deeper masculine induction, which Mick leads and takes him through. Paul's position in the arms of Helen later that night reflects this integration and mirrors that of Carole when she was masturbating at the Club.

Paul has a step further to go, which occurs in the final scene. Carole now appears as the goddess, with an erotic dance that borders on the timeless; a characteristic of the archetype, you may recall. The play between Carole and Helen is of interest as Carole is able to display this newly found depth with her sexual treatment of Helen. Paul is then brought into the scene and reflects on this subtle transition with his increased focus on Carole and which Helen knowingly supports, as does Mick with his watching and admiration. Yet Mick might be more proud of Paul, as it seems his protégé has matured and is also demonstrating his archetypal masculine qualities in the way he engages and plays with the women.

As a passing comment, and beyond the relative lack of sexual description in the final scene, you might have noticed there was no anal sex. I wondered why this would be, and came to the conclusion that it was – obviously – unnecessary. But why? One reason, from the porn perspective, is that Paul has already arse fucked both Carole and Helen, but that seems a little trivial. I then realised it was because of Mick's actions in the preceding scene, which had served as an initiation for Carole into a higher state as evidenced by her response. In this respect, I wonder what state this is?

Maybe that's all a little quick, so let's backtrack a little. We have put Carole and Paul in the 'post-romantic' phase of their respective psychosexual developments, and they seem to be developing deeper connections with their own gender identity, or masculine and feminine principles. In Tantric terms, they have been creative in their sexual development and explored it in a ritual context. These are characteristics of the fifth and sixth chakras, and I would think from the context of the movie that the final scene has them in a kind of dance, literally and metaphorically expressed by Carole, where they are engaging the sixth chakra or, in alchemical terms, adult and undifferentiated love.

I feel that the various elements that lead to this conclusion are embedded in the Club scenes that, as a setting, remind me of the alchemical athanor, flask or container. Whilst there are elements of all the porn combinations there – threesomes, gang bangs and orgies – these do not remain in the lower three chakras of the instincts as routine porn would have them. The settings, ritualisation and symbolic expression give these energies a more coordinated and creative feel, which is the purpose of both Tantra and alchemy.

So, seemingly complex energy patterns are explored in a Dionysian manner. Were they to lack this co-ordination as contained within the patterns of both Tantra and alchemy, they could be destructive rather than creative. Maybe this is why such activity seemingly remains within porn and may serve a function by at least allowing the consumer access to its expression in a semi-ritualised manner. These patterns move our couple from the disenchantment post the fourth chakra to the precipice of the sixth (at least), which Carole has already tasted.

From this point I am going to shift the emphasis from Tantra to alchemy as the main pattern in which to context the ongoing development. I hope I have proven by now that they are essentially synonymous, alchemy being a Western Tantra. The fact that Tantra seems more elaborate, with its seven chakras, is relative, as alchemy has these embedded in its patterns in a somewhat more mysterious manner. We can easily see that the second chakra and the first conjunction, the fourth chakra and second conjunction, the sixth chakra and third conjunction, and the seventh chakra and the fourth conjunction resonate deeply. These acknowledge the points of energetic conjunction of the masculine and feminine energies as they ascend the body, tree or mountain.

The first, third and fifth chakras are embedded in the alchemical process with the base material, furnace and creativity of the whole process. A more detailed analysis of alchemy would reveal more and, like Tantra, demands the active participation of the aspirant rather than a theoretical understanding. Both are methods and ways, not religious systems.

In mythology, the contact between Psyche and Eros does not stop in the "happily ever after" of that myth. Were it to do so there would be a certain sterility or rigidity about it. Eros is connected – in Dionysian fashion – to other forces such as chaos and death, issues that delimit the existential position, but must be engaged for spiritual fulfilment. The connection between Psyche and Eros will allow this to develop to happen. The soul unification at the third conjunction (sixth chakra) will allow passage into the fourth conjunction (seventh chakra). The Dionysian energies, which, to the limited view, can be so destructive, as with the king in the tree, can be turned into something quite transcendent. Does the final scene achieve anything like this?

I have suggested that Carole now has had a taste of the sixth chakra and that Paul is gaining an appreciation of this with the scenes in the Club. Helen seems to add a facilitating role in leading him into a deeper relationship with Carole, whilst she is simultaneously withdrawing from his previous contact with her. This is reflected in the various points of eye contact, which then culminate with the breast and facial cumshot and the ultimate connection of Paul and Carole. I am suggesting this is the culmination of their union in the third alchemical conjunction and that Paul and Carole are resonating with Eros and Psyche.

The cumshot has become a porn standard and is euphemistically referred to as "The Money Shot" because it completes the scene and is what the consumer pays for. At least that's the theory, although it is of interest that it was not a feature in the earlier stag movie era. Because its evolution matched that of the rapid increase and availability of porn, along with some of the sexist agendas implicit, it has come to represent male domination and the male definition of the genre. I find this interesting, because a lot of early porn, whilst using the money shot as the culmination of a scene, did not necessarily focus on this being a facial and often chose nondescript bodily areas, such as the belly. A lot of cumshot scenes also reflect the women in a satisfied and self-fulfilled manner that belies a lot of male fantasy, particularly when he (or they) is 'spent' – which provides an interesting and ironic angle on the term Money Shot!

A recent report I read in a pornography magazine on this matter was of interest to me and is fairly representative. It claimed that the facial cumshot was not an act of aggression, but symbolised a man's power and his ability to provide. It actually used the term "primitive" regarding this power and ability, which I found interesting, thus locating it at the instinctual level. However, it goes on to claim that you may not get to do this in your "real life", as women don't like cum in their eyes because of the stinging it causes, and so the girls in the magazine "do it for you". In this, it is like some of the earlier observations we made, something like you're not good enough or powerful enough as a male when your partner won't 'let' you cum on her face. What about the fact that if women don't like cum in their eyes then why should it be acceptable to the models?

There is an implication here they put up with something they don't like, which is demeaning, and reinforces the male perspective unnecessarily from our perspective. (But, of course, not from theirs!) There are some mixed agendas here, most of which we've already discussed, but it does serve well as a marketing ploy and keeps you hooked. You may actually believe the author and not share this with your partner. The comments above indicate levels of instinctual sexism and marketing angles that I won't bore you with; you'll have heard most of it at one time or another, as well as from me earlier. In our scene Carole initially has her eyes closed, so that negates one argument above; she almost seems to have control over Paul's orgasm. Carole is also directing the scene with Helen now the assistant in the whole process. So, am I suggesting there are levels to the facial cumshot not fully realised, compatible with the higher chakras and their symbolic expression? I certainly am, because the instinctual argument, as espoused above, strikes me as limited, exploitative, circular and redundant.

A little regression to Graham and Emily: It is of note that Emily doesn't receive a facial; she only tastes the men's sperm. Her attention to Graham's cock is a little tentative and seductive, and she has only a small taste of things to come – or cum! This is in contrast to the amounts of sperm the other women receive and in varying locations. This may reinforce the idea that their fledgling relationship is also on a tentative footing, which both Tantra and alchemy would predict.

Let's conclude that Carole and Paul are taking the role of the feminine and masculine principles, respectively, and at this level, they become Psyche and Eros. There could be various angles on what the cumshot represents. Carole's forehead is the location of the third eye and symbolic of the level of the conjunction. Her mouth could be the receptive chalice, a deep symbol of the feminine and reflected in both the ceremony of the Eucharist and the Holy Grail of Christian mysticism. (As an aside: it is interesting that the core symbol of the mystical side to Christianity is a feminine one, isn't it?) Her neck and breasts are the pearl necklace of adornment and abundance of the feminine. The higher chakras and their human alchemical conjunctions have been consecrated; it would seem. By now you might be getting used to these sorts of inversions between the obvious or literal and the mysterious or symbolic.

The ambrosia is the "nectar of the gods" and beyond dualism, so does it represent the unified dual potential of male and female, red and white, sweet and sour, blood and honey? If we take the creation motif, as seen with Shiva and Shakti, but present across cultures in various metaphors of the Fall, then Paul's semen could also be seen as the descent of the divine principle into matter. Alternatively, the semen becomes ambrosia and passes into the mouth as the vessel or chalice and, from there, rises through the already adorned sixth chakra and beyond to the seventh in ecstasy.

You may think I'm getting a little fanciful here, well I am and enjoying it! I am also pointing out that the facial cumshot is much more than the sexist and instinctual act that it is routinely portrayed as. In fact, all sexual expression can be, if you haven't got my point in this matter. The above turning of the scene into various differing perspectives from mythology and comparative spirituality indicates that, in appropriate hands, the erotic can be much more.

What do I mean by this exactly? Well, it depends on the people involved, their level of psychological development and other factors, such as the presence of catalysts and mentors. After all, the bread and wine of the Eucharist are mundane physical elements that are ritualistically and ceremonially transformed into the blood and body of Christ, so what stops us looking at the facial cumshot in this expansive manner? I would argue that this is the spirit in which Paul and Carole are engaging this act in, and that it is prefaced by the rituals of initiation and psychic development that have gone before, and to which this now acts as a celebratory outcome.

The facial and mouth cumshot as a sacrament?

Why not!

I would like to round this chapter off with a little further reflection on alchemy. Although it is a long way from complete in the above representation, I think it creates the strong impression that alchemical symbolism can at least match Tantra in its appraisal of psychosexuality. It is also more inclined to the Western mentality, as it has a tradition that underpins Christianity in its mystical dimension. You might appreciate this a little more with a fact that I have not as yet given you. Rather like tracking down the myths in my library, doing some research on alchemy presented many difficulties and I eventually used a relatively simple text along with my own knowledge and experience. This seemed entirely reasonable until I realised there was no mention of the soror mystica or "mystical sister".

The mystical sister is the partner of the adept (meaning "one who is proficient") in alchemy. When I researched this concept further, I was amazed at how much it matched the description of the male and female Tantric practitioners. This provided me with further evidence that alchemy has, at the very least, one path that seeks realisation (or "enlightenment") through sexuality. I would suggest this evidence is now overwhelming, and alchemy can be synonymous with the left-hand path and, therefore, part of the magical tradition.

So, we end up with sex magic, which progresses to love as the various levels are engaged. All the tools, chemicals of alchemy (which might be symbolically seen as the meat, fish, grain, alcohol and sexual intercourse of Tantra), vessels and nectars are embroiled in a mysterious tradition that is all about enlightenment and which is represented by the ultimate and fourth union. This is the production of the androgyne. Before we get to the androgyne, a little reflection. The normal mundane union of male and female is cock in pussy, lower chakras, ejaculation and the production of a child who, being at the mundane physical level, is either male or female. At the higher level the mouth becomes the vessel that connects to the divine, is the chalice that receives the divine fluid and produces the spiritual child, or androgyne of this fourth union, or seventh chakra.

Back one step. If Psyche and Eros represent the feminine and masculine energies at the sixth chakra, then why is there the supplication of Eros toward Zeus in the myth? Zeus is the ultimate masculine principle in this regard and – almost – matches Shiva. What we have in the final scene back at the Retreat is a quaternary that explores these dynamics a little deeper. Helen has retired a little from centre stage yet remains the feminine principle, Shakti or Aphrodite. Mick stands back as the ultimate masculine principle who, like Shiva, remains uninvolved in the action and toward whom Helen will gravitate as her work is done.

Shiva presents a slightly different figure to Zeus. Although portrayed as the ultimate masculine principal Zeus is intrusive in a way that places him slightly askance from the still divine consciousness of Shiva. My impression is that Zeus is, or becomes, the patriarchal principle and foreshadows the aeon of Pisces in the West with all the distortions we have examined in detail in the course of the book. By contrast, Mick is still and quiet, leaving Helen to remain involved up until the last. This is the change that is implied in our culture; that the masculine principle retires from its interference, even dominance and control, to allow the feminine her full expression. Then, and only then, can their union be complete and the fourth conjunction achieved. In this respect, Dionysus, rather than Zeus, is a better reflection of Shiva in the West.

Paul and Carole are at the third conjunction as a result of the creative and ritual acts that have preceded this scene. Their sexual union completes this phase and the resulting tableau represents the transition to the fourth conjunction. All four participants remain in this quaternary with the final initiation that is symbolised by the sexual act and deeply reflective of the images we discussed a little earlier, such as the Eucharist and Holy Grail.

There is yet another level of imagery contained here. The quaternary can also represent a cross, even 'the' cross. The crucifixion is, in my opinion, a deep image of the transition from the third to fourth conjunction. What is missing in our culture is the balancing emphasis of the resurrection to the culturally dominant crucifixion. By now you might not be surprised about this, as our aeon has taken the patriarchal path and created a monotheism that cannot take this final step ... maybe until now, although probably not by its own hand. The resurrection indicates the attainment of the final conjunction and may cause you to reflect as to why Christian monotheism spends so much energy on the crucifixion but relatively ignores the mysterious dimensions of the resurrection.

This is neither the time nor place to go into the psychology of this and further examine the symbolism, which has been done to some limited extent in the above and would take us too far afield. Instead, I would like to focus on the outcome of the resurrection, which in alchemy is the androgyne. I would argue that this is what Jesus becomes post-resurrection. The androgyne is a hermaphrodite, the ultimate combination of the male and female. Within the image of the androgyne is a combination of the masculine and feminine where both exist and yet neither do: A paradox that is symbolic of the divine and represented by the alchemical gold.

Governing this era in history is the advent of the Age of Aquarius. We are leaving a time of chaos and anxiety, where belief dominated religion and such images as the martyr, victim and hope for a saviour predominated. Aquarius is more impersonal, a time of higher logic and ideas governed by unification, brother/sisterhood and cooperation. It may also manifest the promised love of a Messiah some two thousand years earlier. Well, at least that's the bright side; I suppose it depends on us. The outer planets, which indicate the archetypal patterns, indicate that over the next decade, we will be having a return of the energetics of the nineteen-sixties. Wake up, you old hippy, "the times they are a changing" and maybe that golden era of sexual liberation is returning! Not with the same reactive and revolutionary impetus, but more subtle and integrating. "May you live in interesting times," goes the old proverb.

This era anticipates the androgyne, which, at the mundane level, means an equivalence of male and female, masculine and feminine. Inevitably, this starts from below and the changes are foreshadowed in the sexual dynamics of the age, and doesn't the volcanic eruption of porn indicate this. The challenge is to sift through the dross and work toward what is golden in our sexuality. In occult terms, it indicates the movement of sex magic to love magic. That, after all, is the mystical core of Christianity: Love.

Time to stop as the sun is setting... the sun that is the symbol of this union. We will return when it rises yet again to see how all this has impacted on Brian and Val as a sort of practical application of what we've explored – as if what our porn stars have got up to isn't enough!

The Director's Cut

Part 3

Most of the porn stars arrived at the Retreat on the Friday night and were received warmly by Jan. With the arrival of Paul shortly after breakfast the next morning, the group moved leisurely into the drawing room to begin the debriefing. Carole amused everyone by lightly rubbing her hand on the carpet where some of Graham and Paul's semen had fallen from her breasts, then lifting it and smelling her fingers, to be accompanied by closure of her eyes and a deep exhaled sigh. This brought a smile to all present, although it seemed to Jan that Paul was blushing slightly.

This was hardly surprising; over dinner the previous evening the others had informally started to debrief. This had made Jan feel far more comfortable, as it was obvious that all concerned had undertaken a fair amount of personal integration since their previous meeting together at the Club. When Paul's slight embarrassment subsided, he looked to the others and laughed; Jan then knew he had caught up rapidly and they were ready to begin.

"I've been reviewing some consumer reviews of "Retreat"," Jan began, "which are somewhat contrasting, but mainly endorsing. How do you think the viewer would have taken it?"

"I think in many ways." Paul had leapt in first. *Obviously eager to integrate into the group*, thought Jan. "I suspect you'd have a fair amount of flak from the critics, although I do notice it is also getting a couple of notable nominations. I haven't looked much, as I wanted to do this review first, but I reckon each of us actors may have copped a bit too.

"But the viewer? Could be various responses … there's enough straightforward, raunchy sex to keep most happy, although some sections of the audience may keep the sound down and play with the fast-forward button a bit. I reckon the Club scenes, in particular, would keep the serious aficionado interested and draw them into the ritual action."

"Ritual, Paul?" This was Mick.

"Well, yes, that's pretty much what it is. The patterns are too formalised and I noticed Jan was very particular in our positions and responses as the scenes unfolded. I reckon he did his old trick of planning less than we think!"

Smart, thought Jan, *but he does know me fairly well now.*

"Any gay women out there would have been held by it," chimed in Helen, "and, if not totally anti-men, they'd be tempted to experiment a bit more. I could easily see where I fitted in that transition. So, in that respect at least, they were quite ritualised and provided a few guidelines."

"It brings in a powerful connection between sex and emotions. I suspect that Jan is trying to get a more spiritual perspective and the perceptive viewer would have appreciated that … at many levels."

Carole's expressed the essential unity of what I was trying to do quite succinctly, thought Jan.

Indeed, that was what had happened to Brian, as they would later find out. It had given him a map, which he could take into the future of his sexual explorations without the residual guilt and internal divisions that he felt had always plagued him. In many ways, his dream had helped in that reconciliation process, and he now saw it as a powerful healing endorsement to his viewing experience.

Brian had realised there were two ways he could "read" the dream. The first was more Freudian, and many of the symbols definitely lent themselves to a sexual interpretation but offered only an explanation of his sexual psychology and tended to give it an unhealthy hue, particularly the "vice" association. By contrast, the religiously oriented nature of many of the images inclined him to a more Jungian perspective. Although this gave him a better spiritual perspective of his life and direction, it left him a little dissatisfied as well.

Somehow, he felt the two approaches were missing something because he found it difficult to reconcile them; he didn't want to reject either, as each felt valid; it was just that what seemed like an essential unity evaded his grasp. It wasn't until he started exploring Tantra and then Western psychosexual mysticism that he realised what this dissatisfaction was. At that stage he started to flirt with a non-dualistic view of the dream; that is, it could be sexual and mystical, personal and transpersonal, in a paradoxical and creative way. With this map he then engaged a more Tantric and later an alchemical map and found the images and patterns fitted well both into his dream and his life.

Brian went back through the dream in more detail and took these details into his contemplative space. The outcome gave him a basis to heal beyond the residual guilt, anxiety and fear of his troubled childhood. Val certainly wasn't complaining.

Jan realized they could discuss the consumer's perspective much further. This would have been useful, but it would detract from the main purpose of the meeting; it would be a future event.

"I've already put Mel on to keeping tabs with all the various levels of feedback. I just wanted some initial reflection on how you may have thought it would be received. Like you, Paul, and maybe others here, I've tended to keep only a cursory glance at the feedback at this time."

Mick interjected: "I'll be quite honest. Whilst that's frequently a consideration in shoots, often endorsed by a director with comments like, "a grimace and eye-roll now, Mick, let's give the punter some sense that this is really turning you on", I didn't find much time for that in this shoot. I wondered why and realised that when I get such prompts my heart's not on the job and maybe the shoot is a bit of a dud. What I found in "Retreat" was that you were so focused on our involvement in the process that it hardly seemed like a shoot; it was as if I really entered the part and became it. The potential viewer felt well and truly out of the loop at that time."

With that response and the various nods and acknowledgements from the others, Jan felt he could move on.

"Well, that's great to hear, but what I'd really like some comment on is how the actual sex affected you, if you 'got into the part'? I know that none of you did anything you haven't done before, sometimes frequently! It is just that maybe with these parts and context, it was a bit different?"

"I'll say it was!" Carole's reply was almost instantaneous.

She has a story, thought Jan, *I hope it's what I sense it might be.*

"I've never been into women like that before. The girls from the bar teamed up in such a way I could lose myself and not have any of the lingering inhibitions I usually have when I have a cunt in front of me, or a woman's tongue in me. I've given it a bit of thought: It wasn't the anonymity factor of being with a couple of girls I've never had before; it was more the fact that the two were like twins dancing around me. I didn't give the fact that they were girls a thought after a while, plus the fact I'd been well and truly loosened up by the guys."

"Was the orgasm real?" Paul asked this ... obviously they hadn't caught up independently since the film finished. Jan's brow furrowed, as this surprised him. He wondered why they had not …

"Sure was, although different from with a guy, somehow more liquid; but that could also be because it's the first time I've ever come with a woman, or women… and on a set too!"

"Do you routinely come with guys on a shoot? 'Cos sometimes you act so well I can't pick the difference!" Mick jutted in this time.

"Depends on the guy, the shoot and the director. If there are too many cameras on my face and fanny and too many instructions being barked, it's difficult; but if I can get into it as well as the guy – or guys – then it's usually a breeze. I didn't come with the dildos, that was an act, but that's because I prefer anything inside me to be hot!"

Jan was secretly hoping that Mick and Carole would then explore the upstairs scene a bit further, but he would have to wait as Carole jumped to something surprising.

"Mind you, my response always depends on where I am in my cycle."

There was a collective look of surprise in the room to Carole's comment, maybe with the exception of Helen. It seemed to leap out of her mouth almost unbeknownst to her as well.

"You don't take the pill, then?" Helen was the least surprised and her response invited a dialogue between them.

"No, haven't for several years now. I took it for a couple of years as a teenager and then stopped when Gary and I got hitched up. I stopped then as kids were on the agenda, before I found out he preferred men. That's when I went a bit loose and Rick came on the scene. He was all man and that was fine, but maybe a bit of an overcompensation. When he introduced me to this industry, I was only a bit hesitant, as it felt like a great way to extend my boundaries – at all levels – and I had Rick to kinda ease me in without too much trauma or too many predators hanging around.

"I hadn't restarted the pill with Rick; partly because I am so much more sexually responsive off it and partly because he reassured me about his control. I realised later it was an adjunct to his profession!"

"Well," Mick interjected, "it helps a lot to have it. I saw many a guy lose more than his load because of lack of control!"

"We'll come back to that," commented Jan. "Go on, Carole." He was concerned she might lose momentum and become diverted from an important area; also, Mick didn't show any such hesitation with his comment, so he could wait.

"I've also learnt to keep an eye on my cycle. I had a teenage pregnancy that ended up in an abortion and that was a bit traumatic, so I didn't want to repeat that. I also wanted to keep my body clean and explore my sexuality further. Whilst the pill offers that security, it's at a price – for me, at least."

"Me too," said Helen," but I still use it periodically to control my cycle around shoots. I know some girls use it continuously, which doesn't seem too smart. You don't use it at all, Carole?"

"No. I really enjoy natural periods, too; there's something about the release and flow that's different off the pill. It's not just that I know the guys in the trade have good control … usually, it's also 'cos my sex life doesn't stop on a set. I know when my ovulation is happening, so I avoid any risks absolutely then and that includes a break from shooting, which I'm pretty good at organising. I also have some spermicidal cream if I sense a leak at a potentially risky time, though this is usually just for personal insurance. Heh, I feel better now I've got that minor secret off my chest! I've managed to keep it closely guarded it seems by the look of your expressions.

"It might not be too politically smart to say this in public, but condoms just don't cut it either. In the business, my experience is that when condoms are routinely used the sex within and between the porn stars is also a bit average." This last comment invited some reflective nodding from the others.

Jan felt rewarded with this expression. He was intrigued; he was directing the conversation toward their actual physical responses to the sex in the scenes, but these guys were moving into a range of deeper territory.

"You're playing a bit on the edge there, gal," Helen responded to Carole. "Gotta admire that; my control freak nature won't let me go that far! I must agree with you, though, there's few guys I've done scenes with who I'd prefer had a condom, but it's usually because they don't turn me on too much rather than for the safety angle."

"I wouldn't have spotted you for a control freak?" Paul commented.

"You should have seen me as a teenager!" was her immediate retort. "Then again, with the sexual shit in my family it's not surprising, although it took me a few years to get the connection. In many ways this business has been really healing and helped me reconcile a lot of the trauma and wounds with the experiences I've been through. It's been a kind of therapy for me; I've been almost able to select roles that reflect where I'm at personally."

Jan jumped in: "Anyone else feel the same?"

A collective nodding greeted his interjection, with Paul adding: "Yeah, I flirted on the 'am I gay' thing for many years after my particular and peculiar childhood. Acting helped me explore this at a more mental level, but I actually came into the industry because I realised that this exploration needed to be more experiential and practical. I actually didn't need to do any gay scenes to find out further, as the first threesome I did with a couple made me realise women were my thing." He didn't add, at this stage to all assembled, that Jan had been a significant guide and mentor in this transition.

Jan noticed Carole was looking at her coffee cup. He knew

that meant she was deep in thought, but also avoiding Paul's potential gaze. Indeed, Paul was looking at her when he made the last comment.

"Mick, you were saying …?" Jan moved things on.

"Yeah, control. I read a coupla books and took some instruction from a Taoist on this, when I felt that I was in danger of coming too quickly in scenes. He taught me about the various pelvic muscle groups and how to independently control my arse and cock muscles; even to the muscles that moved my cock and the ones that lifted my balls that helped me hold back on coming. In fact, if I do the last long enough I can go on indefinitely, which can be a drag when the director wants me to shoot!"

Again, the smiles and some laughter. They knew that Mick had a reputation for plenty of semen and this added a lot to an appropriate scene. Mick then added, to some surprised looks, that he had some similar questions to Paul when he started in the business, but rapidly realised it was the ignorance of his upbringing that produced this rather than the trauma that was Paul's experience. In this respect, Mick's settling of such issues was much easier and his feminine nature, gentle and deep, then came into play in some subtle ways, as Jan had noticed in "Retreat".

Time for a break, toilets and further coffee, although Helen's was a peppermint tea.

"I think you've been angling for our sexual responses," Carole was looking directly at Jan, "and we may have moved more into our emotional ones, plus relevant associated areas."

Jan noticed she was being concise, and particularly with her words. "I suspect that was your intention anyway, but I do want to return to the actual sex. I don't think anyone here was really challenged by the sex itself, but I've had a lot to digest since those last scenes."

Jan responded after a pause: "What in particular?"

"Well, Mick's cock in my arse was a surprising challenge. I know he has a good size cock, maybe a bit thicker than Paul, though not as long. When it went in my arse upstairs, I felt tight, even though I wasn't. I'd been well and truly worked up by the guys and then 'come' with the girls – a first in itself – then when Mick stuck it in, it felt really huge. I focused on my arse muscles and did a reverse of what Mick was talking about, relaxing them as if I was having a shit, but that made no difference.

"I realised later it was because of the space I was in. I felt Mick's cock was opening me up in a new way and when the muscle relaxing didn't change anything, I decided to go with it. At first this was painful, but a pain that had an exquisite edge to it. Then I felt this heat going right through my body and into my head, then it seemed to shoot out of the top of my head and I think I lost it for a while."

"It's funny, I felt something similar at the end of our last scene, Carole," Paul chimed in and looked directly at her; she responded in kind. "Even though I came, I didn't in a funny way. I was kind of detached and the cum seemed to go through me and I could almost feel it in my body where it was coming on you."

"I noticed you were crying," she responded.

"Yeah, didn't want Jan to put the camera on me then! Then why should he, you were radiantly blissful and the object of attention."

The pause was immense as tears came to Carole's eyes. Paul was quite still and looked immensely proud. He now radiated to the room the same feeling that he had experienced from Carole in the scene and everyone became caught up in it.

All were quiet as Jan gently started to talk about the ritual context that had emerged in the scenes. He explained a little about the spiritual dimensions to sexuality that he was exploring personally and now professionally, and how he had tried to fashion these into "Retreat". The discussion remained open and he was able to share more in a manner that Paul was familiar with.

Jan knew he was giving them a condensed lesson in the deeper psychology of sexuality and also instructing them further. This was augmented with some further suggested reading and he then brought the meeting to a relative close. He knew they would have a lot to think about and digest, but it was imperative they grasp this framework if Voluptas was to be even considered. He explained that the next day they would run through some preliminary structure and content of the first in the series, so they could take a break for the remainder of the day.

"Well, tonight is going to be interesting!" Jan's comment caused Carole and Paul to look at him somewhat quizzically.

He noticed their surprise: "Sorry, I'd better explain. Tonight Mick, Helen and I are going to work at the Club because we have some special guests coming to the restaurant. I thought I'd go as chef and let these guys do the bar and waitress bit. After the scene in the kitchen, I think they'll fit into the part quite easily!

"Our guests will have a surprise to negotiate; it's all part of the wider vision of and for Voluptas. Carole, can you and Paul come as well? Not to work, but as guests. I feel you have a lot you may want to share."

12

Where to from here?

The kids had settled down after some chips and a drink from a Roadhouse so now Val could allow her thoughts free rein for a while. Her decision to take a few days out from the marriage had been helped by associated business issues, though not entirely necessary on their own merit. Both Val and Brian knew this to be the case, even though it was not discussed. It is not that she felt the marriage was in jeopardy as yet; it was just that there was some confusion and miscommunication.

This confusion stemmed mainly from where they were going as individuals beyond the obvious issue of their respective careers. These careers had always had differences that probably helped their relationship because they were two strong individuals and, therefore, had separate territories in which to express this. No, the confusion was more subtle and deeper than that. One reason she had taken the kids away with her is that she wanted to explore her feelings about her relationship with them separate from Brian's presence. Of course, there were some 'issues' with them, particularly Clare, but nothing had emerged about these relationships that surprised Val or gave her any further input into the confusion.

So, it was the relationship. The sex had always been fine; it was an undeniable part of their initial attraction, even with the age difference, and had been consistently good. Whilst it was something they often fell back on in times of difficulty neither was under any illusion about this, it seemed a case more of getting back to the foundations and common ground to explore what might be happening elsewhere. Both she and Brian enjoyed playing at the edges a little and both had such exploration as prior experience. This was probably a significant mutual point to their attraction, as earlier relationships had often been imbalanced at this level of exploration.

Brian had also introduced Val to pornography. Well, not entirely, there had been that kinky Malcolm, but his porn was not to her taste – literally – as pissing wasn't her scene, although she did try it to find out. The fisting and desire to introduce toys much bigger than a dick made her feel more than a little frightened. Brian's tastes were much more acceptable and made her realise that she enjoyed some of what Malcolm had tried to introduce in this different context. Malcolm's compulsive use and tastes had caused her not to pursue porn further, even though it piqued her interest, she really didn't know how to explore it and was not that Internet savvy.

Brian had no such difficulty and had calmed her anxieties about this masturbatory dimension to his life. Val received the benefit, as he was careful in his introduction of new or extended themes in their sexual life. Her gentle reintroduction to some themes that Malcolm had employed was more commensurate with the nature of their sexual contact at the appropriate time, as well as lacking the abusive edge she had experienced before. She was able to join Brian in this further exploration and discovered a pain and pleasure edge to her sexuality that she had not previously realised.

Simultaneously, the romantic edge waned; you might expect that with the advent of two children, although the love remained and sustained them. Sexually, there were times when the attention drifted, but an early caveat in their marriage and reinforced by Brian's prior experience was that any such attention should be communicated between them and prior to any action being undertaken. This was appropriate, as there were a couple of times when a sexual attraction may have extended to a clandestine affair that could have unnecessarily threatened their relationship.

Partly because of this, and also because of the exposure to sexual complexity, they had confronted any looming attraction with a third party with the ethic of their marital sexuality. On occasion, this meant that a third party joined them in the marital bed. Whilst Val had been a little nervous of this at first, it was with a man whose reciprocated attraction Val had declared to Brian. Although she initially wondered whether Brian's offer to invite David into the bed was to save the marriage and indicated his vulnerability, she was excited by the possibility. More than excited, she revelled in it and experienced sexual attention not otherwise possible. It was David who found this too much, so maybe Brian had been cunning after all? She had to love him, if that was the case!

It seemed to both of them that the undercurrent that most sabotaged their occasional threesome was the emotional agenda of the third party. Confrontation of this agenda with a sexual invitation into the marital bed often stopped the innuendo and sexual games dead in their tracks, and usually, the invitation wasn't taken up! When it was then the "play" factor often sustained the contact for a while, but it wasn't until they got to know Peter and Margot that Brian and Val felt they had met their match. This relationship was sustained episodically over several years and always remained fun and exploratory, but they had not been engaged for a couple of years now. It had just drifted, really, and Val sensed that both she and Brian had moved beyond the need for such exploration on the terms that it had been up to that point in time.

Throughout this period, Val noticed that Brian's interest in porn and erotic art continued but became a little more refined, although she reasoned that it could also be because the industry was 'growing up'. She was further surprised when their relationship resumed its monogamous state that his consumption did not increase; in fact, it seemed to decline somewhat. *Well, that might be okay*, she thought, *but so had their sexual experimentation declined and that wasn't okay! As dragging a third party into bed wasn't the answer, would a more active encouragement of his consumption help this?* Her thoughts drifted and she realised that didn't feel right. So maybe she was now in the throes of the impasse and nothing seemed to engage her as a solution.

One thing that was quietly dawning on her as she reached the end of the highway was that her reflections had been mainly in terms of Brian and his position with respect to the intimate dimensions to their relationship. What exactly was her position? Had she ever defined it? *My god*, she thought, *is this it ... haven't I clearly defined my position and where I am going here?* A wave of panic surged through her body. Of course, she had taken the initiative and made her sexual demands clear, even extending to pushing Brian's boundaries on more than one occasion; yet this was something more subtle, made hazier by the lack of any map she could refer to from her past. She pulled into the drive.

Brian's thinking had been along different lines. The dream had confronted him with where his life seemed poised from a spiritual perspective and how this radiated out to his work. Also, this was where he positioned Stephanie, not misinterpreting the dream as a justification to fuck her or bring her back for mutual pleasure with Val, but as a muse in his working situation. He clearly knew what this meant, that his professional direction required a change that was long in the gestation – a generation maybe – but for which he now felt ready.

Brian had known that this was impacting on Val and he

couldn't entirely insulate her, as his mood was too deep. He also tried to tease out the issues that pertained to his marriage that were a concern, aware that she may interpret that as the entirety of the problem; it was a risk he felt he had to take and that her period away was for her to look at this. It was incumbent upon him to differentiate these factors so that any decisions would be as clear as possible. He spent an hour on the phone that morning discussing the implications with Steph, who would put on her Personal Assistant hat and start the restructuring process.

That much seemed clear: The worn-out man was himself and in need of renewal, and that this professional direction needed to come from a fundamentally spiritual perspective. And this spiritual perspective was ... well, it seemed fundamentally based in alchemy and this made both personal and professional sense to him; Tantra gave him some practical bridges into a Western esoteric art that he had flirted on the edges of for some considerable time. He also had an intuition that the dream related more deeply to the core of his personal development and that this could not be so easily differentiated. It was of a fundamentally psychosexual nature and therefore involved Val, his life-mate. He knew where to start: they would watch the "Retreat" together that evening without prior discussion. When Val entered the house and the greetings were over, she felt happy and relieved with the plan because it did not put a premature demand on verbal expression.

I hope by now I have stripped away all that is degenerative about sexuality as reflected in pornography and arrived at the erotic and aesthetic dimensions of sexuality; if not entirely that, then at least made some significant steps in the right direction. We have arrived here without undue description or illustration, such that I experience little that is directly pornographic in the preceding pages; maybe some that are erotic, but a significant amount that is educative.

Now these words 'educate' or 'education' has tracked me through the course of this book. Not that this was the intention when I started, as this book seemed fun and started as a bit of a lark in response to some personal provocation, but it developed a seriousness that surprised and still surprised me. The 'education' aspect was because of a work I have been simultaneously completing for publication where the words 'education' and 'training' were the most surprising and significant components of the reviews I received. Am I a teacher? I never thought so ... I'm a practitioner, a deliverer of services, I don't teach.

As I've done on several occasions to date I turn to the dictionary: why do I do this? Well, I've found it a very rich source as it contains elements that stretch back in time and provide a depth within words we commonly use and frequently trivialise. I have made reference to this with the words 'cult' and 'myth' that are not only flattened of any depth but also, more disturbingly, given a meaning quite contrary to their original intention. Before I do turn, there is a little further irony – by now, you realise I just love synchronicity – because when I went to the dictionary to look up 'educate', the first word I came to was 'climax'! Need I say more?

Back to educate: "... give intellectual and moral training to" and "... development of character and mental powers." Do you see the deeper issues here? Not just mental training but mental powers and not just mental, also intellectual. You might like this; I certainly do. Intellectual ... "enlightened person." What about the "moral training" bit? Are we or are we not more into soul territory here and well beyond reason, instruction and formulae?

At university, I had two tutors, one for my studies and a second designated moral tutor. So, maybe I am a teacher after all and just maybe this is an educative work. Climax? I won't grab my dick or rush off in search of my partner, as I recognise this will be the last chapter when I had intended two, which I now see as unnecessary.

The essential conundrum pornography leaves us with is the issue of the literal versus the symbolic. At a much broader and deeper level, I also see this as a major concern in Western culture, and in this, I am far from alone. To begin a further exploration of the paradoxes inherent in this equation, let's start with an orientation that commences with the symbolic.

It is the metaphoric and symbolic dimensions that I have tried to access from fairly early on in this exploration. So, once the current social, psychological and political issues regarding porn were out of the way I launched into a creative act – "The Weekend Retreat" – which surprised and excited me. By surprised, it was because, beyond a certain point, it was not planned, and by excited, I mean that literally, I became aroused, sometimes sexually, but mainly in a joyful and playful way. I don't see these responses as negating the creative act; in fact, I think they are essential ingredients of any act of creativity. What was more surprising was that when I came to unravel "Retreat" I found it to be deeply symbolic of psychosexuality and to connect to further dimensions in the Great Chain of Being, the higher chakras, alchemical conjunctions, spiritual insights or whatever. It certainly wasn't limited to the instinctual and the literal.

Yet the "Retreat" can be looked at this way. It is a literal description of sexuality that can be called playful, Dionysian or promiscuous; depending on which hat you might be wearing. It can be seen as sexually stimulating and leading to masturbation, be evocative and an enhancement to lovemaking, or depraved; again, depending on the hat. So, does it come down to the viewer? Well of course it does, but it also comes down to how the creative product engages the viewer and where that may lead.

Of course, with the mass of routine porn, this is to masturbate and maybe a tad of instruction. It is stripped of any symbolic import, unless inadvertent. It is designed to engage you in a repetitive cycle of viewing and consumption to the point of compulsion, even addiction, then again, so can chocolate. Yet if the symbolic dimension is engaged, which creativity will do, then the sexual energy can be drawn out of the cycle of repetition and, like Kundalini, begin the ascent up the Great Chain as symbolised in Tantra by the spinal cord. As this happens there is a transformation of the energy into a more soulful and then spiritual perspective.

That's all very well, wise guy, you may be saying, but what about the issue of whether porn should be taken literally or not? You're going to love my answer, because it all depends on you. As you may have seen in the previous chapters, there are two paths, what I have called the "left" and "right-hand paths", as symbolised with the Kundalini energy and her ascent. The right-hand path remains metaphoric and engages the imagination in an ascetic and inner mode. The left-hand path moves into the literal and, from there engages the imagination and symbolic realms; it is more active, ecstatic and magical.

Both these paths are equally valid. In the West, we have given stress to the right to the exclusion of the left. Although, more than that, we have become disconnected from the realms of the feminine, the body and our sexuality that are the essential foundations and ingredients of any personal and spiritual evolution. The left-hand path is, therefore, more in need of resurrection, but because of its relatively neglected and denied position, it is the more potentially explosive in a myriad of ways.

It is not surprising that these approaches have, until recent times and the advent of the porn eruption, been the province of magical traditions and it is these that might need some restoration to encompass these energetically sexual approaches.

Porn does not routinely and commercially do this; it is not what the main bulk of the industry is about. But what it is doing is demonstrating to the public the range of sexual activity that may be routinely possible – an instructive function – to activity not routine, but potentially accessible. What porn lacks, and the "Retreat" tries to restore, is some of the containment and pathways of exploration that are necessary for such activity to become creative and spiritual, should the left-hand path be chosen.

What I have implied in this work is that Brian and Val have taken this instruction on board in various dimensions of their lives. What they probably lacked in this was the ritual containment and guidance that could have educated them further, which such movements as the magical tradition and the Dionysian mysteries of the past can educate us in. In this sense, it is more the second half of the movie that could be most instructive to them, or even educative in the genuine sense. We'll return to them to see where they take it.

As they moved through the next few hours there was a lot to share, yet it remained deliberately circumstantial, as Brian knew the movie might be the trigger for the deeper issues they needed to engage. Their communication had moved from the rounds of discussion that were always in danger of leading to blame and accusation. Both had become independently clear that certain issues that had entered the fray, such as work or the kids, were not the fundamental issues. Brian had come to realise that he was undergoing a major change in his life and had already addressed this at the professional end of the spectrum; he was now doing it at the personal. For her part, Val realised the depth of Brian's change and hence his mood, but also that she needed to be more actively engaged in the process. So, when Brian had suggested watching "The Weekend Retreat" as a sort of circuit-breaker, she readily endorsed this, when in the past she may have been less enthusiastic or dismissive, as she had seen a lot that was repetitive and boring.

Encouraged, Brian put on the movie after the kids were sound asleep and the door locked. Val was blown away. She enjoyed the first half anyway, but the second seemed to open up a veritable Pandora's Box of goodies rather than ills. They finished the movie, silently made love and went to sleep. Brian didn't dream that night; he'd probably had enough. Val's dreams were fleeting; she recalled directing people around a movie set; presumed this reflected the movie, but also thought it may indicate that she needed to take a more active direction in her erotic life. It reinforced the reflections she had made on the drive home.

Over the next few days, their discussions were interactive and exploratory. Brian picked up a book called "The Porn User's Guide to Enlightenment" that seemed to confirm and reinforce their position. It gave him added strength for what he perceived as being the next step. There was also a useful reading list at the back for them both to refer to and use, as well as a website that indicated there were places in the West that were exploring these dimensions in an educative and interactive manner.

Val called Margot and they met for a drink after work one day, asking their respective partners to sort out the domestic issues of the evening. Margot was understandably surprised to hear from Val, as their relationship had become defined by the sexual encounters, and so she presumed the request for a meeting was something in that area, but was discreet enough to await their meeting. Her curiosity was definitely aroused ... and you may further wonder what their respective partners were imagining!

"Well, my love, you have my curiosity running hot, after all this time as well!"

"I thought I would," replied Val, "but I wanted this to be face-to-face."

"Understood, so spill the beans."

Val told Margot that there was no prepared speech, but a request for some feedback and possible assistance. Val was aware that Margot had been involved in the feminist movement for some years before she had met Peter, whom she told Val and Brian in the past had 'tamed' her! Margot's involvement had extended to a couple of years of lesbian encounters until she realised that "cocks rather than cunts were my preferred option." Of course, Val had known of this in the mutual encounters that the four had experienced together, but she had only entertained contact with Margot as part of the 'play'.

Margot was a little surprised: "You mean you want more intense girlie stuff now, my love?"

"Well, I'm really not sure ..."

Val conveyed to Margot where she and Brian were 'at' in their relationship, but also about the movie. What had affected her most was Carole's involvement with the girls at the Club, but more significantly with Helen back at the Retreat. There was something about all this that she couldn't let go of and it kept circulating in her mind.

Margot explained that the only girl-to-girl encounters that she had been involved with had also been with Peter present since she met him, but she had a sense that Val was wondering whether some more exclusive contact was what she craved. Margot also explained that since the relationship with Brian and she had waned that Peter had suggested a couples' club, which they had joined. Margot said that any exclusive stuff with another woman – or more – was usually on a stage in front of a live and intermittently involved audience! Val was not sure whether Margot was serious or not and didn't follow this comment with any further question. Instead, she got right to the point: "I want to explore women's sex with you, Margot."

Margot had guessed it might come to this. She was pleasantly surprised; the thought of Val all to herself was appealing and exciting, but she'd always considered that beyond Val's range. Margot was also impressed by Val's newfound directness; she had thought that if she decided to explore that outcome before she might have to lead Val to it.

Now this was all outside the usual parameters of their sexual engagement, but Val was insistent and Margot was excited. They agreed to go back and discuss this with their respective partners and gauge the outcome. Neither man seemed to baulk at the possibility, but each said they wanted to talk to the other. When this occurred, Brian realised that Peter had more confidence in this issue than he had; in fact, Brian was somewhat anxious and fearful for his relationship with Val. Peter's comment was that he wanted to weal the camera when the official 'take' came up for recording!

All the jokes notwithstanding, the men agreed to let Margot and Val have their time and space together. Peter mirrored these occasions by coming around to Brian's house when he was doing the child minding and they came to share a lot about their male experiences at a personal level. Brian, who had never had a gay encounter, was surprised to find that Peter had several during his sexually formative years, but none since he had moved solidly into heterosexual relationships. Certainly, Brian had never felt threatened by him in this way in their various encounters and Peter explained that it wasn't something he felt any need to bring into them either.

Brian did get a picture of the couples' club, which was called the "Dispensary". The founder was a Pharmacist who was taking a light-hearted poke at his profession – and probably elsewhere as well! His experience in various Asian cultures was of considerable assistance in the founding. There were some fairly strict rules, such as couples always arriving and leaving together and no contact of a sexual nature beyond the club. Somewhat surprisingly, there had been only one occasion when a couple had left their respective spouses as a result of meeting there. Given the years and numbers involved, this was considerably less than one would expect in the mainstream. It also spoke a lot about the maturity of the club members and that they were well scrutinised prior to joining.

Brian guessed that sooner or later, Peter would invite him and Val. In the meantime, he was dealing with the anxiety he had about Val and Margot by researching some of the material he came across in "The Porn User's Guide" and was particularly impressed about Tantra on first reading. He decided to independently research this further and to engage in some of the spiritual practices he subsequently found. He was pleasantly surprised that Val showed an interest and usually joined him in the meditative practice and physical exercises he was undertaking.

In reality, the marriage was never in question in Val's mind, and Margot was relishing her Instructress role. We also won't go into any detail here; partly because the sexual content has already been described by the encounters of the various women in "Retreat", but more so because it is a feminine mystery process of initiation. The encounters went on for a few months, and then, seemingly out of the blue, Val announced that they had finished. Margot showed no surprise, Peter was vaguely amused and Brian quietly relieved. Although this anxiety had been somewhat allayed by the interesting dimensions that were occurring in his lovemaking with Val.

Of course, the invitation to the couples' club followed and, of course, Val and Brian joined. What both of them appreciated was the emotional maturity of the members. There was a dispute and grievance process that was rarely engaged because of this and they felt that the members were there to explore a range of their sexuality that couldn't be achieved elsewhere. Yet there was something missing and both Brian and Val could feel it, even if they couldn't at that time explain it. In the meantime, they enjoyed what the club had to offer, in particular the theatrics. One of the most enjoyable features was that a person, or sometimes a couple, chose a particular scenario not unlike a porn scene, as well as the various invited performers. A script of sorts was kept to and the remaining members formed the audience, although they were aware they could also be called on as participants at any time. Brian could easily recognise elements of ritual here, as portrayed in "Retreat", as well as what he was discovering in his spiritual research. Val discovered herself to be a performer of quality and even got into directing others.

Whilst the couples' club had other rooms for restricted purposes, it was only the dungeon that Val and Brian made use of, and only at times when the atmosphere was 'soft'. They were both aware that the dungeon was used for 'harder' purposes, but that was not of interest, nor were the rooms where the content became a little more perverted. Val, for one, had experienced her fill of fists, big toys and urine. Yet they both understood the purposes of these different spaces and their presence didn't create any conflict for them.

Instead, the conflict came from where the couples' club was strategically and psychologically situated and what was emerging for both of them. Their relationship had deepened and their independent careers had taken imaginative and creative turns, pleasing to both. The children were growing, and were aware that they had some fairly "far out" parents, but not aware of their activities, they simply enjoyed the psychological and social spin-offs. The conflict was that both Brian and Val had a sense of something more that they were looking for and that the club was not serving this. They had taken their sexual experience in those terms as far as it could go. Both were bringing their energetic discoveries back to their intimacy, which was now significantly more than just in their lovemaking. Both were also recognising through their spiritual enquiry and subsequent experience that they needed to put their mature sexualities in a differing context and direction. They asked questions about this of themselves and the couples' club, but none of the members there showed any inclination to take the experimentation further.

Was this it? Was this the end of the exploration? They made a choice. What they realised was that in the absence of any person, place or institution that could guide them further, they were thrown back on their own resources. These were now considerable, and they were hardly unhappy; they just felt they were on a quest and wanted to continue the exploration. They also had come to a spiritual truth: there was no need to go out and chase any further alternatives. If they remained true to their practice, then any such alternatives would come and greet them. In the meantime, they had more than enough information to work with.

One interesting feature was the porn. The director of "The Weekend Retreat" had not, as yet, brought out a follow-up or sequel. In fact, there was no other work that Brian could find. This was a little disappointing. He did find Carole, Paul and the others in movies subsequent to "Retreat". He almost invariably enjoyed these and Val was quick to note that he rarely, if ever, brought a DVD that did not contain at least one of them. The strange thing was that they were rarely alone in any movie, there always seemed to be at least one of the others there. Was she right in this? She did a check: in fact, there was always more than one. *Interesting*, she thought.

There was also something subtle that both became gradually

aware of. When the main porn stars of "Retreat" were in a movie then the quality and style of production had a vague similarity to that seminal movie. This was irrespective of the production company, producer or director, and even the more forceful stars in porn. It was as if they quietly affected everything around them. Their acting also seemed to flow on from what they had portrayed in "Retreat". Brian took some old movies out that contained any or some of them. He was sure that these changes had only been since "Retreat" as far as he could tell. Anyway, he enjoyed what he did get, his porn budget was less, but he'd still like another production from that director!

Where does porn fit into Brian and Val's life now? I think the above may adequately describe it. Porn has been a significant feature of Brian's life and probably will always remain so. Yet now its place is quite restricted and reflective of his – and Val's – psychosexual level of development, which is how you'd expect it to be. He has also become more conversant with eroticism at large and erotic art in various forms: images, poetry and prose. He has also extended his interest into the historical and cultural aspects of the erotic and beginning to connect it with the magical and other spiritual traditions of his own heritage. He doesn't deny that Tantra has been of significance and even essential to his enquiry, it is just that he thinks there may be traditions closer to home that would suit him. I would agree, and he has picked up the hints about alchemy reading this book.

Here's to you Brian!

Let's not get too puritanical with these higher dimensions. Remember, they are inclusive of and transcend all that passed before, but that does not equate to what has passed being redundant or denied. There's always a place for good sexual raunch, even in the best porn movie!

Psychosexual development, to a greater or lesser extent, is

under our personal control. It is a challenge, even a risk to open up to sexual dimensions that are denied and even denigrated in society. I trust I have put this denigration on a firmly dysfunctional footing so that the denial can be negotiated, even though it requires courage and facing some fears. However, the trend of the time is with us in this regard. It is not so long ago that a book such as this would have attracted charges of obscenity. "The times they are a-changing!" sings Bob Dylan and in this realm, he is certainly right.

Yet we always have to negotiate the fine line between the literal and the symbolic as well as appreciating their interconnection. If I were to tell you that my perspective is to see the literal as part of a reflection of the symbolic, or one expression of it, then does that help? If I use the metaphor in a sexual context and indicate that sexuality is initially and fundamentally feminine and that masculine sexuality is one expression of it, does that help any further?

Remember Teiresias ...

The question of whether to take a literal approach to psychosexual development is a big one. If you want to argue that my position in this book is that it often requires literal exploration; then you are right. However, this stems from the reinstatement of nature, the body, femininity and sexuality into our psychic economy, then seeing them as the basis of our psychosexual development, its flowering in the soul, and ultimately the archetypal world of spirit (and they're beyond gender). The choice is whether we take the left- or right-hand path; how do we decide? As ultimately both are embraced in the symbolic world and governed by ritual and ceremony then the literal path is but one and a risky one at that, because it is magical and places a demand on us at an individual moral level that the right-hand path can often comfortably slide by ... even if this might be a 'sin of omission'.

Here is an overarching general principle, which I will back up with some examples. If we attend to our psychosexuality, it is a sure avenue to an appreciation of the soul. At this point, we stand between the worlds; let's call them the spirit and the external world. If we see the world as a mirror of the spiritual, it might ease any existential anxiety you may be experiencing. Then we listen to the imaginings and ideas that permeate the soul and our individual reality. These are the messages of spirit and if we have taken responsibility for our psychosexuality to date it behoves us to simply listen.

Listen to what, you may well ask? Well, from the inner perspective, it is images in the form of dreams, visions, intuition or flashes of insight, but first, you must trust them, and that's no easy task. So even prior to that the message is to listen and listen again, then watch your life and how these imaginings are informing you. Then you gain trust and can engage with them more actively in contemplation, meditation and even ritual. These images are mirrored in the world. You may see them in a chance encounter, things that "happen in threes" or the rumblings of the deep synchronicity that unites the spirit and physical worlds, which we may recognise and often trivialise as mere "coincidences". These dimensions comprise a book, at the very least, but are a significant part of any spiritual training and its ritual expression.

So how does this instruct you whether to fuck the woman or man you fancy or appreciate the attraction entirely at the imaginary and symbolic level? I am of the firm conviction that if you follow the above guidelines and put your own personal needs, desires and trips on hold, you will be 'told'. Maybe that is the place for decent psychotherapy, to get the 'trips' out of the way so that you can listen and not be confused. Or maybe you've got to let the trips dictate for a while until you see the difference. This is where those who have trodden the path before you are of great assistance. In the East, they are called Masters or Gurus. In the West, we pasture them out after mid-life for some of the reasons we've explored earlier; a crying shame, really, as we have an urgent need for such eldership at this time of great change.

This is what is known as an "Antinomian" position. Antinomy: "Contradiction in a law, or between two laws; conflict in authority; paradox." (Oxford English Dictionary). This sums it up fairly well, doesn't it?

However, the antinomian position extends that a little: "Opposed to the obligatoriness of moral law. One who maintains that the moral law is not binding on Christians." (Also OED). Once you have your head around the little twists and turns, such as reading "moral" maybe as "ethical" and "Christians" as "mystics", you get something like this: Antinomian means acting from a position of spiritual unity and grace that dictates one's rights, responsibilities and actions, which may appear to conflict with conventional ethical, institutional and religious standards. A highly exalted position? Maybe, but maybe also one to attain to? It is also a far cry from the commonly held criticism that such a position is a license to sin without consequence.

Brian and Val have tended their resignation to their brief involvement in the couples' club but are given emeritus status by the founder and, in the future, will occasionally visit for a drink and light socialisation. The relationship with Peter and Margot has attained a similar status, as well as a care-taking dimension to Brian and Val's children and, as an involuntary childless couple; this has become an added joy. For these months, Brian and Val have been engaged in their spiritual practice, aware that this may be the entirety of their psychosexual future together, a fact that caused them no distress. Except spirit had other plans ...

It was their anniversary and they planned a big day together, with the children at Margot and Peter's house for the weekend. The day started casually with a light lunch and a shared bottle of champagne, which led to an afternoon of lazy chatting in a discrete part of a local forest that Brian had sourced and ritualised. He had never seen anyone else there and they were in such a position that he believed they would know well in advance. Val had no anxiety as she lay with Brian idly playing with her arm and the subsequent afternoon doze was tranquil.

Val awoke from her light slumber to hear birds talking, flitting and playing in the trees above her. She saw little as the sun obscured her gaze and created a certain surreal feeling to the setting. She looked to one side at the purple rug on which they were lying, still clothed she believed. Brian moved above her from her left. He now had only his unbuttoned shirt on and he was gently removing her panties as well as lifting her skirt above her waist. She had no complaint. Brian moved her knees apart and inserted one finger in her cunt, just long enough to start the moisture flowing. Then he inserted himself, bringing his pelvis firmly against hers and lay against her for a short period, gently ruffling her hair and kissing her ear.

She was relaxed and still a little dozy and he was moving his pelvis in a soft manner against hers. She felt fluid and inviting and moved her legs up to gently rest over his. As his pace increased these same legs made their way up and out with her calves over the back of his thighs and her hands resting on and lightly gripping his firm buttocks. She had always enjoyed the shape of his arse and there was a sexual security in holding it like this. He had one arm behind her neck and the other was now playing with one of her now-exposed breasts.

Then he raised himself on his elbows, she felt a loosening in her pelvis and they both heard the audible clicking as it opened yet wider. It had begun. Deep in the recesses of her cunt, filled by his manhood, Val felt the previous warmth to become hot and intense. He started moving harder, not with the frenetic thrusting of youth, but the deep penetration of maturity that entered, rocked and rotated her vessel. He was yet harder. She looked into his eyes and almost didn't know him. His returning gaze was fixed and almost alien. He looked like another, whom she briefly wondered about as she met a deep thrust. He was someone else whom she knew dimly yet deeply. He was in that zone that was frightening, yet exciting. She gripped him tighter and answered with her own rhythm. Her eyes closed and she gave little gasps as the heat pulsed its way up through her body from somewhere deep within.

Val felt his cock briefly, it seemed to coil within her and she didn't know its position, it seemed both to fill her and yet not to be there. His face took different guises; she responded with a laugh to some and shock to others as, all the while, the intensity rose, and their bodies came together even tighter. There was a gag in her last gasp. He took his hand and gently gripped her throat, such that she was initially shocked yet became more excited. Her head began to pulsate, seemingly in unison to the image of this man, known yet unknown, and more than a man, who challenged her every movement and drove her relentlessly onward as she drove him in return. She sensed the edge. Her eyes were closed. The noise coming from him was strange, like a foreign tongue. She listened to its sweet music, a lullaby of an ancient time. They danced and as two spheres melted into each other and she was over the edge.

They found each other in that strange hinterland. They knew each other and always had. Products of a greater source they were beyond the fear and chaos, and they gently danced, formless, through the breath of the stillness. Then they were beyond even that and as one; a oneness that included all existence, which effortlessly ceased to be.

As they both quietly came back, they looked at each other as if for the first time. Once again, he was Brian, and she was Val. Once more, the familiar assembled around and embraced them. Simultaneously, a smile passed their lips as their eyes familiarised each other. Brian gently rolled back to his earlier position as they watched the sun dance through the trees and the birds celebrate.

"So, where to this evening, lover?" asked Val, replete with love.

"You know that restaurant called "Pandora's Box" that we've often seen and remarked on, but never quite managed it?"

"The one on the foreshore, part of that big function complex?"

"That's the one."

"You thinking of there?"

"Already booked, love. Peter has taken Margot there with his in-laws. He reckons the atmosphere is soft and gentle, but a little "unnerving" was the actual word he used."

"You want to unnerve me on our anniversary, you bastard!"

"No ... well, not that way! It's just that when he described it like that, I had a sense that it may be just the place for us. Only a feeling but I'm willing to back it."

So, later on in the early evening, dressed casually yet elegantly with a mild 'edge', supposedly for each other's eyes only, they set off to the restaurant.

The atmosphere certainly was soft, the music gentle and unobtrusive, and the lighting low around the tables. Val and Brian were shown to a table overlooking the river and settled into the cocktail they had brought with them from the adjoining bar and studied the menus. It was relatively early; they had been nearly the first to arrive, and people were still entering, as were some of the staff. Brian found it difficult to appreciate what Peter had meant by 'unnerving', as he felt relaxed and appreciated the atmosphere plus Val's quiet radiance, which he usually noticed after they had made love.

It was now nearly a year since Brian had received and they viewed together "The Weekend Retreat". Their lives had certainly been interesting since then and both were inclined to see that the movie had been influential in this regard, maybe more than simply coincidental. Probably the most significant change had been that Brian had pursued the work of high energetic states in his neurophysiological research and was exploring the whole issue of ecstasy and consciousness. He had always had a notion that the Western approach to personal and spiritual evolution had a strong ecstatic basis; now, the experiences of his personal life had flowed into his work and teaching. Val had joined him in this and they had set up their own business with respect to this, as there seemed an increasing demand for such exploration that was not accommodated in the mainstream culture. This had almost happened accidentally and both felt fulfilled that their work was reflecting their personal beliefs and ethics.

Their relationship reflected this. It had come to a place where they were both individuals yet shared a common ground that was implicit. The anxieties associated with relationship fears, jealousy, possessiveness and the like were now gone. Both had recognised that their path was one of personal exploration that included a full experience of their respective and collective sexualities. This had gone through a fair amount of personal examination, as the desire for simple indulgence was well-sated and any motives for such a continued outlook required close inspection. Both felt that their paths were guided by a spiritual intelligence that was almost taken for granted, even when this seemed to directly challenge their relationship.

There was a sense of aloneness though. They had each other, but had come to a place that few around them seemed to understand or want to share. This, of course, had given them good cause for reflection, yet all the signs were for them to continue as they were. The last few months had also been characterised by a fidelity that was different, as they had not met anyone with whom they felt to share their psychosexual experience, even in a platonic manner. Brian wondered whether his teaching role, which was now more of a mentorship, might include this in the future, but at this time, this was merely reflective and certainly not something he was going to actively promote unless he was given an indication otherwise.

Their conversation was light and reflective, covering the above territory with questions of each other and shared opinions. They were now well into the evening and the wine had mellowed them with the music fostering a drift in their chatter to humour and even teasing of each other. Brian put down his glass and gazed whimsically past Val's shoulder and was quietly taken aback. There was a table at the rear of the restaurant where a couple were also engaged with each other in a manner that reflected them. The man was more visible to Brian, as he picked up his wine glass, looked at Brian and gave him a silent toast followed by a smile. The man looked astonishingly like Paul from the "Retreat" movie. He said nothing to Val.

Brian was waiting to see the woman's face, as she had her back to him. His frequent looks there attracted Val's attention and she queried him. With a slight hunch of his shoulders, he remarked on the association in a dismissive manner. As the route to the toilet would take either of them near to this table, Val suggested she powder her nose. Brian smiled as Val left and walked past the table with a discreet glance.

Inside, Val gave the mirror a disinterested gaze as the door opened behind her and she caught the rear of the elegant, shapely brunette just as she went into the toilet. Val left and walked past the table back to Brian. Obviously, she was disappointed, as she had hoped to look at the women on the return to her own table. Certainly, the man had looked like Paul and his enigmatic smile hadn't helped her confusion. She communicated this to Brian on her return and both waited eagerly for the woman's return. After what seemed like an age, she came out, and now the whole atmosphere became a little surreal, as she definitely looked like Carole. Although she didn't look at their table, Paul raised his glass and offered another silent toast.

Brian looked at Val; they were certainly unnerved and sought an explanation.

"My arse is still tingling, sir."

Brian was startled out of the trance state he was in. He looked up to the blonde waitress who stood at his left shoulder. Now he was completely aghast, as it could have been Helen who uttered the comment.

"I'm sorry?"

"I asked whether your glass needs refilling, sir?"

"Yes, thank you." He looked at Val. She was looking at Helen with her mouth open and very slowly returned her gaze to Brian, as the waitress moved away. Both remained speechless as Paul and Carole quietly got up, tended to their bill and left. Brian and Val were back at the "Retreat", and silently, both were waiting for Mick.

He, of course, arrived in due course with the dessert menu and an enquiry about port. His waiter's outfit seemed identical to the one he was wearing when he arse fucked Helen. By now, although still quite speechless, Val and Brian took it all in their stride and even exchanged a smile. They both saw him give Helen a slight slap on the bum, as he resumed his place behind the bar and started to wipe a glass.

Although they had been unnerved, probably qualifying Peter's intuitive assessment, both Val and Brian now felt strangely settled. Of course, they discussed what was happening around them and initially asked each other questions that anyone would ask. Were they imagining it? Maybe they were here to do a movie and they had just chanced upon them? These queries slipped into the distance as they both realised this was the work of spirit. They settled to their dessert and port and engaged each other in a light and even whimsical manner.

Brian led Val to the cloak stand where Helen retrieved Val's coat and silently helped her into it. Brian went to the till and Mick presented him with the meal account. As he was settling the bill with the usual interchanges of "I hope you enjoyed your meal, sir?" and the like, Mick turned as the door behind him opened. There was Jan, dressed in a chef's outfit. Brian, by now completely comfortable with what was happening around him, acknowledged the meal and the particular culinary aspects he had discerned. He believed Jan to be the real chef of the restaurant, as he had no idea what the director of "Retreat" actually looked like. The comments from Brian, the chef/director acknowledged with a smile, not wanting to take too much credit for a meal he had not actually prepared!

"I'm pleased sir, but I'm also here for another reason."

"Yes?"

"You and your good lady are our one thousandth guests, and you may not know it, but when we opened "Pandora's Box" we advertised this figure for a gift."

"Well, that's a bonus. What might that be?"

"A weekend at our affiliated retreat."

Epilogue

As chance would have it – although the god who governs such coincidences is a greater god than we recognise – as soon as I had finished the main draft, I was given a book by Colin Wilson called "The God of the Labyrinth". Although I was aware of many of Wilson's works, I had, somewhat surprisingly because of the subject matter, not come across this one from 1970.

Wilson's work has had a seminal effect on me. A book in the post, being the lady's personal copy of "The Outsider", followed a brief affair that ended a long-term relationship: I realised my life was about to undertake a huge change. The people described in this anthology felt like spiritual brethren and I started to see that the affair was an induction, which the lady concerned confirmed at a subsequent meeting. As I started to read "Labyrinth", by contrast a (supposedly) fictional work, I was plunged into an acute infective illness requiring intensive treatment, but continued my reading. The completion of the book marked the end of the severe part of the illness. So which god was talking here? The god of chance certainly, but maybe also the god of the labyrinth?

Wilson's book is an accelerated ride through sexuality, its place in our lives and ultimately our cultural future. Like my work, Wilson adopts a Western orientation and takes sex into what I have termed "psychosexuality", even to the archetypal level. Reich's work is also semi-fictionally introduced into the text. Wilson, at that time, felt compelled to negotiate potential charges of pornography that are discussed in the book and which I note have a similar ring to my arguments on this issue;

I felt vindicated. What this 'chance' reading also did for me, even though it is a parallel and complementary work in many ways, was make me realise that, with my definition of Pandora's Box, I hadn't just opened it – I had gone inside. Like my first contact with Wilson, I feel my life is to undergo a change.

When I awoke from the final delirium of the illness, I had patterns, images, and ideas of where I could take this present work further. When this fever subsided, I realised that it was not about further comment in an epilogue or a discussion or even a comparison with Wilson's ideas. It was about future works, but it was also about how this would reflect in the way I conduct my life and its professional expression.

Sex is at the core of all this, the energy of which is not simplistically a by-product of our physical condition. It is the inkling of the divine that lives deep within us awaiting awakening and flowering. It is life-affirmative, carried by enthusiasm and passion, maturing into the wholeness of our individual psychosexuality and our collective existence as love. If pornography has the capacity to, at least, put us on the right path then who has the right to refute us that direction? Sexuality is God-given, not simply for procreation; our future as a species may depend on this simple insight.

Then a further twist of fate: After completing the proof-read of this work, I came across a studio of pornography, based in Britain, which seemed to blend some of the raw instinctual elements of sexuality with a creative, erotic perspective and sometimes purposeful narrative.

One film, in particular, appealed to me. Ironically, it was by a director I had not come across before and described a young woman's experience at a 'getaway', where she was unaware of the sexual undercurrents that already existed there. There were some performers I had come across in other porn productions, but, significantly, a core group I had not. The scenes do not specifically follow the rote formulae of mainstream porn and explore some sexual themes in an unusual and creative manner. The young woman seems to undergo an initiation of a sexual nature in her time there and leaves a different person. There is also a significant component of ritualisation.

Whilst the acting was not of a high standard and did not reach the complexities that are contained in my fictional account, there is a clear move in that direction. Some of the limitations in the acting would be because the porn stars would not have this as a significant component in routine involvement in the industry, as well as the fact that in this movie, they are from a broad spectrum of nationalities, making the narrative problematic.

I found this fascinating, but I was also a little more fortunate than Brian, as this director has made at least one other film! (Yes, I will be getting it ...) Yet what surprised me, beyond the 'endorsement' of the fictional account of the "Retreat" and many of the conclusions drawn from this, was the synchronicity of the event.

The spirit of sexuality is alive and well, it would seem!

Postscript

You may recall this passage from chapter one ...

> *"We at Private wish to promote a more liberal attitude towards sex, and a better understanding of all sexual inclinations. We believe that sex is both natural and enjoyable, and therefore it is most definitely wrong to attempt to hide or feel ashamed about it. Furthermore, we know that good erotography has a positive and stimulating effect on human sexuality."* (Quoted verbatim and in total.) *At this early stage of our exploration, you may agree or disagree with this statement. Maybe you might like to take a note of your reactions and opinions regarding it and then compare when you re-read it, having finished this book.*

How does this read now?
Here's my evolving version, by way of a conclusion:

> *Sexuality is our birth right and a pathway to redemption that is both creative and exciting. It is a rich and varied tapestry that can deal with and transcend issues that would chain us to an unproductive existence. It unites all of life in a journey towards our highest personal and spiritual fulfilment and realisation. Ultimately it is the gift given of the gods for our journey home.*

About Drew Wynn

Drew has spent his life preoccupied with sex, for which he makes absolutely no apology. In this book, he presents a distillation of his ideas and feelings, fashioning them into a creative whole that he wishes to share with the troubled majority of the population in these matters.

Whilst this work contains rather controversial though topical subject matter, it continues his series of writing and other creative output in this exciting field. An earlier work, Sex and the Supernatural, explored sexuality in the supernatural and parapsychological fields. The series then continues to show how a re-visioned and revitalised view of sexuality can creatively inform Western culture and the mental health field, in particular. That this position needs to reconnect with our Western spiritual heritage he sees as fundamental and is a major theme of the present work.

A medical practitioner with considerable experience in mental health, Drew has extensively explored differing cultural and historical perspectives of illness and health. This background has allowed him to see the dysfunctional perspective Western culture has toward sexuality and the void that exists in regard to its place in health, illness and disease.

Drew believes that we need to move beyond these cultural distortions and that medicine in the West needs a reintegration of sexuality from more than the objective, scientific and even demeaning position it has gained in recent generations. He further sees as fundamental and more than a coincidence that the spiritual bereftment of the West parallels the lack of integration of our sexuality.

Bibliography

There is, of course, a mass of material in the marketplace regarding sexuality and pornography. The list, below, is what has informed me personally over the years and has been the background to this work. It is certainly by no means exhaustive and, although seemingly historical, some of the older works still stand out and have not been superseded, in my opinion. Although I, obviously, do not agree with much of the material in these books, they do serve to cover the field and provide a platform for further exploration.

I have made little use of the Internet for this work – apart from accessing pornography! Yet the potential beyond this is obvious: For example, Llewellyn Publications cover these related fields extensively and are worth a Google. For those unacquainted, the pornographic material online is vast and extensive. I do not want to provide advertising in this area, but strongly recommend you begin with reputable producers.

The Thames and Hudson series are an excellent introduction to the esoteric arts associated with psychosexuality, with works that expand and extend on the above themes. They comprise a limited introductory text with many illustrations in a large paperback format.

Klossowski de Rola, Stanislas. *Alchemy: The Secret Art*. London. Thames and Hudson, 1973

Mookerjee, Ajit. Kundalini: *The Arousal of the Inner Energy*. London. Thames and Hudson, 1982

Rawson, Philip. Tantra: *The Indian Cult of Ecstasy.* London. Thames and Hudson, 1973

Tantric oriented works associated with sexuality:

Avalon, Arthur. The Serpent Power. New York. Dover Publications, 1974

Danielou, Alain. The Complete Kama Sutra. Rochester. Park Street Press, 1994

Hyatt, Christopher S. Secrets of Western Tantra. Tempe. New Falcon Publications, 1989

Meldman, Louis William. Mystical Sex. Tucson. Harbinger House, 1990

Mumford, Dr John. Ecstasy Through Tantra. St. Paul. Llewellyn Publications, 1988

Rajneesh, Bhagwan Shree. Tantra Spirituality and Sex. Oregon. Rajneesh Foundation International, 1997

More exclusively Tantric works:

Krishna, Gopi. Kundalini: The Evolutionary Energy in Man. Boulder. Shambala, 1971

More specifically sexual texts:

Anand, Margo. The Art of Sexual Ecstasy. Los Angeles. Tarcher, 1989

Douglas, Nic and Slinger, Penny. Sexual Secrets. Rochester. Destiny Books, 1979

Losowick, Lee. The Alchemy of Love and Sex. Prescott. Hohm Press, 1996

More academically and scholarly sexual texts:

Evola, Julius. Eros and the Mysteries of Love. Rochester. Inner Traditions, 1991

Feuerstein, Georg. Sacred Sexuality. Rochester. Inner Traditions, 2003

Fradon, Ramona. The Gnostic Faustus. Rochester. Inner Traditions, 2007

Versluis, Arthur. The Secret History of Western Sexual Mysticism. Rochester, Destiny Books, 2008

Works on and about pornography:

McKee Alan et al. The Porn Report. Carlton, Vic. Melbourne University Publishing, 2008

Stoller, Robert J. Porn: Myths for the Twentieth Century. New Haven. Yale University Press, 1991

(Stoller has written several psychoanalytically- inclined works on pornography)

Williams, Linda. Hard Core: Power, Pleasure, and the "Frenzy of the Visible". Berkeley. University of California Press, 1989

Williams, Linda. (Ed.) Porn Studies. Durham. Duke University Press. 2004

Alchemy and Magic:

Aswynn, Freya. Northern Mysteries & Magick. St. Paul. Llewellyn, 1990

Danielou, Alain. Shiva and Dionysus. New York. Inner Traditions, 1974

Harpur, Patrick. Daimonic Reality: A Field Guide to the Otherworld. Ravensdale. Pine Winds Press, 2003

Harpur, Patrick. The Philosopher's Secret Fire. London. Penguin, 2002

Ramsay, Jay. Alchemy: The Art of Transformation. London. Thorsons, 1997

Thorsson, Edred. Northern Magic. St. Paul. Llewellyn, 1993

Other approaches to sexuality:

Foucault, Michel. The History of Sexuality, Vols 1-3. London. Penguin, Various (Philosophy)

Taylor, Timothy. The Prehistory of Sex. New York. Bantam 1996

(Archaeology)

Reich, Wilhelm. The Function of the Orgasm. New York. Pocket Books, 1975 (Reichian)

Singer, June. Energies of Love: Sexuality Re-visioned. New York. Anchor Press/Doubleday, 1983 (Analytical Psychology – Jung)

Stoller, Robert J. Observing the Erotic Imagination. New Haven. Yale University Press, 1985 (Psychoanalytic)

Depth Psychologists:

Jones, Ernest. The Life and Works of Sigmund Freud. Hammondsworth. Penguin, 1974

Thomas Moore. (Ed.) A Blue Fire. New York. HarperPerennial, 1991

(A selection of writings of James Hillman's Archetypal Psychology.)

Reich, Wilhelm. Selected Writings: An Introduction to Orgonomy. New York. Farrar, Straus and Giroux, 1979

Whitmont, Edward C. The Symbolic Quest. New Jersey. Princeton University Press, 1969

(A classic introduction to Jung's Analytical Psychology)

Postscript: Freud, Jung, Reich and Hillman have published extensively.

Mythology and Sexuality: Bates, Brian. The Wisdom of the Wyrd. London. Rider, 1996

Johnson, Robert A. She (1976) and He (1977). New York. Harper and Row

(Based on Jung's psychology applied to gender)

Other works referred to in the text:

Fischer, Roland. State Bound Knowledge.

In: Understanding Mysticism. Richard Woods (Ed.). London. Athlone Press 1981.

Erotic works of note:

Bataille, Georges. Story of the Eye. London. Penguin, 2001 (Contains a monograph by Susan Sontag, The Pornographic Imagination, and Roland Barthes, The Metaphor of the Eye.)

de Sade, The Marquis. The 120 Days of Sodom and Other writings. London. Arrow, 1990 (With an Introduction by Simone de Beauvoir.)

Houellebecq, Michel. Platform. London. Vintage, 2003

Nin, Anais. The Diary of Anais Nin, Vols 1-7. New York. Harcourt, Various

Thomas, D.M. The White Hotel. Hammondsworth. Penguin, 1981

Wilson, Colin. The God of the Labyrinth. St. Albans. Mayflower, 1974

Postscript: The above selection is highly selective, reflects the text and is designed simply as an introduction to the classic erotic works of literature. Sontag's monograph in The Story of the Eye gives an anthology of major works in the text. De Sade's work is historically a classic, more than erotically. Other major writers in the fields include, of course, Henry Miller and D H Lawrence amongst others and are highly recommended. There has been a huge increase in the number of popular modern erotic and pornographic works now available; these have been excluded from the above, as the field has been restricted to historical and erotic classics only.

www.ingramcontent.com/pod-product-compliance
Lightning Source LLC
Chambersburg PA
CBHW032047020426
42335CB00011B/228